"This book, with Bill Cavanaugh's *Torture and Eucharist*, represents a more challenging stage of and for liberation theology. Bell's extraordinary analysis of the capitalist captivity of Christianity makes chilling reading, but at the same time he helps us see how what appear to be weaknesses may represent the gift God has given us to resist the powers."

Stanley Hauerwas, *Gilbert T. Rowe Professor of Theological Ethics, Duke University*

"Christians have often naively ignored the powers and principalities that shape our actual desires. We have too often imagined that it is easy to learn to desire, love and know God. In this powerful, stimulating and insightful book, Dan Bell demonstrates the challenges that capitalism presents to Christian faith as an extraordinarily powerful force shaping our desires and distorting understanding of God. Bell's constructive theological confrontation of Christianity and capitalism engagingly challenges us all to more rigorous thought and faithful living."

L. Gregory Jones, *Dean of Divinity School and Professor of Theology, Duke University*

"Dan Bell's book launches an incredibly serious theoretical and practical challenge to the direction of 'liberation theology,' but a challenge that is at every turn against capitalism and for the poor. In Augustinian fashion the technology of desire that is capitalism is opposed to the shaping of desire for God that is Christianity. From this opposition – supported by discussion of a host of figures from Bernard of Clairvaux to Foucault – Bell argues for the profoundly political character of Christianity itself. The logic of forgiveness is then read as central to the politics that is Christian life and as founded in trinitarian theology.

The combination of the theoretical and the sheerly 'practical' is one of the great strengths of the book – Dorothy Day out-thinks Marx and Adam Smith! The book should – if possible in combination with Bill Cavanaugh's *Torture and Eucharist* – be compulsory reading not only for all who are concerned with political theology or liberation, but also for all concerned with ecclesiology and the very nature of desire."

Lewis Ayres, *Assistant Professor of Historical Theology,*
Candler School of Theology, Emory University

"This book is an important entry into a major debate and even those who disagree with Bell will not be able to ignore his argument."

William T. Cavanaugh, *Assistant Professor of Theology,*
University of St. Thomas, St. Paul, MN

LIBERATION THEOLOGY
AFTER THE END OF HISTORY

What has become of Latin American liberation theology in the wake of capitalism's triumph? What has happened to the "irruption of the poor"? More importantly, has Christianity been exhausted as a font of resistance to capitalism? What resources of hope remain?

Liberation Theology After the End of History assesses the pathos and promise of Latin American liberation theology's vision of Christian resistance to global capitalism. Drawing on the postmodern critical theory of Gilles Deleuze and Michel Foucault, Daniel M. Bell, Jr. casts capitalism as a discipline of human desire. In this situation, argues Bell, Christian resistance must take the form of a counter-discipline, and in defense of this claim he takes up the liberationists' vision of the Church of the poor, arguing that, ironically, it is a refusal to cease suffering that portends the liberation of desire from its capitalist captivity. The result is the most thorough account to date of the rise, failure, and future prospects of Latin American liberation theology.

Daniel M. Bell, Jr. is Assistant Professor of Theological Ethics at the Lutheran Theological Southern Seminary. He has previously published articles on Latin American liberation theology in *Communio, Modern Theology, Journal for Peace & Justice Studies,* and *Journal of Religion & Society.*

RADICAL ORTHODOXY SERIES
Edited by John Milbank, Catherine Pickstock and Graham Ward

Radical orthodoxy combines sophisticated understanding of contemporary thought, modern and postmodern, with a theological perspective that looks back to the origins of the Church. It is the most talked-about development in contemporary theology.

CITIES OF GOD
Graham Ward

DIVINE ECONOMY
D. Stephen Long

RADICAL ORTHODOXY
edited by John Milbank, Catherine Pickstock and Graham Ward

TRUTH IN AQUINAS
John Milbank and Catherine Pickstock

LIBERATION THEOLOGY AFTER THE END OF HISTORY
The refusal to cease suffering
Daniel M. Bell, Jr.

LIBERATION THEOLOGY AFTER THE END OF HISTORY

The refusal to cease suffering

Daniel M. Bell, Jr.

London and New York

First published 2001
by Routledge
11 New Fetter Lane, London EC4P 4EE

Simultaneously published in the USA and Canada
by Routledge
29 West 35th Street, New York, NY 10001

Routledge is an imprint of the Taylor & Francis Group

© 2001 Daniel M. Bell, Jr.

The right of Daniel M. Bell, Jr. to be identified as the Author of this Work has been asserted
by him in accordance with the Copyright, Designs and Patents Act 1988

Typeset in Baskerville by
M Rules
Printed and bound in Great Britain by
Biddles Ltd, Guildford and King's Lynn

British Library Cataloguing in Publication Data
A catalogue record for this book is available from the British Library

Library of Congress Cataloging in Publication Data
Bell, Daniel, M., 1966–
Liberation theology after the end of history: the refusal to cease suffering/
Daniel M. Bell, Jr.
p. cm. – (Radical orthodoxy series)
Includes bibliographical references.
1. Liberation theology. 2. South America – Church history. I. Title. II. Series.

BT83.57.B445 2001
230′.0464′098–dc21   2001019310

ISBN 0–415–24303–3 (hbk)
ISBN 0–415–24304–1 (pbk)

To the community of Lutheran
Theological Southern Seminary

CONTENTS

ACKNOWLEDGMENTS

In the course of preparing this work, I have been reminded relentlessly that I am only able to do what I do because of the labor and sacrifices of so many others. My family has been supportive and encouraging in countless ways. Professor Donald Musser, of Stetson University, introduced me to the beauty of theology. The many who contribute to A Foundation for Theological Education and The United Methodist Church made possible the fellowships I received from those bodies. The friends who have blessed my life during the years of this work – at Duke University, Truman State University, Monmouth College, and now at Lutheran Theological Southern Seminary – have been an invaluable and irreplaceable source of encouragement, insight, and inspiration. Those who read earlier drafts of this work deserve special mention: Bill Cavanaugh, Rodney Clapp, Jim Fodor, Steve Long, Sujin Pak, and Joerg Rieger. Gratitude is also due Graham Ward, John Milbank and Catherine Pickstock, whose enthusiasm and critical insight saw this through to completion and made it a much better work. And my thanks go to Amanda Warner for her work in preparing the index.

A prior incarnation of this text served as my doctoral dissertation at Duke University, completed under the guidance of Stanley Hauerwas. Stanley has been wonderfully supportive and instructive throughout the course of this project. I am also grateful to Mary McClintock-Fulkerson, Ken Surin, Willie Jennings, and Greg Jones, who have been generous teachers and helpful interlocutors.

Although he died when it was scarcely begun, Fred Herzog exerts a special influence on this work. In the way he lived his life he showed that it just might be possible to "seek first God's Kingdom and God's righteousness," to remain faithful, even in the academy.

Finally, I give thanks to all those who have allowed me to share in their lives at the Community Shelter for HOPE, Guess Road Correctional Facility, Central Prison (all in North Carolina), the Habitat for Humanity projects in Missouri, Illinois, and South Carolina, and the communities in Costa Rica, Honduras, and Mexico that so generously welcomed me in recent years. They continue to remind me of what is truly important.

Rudimentary versions of parts of the argument in Chapter 2 of this book appeared in two journals. "After the End of History: Latin American Liberation Theology in the Wake of Capitalism's Triumph," *Journal of Religion & Society* 2 (2000): 1–10 (first published by the *Journal of Religion & Society*) and "Men of Stone and Children of Struggle: Latin American Liberationists at the End of History," *Modern Theology* 14 (January 1998): 113–141. Copyright © Modern Theology, 1998.

INTRODUCTION
The end of history

In 1989 Francis Fukuyama, an official at the US Department of State, heralded the arrival of "the end of history." By this he meant the unabashed victory of economic and political liberalism on the stage of world history, the triumph of consumerist Western culture, the total exhaustion of viable systematic alternatives to Western liberalism. History, said Fukuyama, was ineluctably moving in the direction of the "victory of the VCR," that is, toward a universal homogeneous state characterized by liberal democracy in the political sphere combined with easy access to VCRs and stereos in the economic. The crumbling of the Berlin Wall marked the revelation of liberal democracy and the free market as the paradigmatic form of human society, as the regime that best "satisfies the most basic human longings."[1]

Many Christians have greeted this development with deep satisfaction, believing that capitalism is quite compatible with Christianity. Accordingly, with great joy they announce that "we are all capitalist now" and happily join the chorus of voices celebrating the "capitalist revolution."[2] Others, however, lament this development, believing that capitalism, far from accommodating Christianity and marking the culmination of history, is actually antithetical to the faith and an obstacle to history's true end.

My argument takes as its starting point the latter position. My basic premise is that the end of history has not been brought near by the boardrooms of New York and Tokyo or the staterooms of Washington DC and Mexico City, nor does human desire find its satisfaction in the capitalist market. Rather, history discovers its end far from the boardrooms and away from the marketplace, on a hill where a poor person, uttering the words "forgive them," was crucified.[3] In other words, broadly conceived this project is about the contemporary struggle between capitalism and Christianity over the end of history, over the redemption of humanity. Does capitalism exhaust the horizon of human emancipation? Must we all bow (or at least slouch in our recliners, remote in hand) before the VCR and prostrate ourselves to the forces of Wall Street? Or can Christianity fund resistance to capitalism? Is Christianity capable of liberating human desire from capitalism? In other words, what comes after the end of history?

According to traditional accounts of Christianity, although the end of history is found outside the city gate among the crucified, history does not end with the crucifixion. From the depth of that space of exclusion the crucified one was raised. Hence, for an answer to the question "what comes after the end of history?" I turn to what is going on outside the city gate today, to the contemporary spaces of exclusion. In particular, I engage the Latin American liberationists and their account of the "Church of the poor" that has emerged in recent decades to contest capitalism's ascendancy. As a result of their work among the impoverished masses of Latin America and their provocative articulation of a "preferential option for the poor," the Latin American liberationists have consistently posed the question of Christian resistance to the capitalist order in the most compelling of terms. Consequently, their work – and the life and activity of the poor Christian communities in their midst as articulated by the liberationists – serve as the primary foil for this project.

Recently, however, Latin American liberationists have acknowledged that their revolutionary efforts are in disarray. In the wake of the electoral defeat of the Sandinistas, the intensified siege of the Cuban revolution, the collapse of socialism, and the subsiding of revolutionary currents, Latin American liberationists share a generalized sense of crisis among those forces that had hoped to usher in a new era on the revolutionary wave of the "irruption of the poor." Hence, with the chastening of revolutionary expectations, Fukuyama's end of history raises the specter that the triumph of capitalism not only marks the culmination of history, but of Christianity as a credible source of resistance to that order as well. The present age may well be remembered, in the words of John Kent, as "the end of a line of growth, an end which neither Marxism nor Christianity can prevent, not even when they combine in 'liberation theology.'"[4] Is it possible that capitalism has succeeded where two millennia ago the powers and principalities failed? Has the stone been rolled back in place, with the crucified left to languish for ever?

In this situation, Kent suggests, a theology of survival – one more akin to diplomacy than ideological crusade – may be more to the point than a theology of liberation. Hence, the subtitle of this project. While the phrase "the refusal to cease suffering" is fraught with difficulties and does not immediately evoke images of survival, it is my contention that the possibility of Christian resistance to the capitalist order is anchored in those whom Ignacio Ellacuría called "the crucified people" and their enactment of God's gift of forgiveness.

At the heart of my argument is the assertion that the conflict between capitalism and Christianity is nothing less than a clash of opposing technologies of desire. Christianity has traditionally conceived of the human being in terms of desire. Augustine's famous dictum, "our hearts are restless until they find rest in thee" captures this sentiment well. The human being is constituted by desire, the desire of God. The Christian tradition also claims, however, that desire has been corrupted. Sin has distorted desire. Sin captures and bends desire in unnatural directions. It disciplines and enslaves desire. In what follows I argue that capitalism is one such discipline of desire. It is a form of sin,[5] a way of life that captures and distorts human desire in accord with the golden rule of production for the market.[6] Given the horrendous consequences of this discipline for the majority of humanity, it is fitting to call capitalism a form of madness. Christianity, on the other hand, is about the healing or liberating of desire from sin. It is a therapy, a way of life that releases desire from its bondage, that cures the madness so that desire may once again flow as it was created to do.

My argument begins in the first chapter with the display of contemporary capitalism as a discipline of desire. This display in turn begins with a brief introduction to contemporary capitalism by the liberationist Franz Hinkelammert. His analysis of "savage capitalism" highlights themes and issues that will recur throughout the project. Following this, the heart of the chapter is devoted to a more structured account of the way capitalism disciplines desire. Drawing on the work of Gilles Deleuze and Michel Foucault, I argue that savage capitalism's victory is not merely economic, but ontological. Capitalism extends its reign by far more than merely fostering a particular mode of production and division of labor; it is best understood as an ensemble of technologies that disciplines the constitutive human power, desire. Of particular importance is the recognition that capitalism only succeeds in disciplining desire through the agency of the state-form. Capitalism advances as the state-form delivers desire to its discipline. It is here that Foucault's work on "governmentality" proves perspicacious. His account of governmentality reminds us that the state-form embraces more than "the state," that it includes a vast array of "technologies of desire" operative on the social, cultural, and personal as well as economic registers that together form and govern desire in accord with the demands of the capitalist market.

In the second chapter I consider the powerful witness of the Latin American liberationists and the Church of the poor in their midst. For their efforts to distance Christianity from capitalism, often at great personal cost, they deserve much praise. They have contributed significantly to a widespread appreciation for the connection between the Christian life and struggles against all forms of oppression – so much so that even their fiercest ecclesiastical opponents now proclaim a gospel of liberation (albeit a liberation of a much different hue). They have boldly challenged the Church to leave its spiritual ghetto, where for too long it has remained comfortably complicitous with the powerful while ignoring the cries of impoverished masses. Here, however, I challenge the liberationists' theorization of Christian resistance to capitalism on the grounds that that theorization is insufficiently radical. In itself, this claim is unremarkable; critics of liberationists' social theory abound. In contrast with the majority of the critics, however, I argue that the root of the crisis of liberationist social theory lies in their ecclesiology. The ecclesiological innovations inaugurated by the liberationists to overcome the failures of the New Christendom ecclesiology dominant in the 1960s falter insofar as those innovations remain embedded in the modern narrative that divorces religion from the social-political-economic dimensions of life. As a consequence, the Church of the poor is only indirectly political and politics is conceived as statecraft. This remains true from the earliest writings, with their revolutionary expectations, to the more recent emphasis on democracy and civil society. When viewed against the backdrop of Deleuze and Foucault's work, it becomes apparent that this commitment to an apolitical Church and politics as statecraft cannot help but deliver liberationists into the maw of the capitalist order.

In the interest of revitalizing the liberationists' revolutionary efforts, I conclude this chapter by gesturing toward an alternative account of the Christian community, one that rejects the false and futile politics of statecraft and instead reclaims the Christian community as a public *sui generis*, that is, as a social, political, economic formation in its own right. In other words, my constructive effort to envision Christian resistance to capitalist discipline begins with Christianity's reassertion in the material realm as the true politics. Christianity is the true politics, the true polity, over against the agony of capitalist discipline, in the Augustinian sense that the Church embodies the true form of human social, political, and economic organization because its order is one of liturgy, of worship of the triune God.[7] As will become clear, however, this reassertion of the political character of Christianity is not an instance of wistful pining after a departed Constantinianism or Christendom. Rather this non-identical renewal of Christianity's public presence finds its exemplification in the Church of the poor. In particular, I suggest that there are signs that some elements of the Church of the poor may in fact embody this alternative, setting aside politics as statecraft, and hence may be able to fund resistance to capitalism. This is the first step in reclaiming the particular technologies of desire that God may have provided for healing desire and resisting the madness that is capitalism.

The next step occurs in the third chapter, where Christianity is reclaimed as a therapy of desire that may be capable of both liberating desire from its capitalist captivity and enabling it once again to flow freely as it was created to do. I begin with a construal of Christianity as an ensemble of technologies of desire. Using the example of Bernard of Clairvaux and the twelfth-century Cistercians, I argue that far from being the apolitical custodian of moral values or a preferential option, Christianity is, no less than capitalism, an ensemble of technologies that shapes and forms desire. As an ensemble of knowledges, systems of judgment, persons, institutions, and practices, Christianity governs desire; through a host of technologies such as liturgy, catechesis, orders, and discipleship, Christianity exerts an ontological influence on humanity. It reshapes desire. Following this display, the question is broached, what kind of therapy does Christianity offer to counter capitalist discipline? Specifically, because of the frequency with which it is invoked against capitalism, the question is posed in terms of justice. Is justice the name of the therapy that Christianity offers desire corrupted by the madness of capitalism? Again, because of their prominence in the struggle against capitalism, the Latin American liberationists are the foil for my argument. Against capitalism they proffer a conception of justice as the guarantor of rights. I unpack this account of justice by situating it within the tradition of Catholic social teaching on justice, highlighting both important similarities and differences. Finally, I offer an analysis that reveals several theological and practical difficulties with justice so conceived, difficulties that suggest that far from liberating desire from capitalism, the liberationists' vision of justice can only accentuate the terror of the capitalist order.

The subject of the fourth chapter is forgiveness. Here I present the case for forgiveness as the therapy that Christianity offers desire in order to liberate it from capitalism. I begin by arguing that forgiveness avoids both the theological and practical deficiencies that undercut the liberationists' account of justice. Next, I turn to what the liberationists have to say, particularly their reservations and suspicions, concerning forgiveness. This sets the stage for what follows, namely an analysis of forgiveness as an ensemble of technologies of desire that is organized around addressing the liberationists' concerns. This is to say, the presentation focuses on those technologies essential to establishing forgiveness as a form of resistance to capitalism. Central to this account of forgiveness are those whom Jon Sobrino and Ignacio Ellacuría call "the crucified people." In spite of their own commitment to justice as the guardian of rights, the liberationists acknowledge that many of the crucified people who constitute the Church of the poor are facing their oppressors and extending the gift of forgiveness, not demanding what is due in accord with their "rights." More importantly, the crucified people are extending forgiveness precisely as a form of resistance to capitalism. They are enacting forgiveness as a means of liberating desire from its capitalist captivity. Included here is a reconsideration of the place and function of justice, reconceived in terms of the aneconomic order of the divine gift of forgiveness, in the Christian life.

Finally, this chapter concludes this project with an appraisal of the risk of forgiveness. At this point it is clear that the therapy of forgiveness is nothing less than an effort to resist the unjust suffering of capitalism with a refusal to cease suffering. As such it is an odd and risk-laden form of resistance. Because it expects the victims of injustice to refrain from resorting to claims of "what is due" and "rights" in their defense, it is haunted by the possibility that ultimately forgiveness is nothing more than the refusal to cease suffering. Here I confront head on the suspicions that have stalked forgiveness the length of this chapter. Does this account of forgiveness disempower victims and inevitably sanction the impunity of the powerful? I argue that the forgiveness enacted by the Church of the poor does neither, that on the contrary it is an instantiation of a crucified power and of a suffering against suffering. But is this true? My final move is a confession that the truthfulness of the claims I advance for forgiveness, as well as the wisdom of the crucified people's refusal to cease suffering, remain to be seen. Christians await the consummation of redemption, when suffering will indeed cease. Until that time, the refusal to cease suffering is an act of hope. More specifically, it is a wager on God. Is God who Christians claim God is, the one who defeats sin not by extracting justice in the sense of rendering a strict account of "what is due" but by reaching out to the sinner with the gift of forgiveness?

What is the point of this project? I have struggled with identifying what I hoped to accomplish in this work. Part of this struggle involved defining my relation to the Latin American liberationists and the crucified people of the Church of the poor.

Although I critique the liberationists, I do not really have nor do I want an argument with them. Although I have been welcomed and embraced by poor Christians in Central America, I do not presume to speak for them. At times I assumed I was engaged with the liberationists in a common effort to answer the question, how do we proclaim God as savior in the midst of a world suffering from the madness of capitalism? While capitalism has created a certain bond between us, the legitimacy of this assumption rested on the presumption on my part that we shared a common faith, as the author of Ephesians wrote, "There is one body and one Spirit . . . one Lord, one faith, one baptism" (4:4–5). Yet I have come to see the error in this too. In an essay on theology from the underside of history, Gustavo Gutiérrez observes, "The poor of the earth, in their struggles for liberation, in their faith and hope in the Father, are coming to the realization that, to put it in the words of Arguedas, 'the God of the masters is not the same.' Their God is not the God of the poor. For ultimately the dominator is one who does not really believe in the God of the Bible."[8]

Finally, I came across an account of an All Souls Day celebration that took place in San Salvador during the 1980s, when the United States was actively supporting the Salvadoran government in a brutal counter-insurgency campaign that, interestingly enough, included the murder of several of the liberationists on whom my work here draws. Jon Sobrino describes one particularly compelling incident at that celebration:

> Around the altar on that day there were various cards with the names of family members who were dead or murdered. People would have liked to go to the cemetery to put flowers on their graves. But as they were locked up in the refuge and could not go, they painted flowers round their names. Beside the cards with the names of family members there was another card with no flowers which read: "Our dead enemies. May God forgive them and convert them." At the end of Eucharist we asked an old man what was the meaning of this last card and he told us this: "We made these cards as if we had gone to put flowers on our dead because it seemed to us they would feel we were with them. But as we are Christians, you know, we believed that our enemies should be on the altar too. They are our brothers in spite of the fact that they kill us and murder us. And you know what the Bible says. It is easy to love our own but God asks us to love those who persecute us."[9]

This project is an attempt to make sense of the card on the altar that read "Our dead enemies. May God forgive them and convert them." It is an effort to comprehend the power present at that celebration, the divine power that enabled the crucified people to reach out to their enemies, the enemies of God, with a love that just might overcome all sin and suffering and usher in an age where all gather round the table of God and share in its bounty as sisters and brothers.

Notes

1 Francis Fukuyama, "Reflections on *The End of History*, Five Years Later," in *After History? Francis Fukuyama and His Critics*, ed. Timothy Burns (Lanham, MD: Rowman & Littlefield Publishers, 1994), 241. Fukuyama's ideas are expounded in his article, "The End of History?" *National Interest* 16 (Summer 1989), 3–18 and the book *The End of History and the Last Man* (New York: The Free Press, 1992).

2 Michael Novak, *The Catholic Ethic and the Spirit of Capitalism* (New York: The Free Press, 1993), 101; Peter Berger, *The Capitalist Revolution* (New York: Basic Books, 1986).

3 Posing the relation between capitalism and Christianity in such starkly oppositional terms may strike some as rather incautious and overstated. My defense of this claim is the unfolding argument of this project.

4 John H. S. Kent, *The End of the Line? The Development of Christian Theology in the Last Two Centuries* (Philadelphia: Fortress Press, 1982), viii.

5 This may strike some as a rather strong claim simply to take for granted. However, far from being an exceptional claim, it is in fundamental accord with capitalism's neo-conservative defenders, who acknowledge both capitalism's disciplinary and sinful character. For example, with regard to the disciplinary character of capitalism, Michael Novak writes that "capitalism is not a set of neutral economic techniques amorally oriented toward efficiency. Its practice imposes certain moral and cultural attitudes, requirements, and demands." Likewise, with regard to capitalism's moral status, he writes, "Capitalism itself is not even close to being the Kingdom of God . . . The presuppositions, ethos, moral habits, and way of life required for the smooth functioning of democratic and capitalist institutions are not a full expression of Christian or Jewish faith, and are indeed partially in conflict with the full transcendent demands of Christian and Jewish faith." See *The Catholic Ethic and the Spirit of Capitalism*, 227–228.

6 This statement deserves a bit of attention. It is commonplace simply to assert that capitalism creates an acquisitive subject that is relentlessly driven to acquire and consume more and more. While it is one of the main pillars of my argument that the logic of capitalist discipline is a logic of acquisition and consumption, it is nevertheless a crude simplification to suggest that there is a single capitalist subject and that that subject is acquisitive. On the contrary, capitalism covers a broad spectrum of subject positions: from the hyper-acquisitive Trumps and Reagans (the latter a trope for the collective subjectivity of an empire), to the bulk of humanity, the "two-thirds" world who although hardly partaking of the fruits of the capitalist order are nevertheless subject to and disciplined by it. In other words, capitalist discipline celebrates consumption, but does not form all of its subjects as consumers. Many who are subjected to its discipline do not so much strive to consume and accumulate as struggle to survive.

Recognizing the polyvalence of capitalist subjectivity highlights the reason for focusing on technologies of desire. What distinguishes capitalism is not the formation of a particular subject, because there is no monolithic capitalist subject. Pressing this point, capitalism is distinguished neither by its formation of subjects with a passion to accumulate and consume nor by its perpetuation of the misery of the majority of humanity. Although perhaps intensified by capitalism, both conditions preceded capitalism.

Capitalism is distinguished by the technologies of desire embodied in the processes of production for the market it oversees. In other words, what sets capitalism apart is the way in which all desire is disciplined by the requirements of production for the market. Consequently, what can be said is that the plurality of capitalist subject positions share a "family resemblance" (to use Wittgenstein's well-known concept): they all are disciplined by the axiomatic of production for the market.

Hence, the focus of this project is neither the kind of subject capitalism produces nor the kind of subject needed to resist capitalism. Rather, the concern here is with technologies that may be able to release desire from capitalist discipline. In other words, the focus is primarily resistance, which undoubtedly will nourish multiple subjectivities.

7   See Rowan Williams, "Politics and the Soul: A Rereading of the City of God," *Milltown Studies* 19/20 (1987), 55–72; John Milbank, *Theology and Social Theory* (Oxford: Basil Blackwell, 1990): 380–438.

8   Gustavo Gutiérrez, *The Power of the Poor in History*, trans. Robert R. Barr (Maryknoll, NY: Orbis Books, 1983), 204.

9   Jon Sobrino, *The Principle of Mercy* (Maryknoll, NY: Orbis Books, 1994), 63.

1

THE INFINITE UNDULATIONS
OF THE SNAKE

Capitalism, desire, and the state-form

Latin American liberationists insist that theological reflection carefully attend to the contours of contemporary reality. Accordingly, I begin this account of Christianity as a font of resistance to capitalism with an analysis of contemporary capitalism. Specifically, the principal task of this chapter is to display contemporary capitalism as a discipline of desire. This display proceeds in several steps. First, I introduce contemporary capitalism by taking up Franz Hinkelammert's analysis of "savage capitalism." Hinkelammert's work is useful insofar as it serves as a salutary introduction both to the Latin American liberationists, who are the primary foil for my argument, and to several themes that will occupy center stage throughout this work. Moreover, given that the benevolence of capitalism has attained the status of a veritable truism today, Hinkelammert's unflinchingly critical (and some might be tempted to add, unnuanced) appraisal of capitalism serves as a poignant reminder that capitalism's triumph has not been achieved without a certain cost being borne by those whom Fukuyama dismisses as still "mired in history."[1] Second, I engage the work of Gilles Deleuze on capitalism and desire. Deleuze's work suggests the victory of savage capitalism is not simply economic; it is, more insidiously, ontological. Capitalism, Deleuze argues, extends its dominion over humanity not merely through the extraction of labor and production of wealth, but by capturing and distorting the constitutive human power, desire. Moreover, Deleuze's analysis implicates the state-form in the capitalist capture of desire, which brings us to Michel Foucault and his work on "governmentality." This complements Deleuze's account and completes the display of contemporary capitalism as a discipline of desire by showing that the state-form encompasses much more than that ensemble of institutions called "the state," that it encompasses a whole host of "technologies of desire": technologies present in the social, cultural, and religious as well as political and economic registers that shape and form desire in particular ways. Finally, I conclude by briefly suggesting why even as we learn from Deleuze and Foucault, we must look beyond them if there is to be any hope of desire escaping capitalist discipline and attaining its true end.

Savage capitalism

Even as Fukuyama lauds neoliberal capitalism as the beacon of prosperity and hope astride the pinnacle of history, Latin American liberationists denounce global capitalism as a brutal and oppressive force responsible for the misery and premature death of much of the world's population. Given that the Latin American liberationists have long been concerned with the expansion of the capitalist order on account of the suffering and misery that it has perpetrated and is perpetuating, this is unsurprising. Indeed one could cogently argue that it is precisely the bold and uncompromising critique to which the capitalist order was subjected by theologians such as Hugo Assmann, Gustavo Gutiérrez, and Juan Luis Segundo that first attracted attention to liberation theology.

In the years since the end of history was announced, one of the bolder analyses of contemporary capitalism to emerge from the Latin American liberationists is that of Franz Hinkelammert. In an article that has resonated in the work of many liberationists, entitled "The crisis of socialism and the Third World," Hinkelammert exposes the underside of the "end of history".[2] In bold strokes that indubitably would inflame capitalism's partisans, Hinkelammert develops three theses on recent changes in the international capitalist order, changes that amount to the advent of a new era he calls "savage capitalism."

Three theses on contemporary capitalism

The first thesis is nothing less than a concession of defeat. Hinkelammert acknowledges capitalism's victory. Capitalism has won. Its rivals have been soundly defeated. "The world that now appears and announces itself is a world in which there exists only one lord and master, and only one system," writes Hinkelammert. "[T]here no longer remains any place of asylum . . . The empire is everywhere. It has total power and it knows it . . . The consciousness that an alternative exists is lost. It seems there are no longer alternatives."[3] For the Third World, this amounts to being cut loose from even the minimal assistance it had previously received. With the ascendancy of the capitalist order, with the extension of its empire, Third World countries lost the strategic importance they once possessed as pawns that the competing superpowers would play off against each other.

The Third World now finds itself adrift in the midst of what Hinkelammert calls "wild" or "savage" capitalism.[4] In the 1950s and 1960s capitalism was tempered by a reformist current that went by the name of developmentalism. At that time, even as the capitalist market was acknowledged to be largely self-regulating, it was nevertheless recognized that the market, left to its own devices, was unable to assure development and solve the grave socio-economic problems that afflicted the Latin American continent. Consequently, the welfare state, public investment, and industrialization by means of import substitution were all accepted components of this "capitalism with a human face."[5] The 1970s, however, marked a shift towards a more extreme, unfettered capitalism. This was the beginning of the era of Milton

Friedman's "total capitalism," of neoliberal economics, and "structural adjustment." This is the capitalism of the era for which Ronald Reagan and Margaret Thatcher are icons: anti-interventionist, anti-reformist, anti-populist. In short, capitalism shorn of its human face.

One of the central precepts of this naked capitalism is an aggressive anti-statism. In contrast to the earlier phase of capitalism, which conceded a necessary regulatory role to the state, savage capitalism denounces all state intervention in the market and sets about dismantling the welfare state and selling off state-owned enterprises. In Latin America this anti-statism was incarnate in the national security states that appeared in the 1970s and 1980s, Chile under Pinochet being the paradigmatic example. This anti-statism, however, is deceptive. It amounts to a minimalist state that only renounces its regulatory and welfare role. While savage capitalism's advocates say they are anti-statist, in truth, what they favor is a "small-state, strong-state."[6] That is, they are advocates of a state that is long on repressive capability and short on social assistance. What is forsaken, in other words, is not intervention, but intervention that obstructs the free operation of the market. The neoliberal state is a police state or anti-state, the function of which is essentially negative. It exists as a repressive tool of the market, used to deliver society to the market.

With the advent of this savage capitalism, states Hinkelammert's second thesis, the population of the Third World is rendered largely redundant. It is no longer needed; it is excluded. Production in the Third World has traditionally developed on the basis of its labor force and its raw materials. Today, however, that labor force is increasingly being rendered superfluous. Advances in productive technology mean that capitalism needs less of the available labor. "The First World still needs the Third World," Hinkelammert writes, "its seas, its air, its nature, even if only as a garbage dump for the First World's poisonous garbage. Its raw materials continue being needed. What is no longer needed is the greater part of the population of the Third World."[7] The market's logic of maximum efficiency entails the sacrifice of redundant populations. Capitalism simply does not need this many people – all these unnecessary, dangerous people. They are excess. Hence, with the arrival of savage capitalism, it becomes a privilege to be exploited: Hinkelammert cites a Latin American saying, "It is bad to be exploited by the multinationals. It is worse, however, not to be exploited by them."[8] Third World countries increasingly find themselves competing with one another for limited openings in the international capitalist market, with the consequence that more and more people are not even able to find a place on the margins of this system. They are excluded, discarded to wander outside the productive system, foraging in the garbage dumps and making newspaper cakes for their children.[9]

In this situation development is not possible for Third World countries; indeed, the central countries consider Third World development on the basis of industrial integration into the world market a threat. This is Hinkelammert's third thesis.[10] Third World development is no longer perceived as a goal to be attained, but a threat to be squelched. With its arrival in the 1970s, savage capitalism did not establish industry that could competitively enter the world market. Rather, it renounced industrialization and silenced the masses with the terrorism of the national security state. Instead of fostering efficient enterprise, it reduced Latin America, once again, to the exportation of raw materials and agricultural products. Instead of overcoming underdevelopment, an efficient underdevelopment was pursued.[11] Even if a few small countries have escaped the First World's grip, the visible tendency in the Third World is away from self-sustainable industrialization. Even those industries that were established in prior decades have been targeted for destruction or stagnation. The First World countries simply no longer see any advantage to be gained from allowing and encouraging this kind of development. Accordingly, savage capitalism opts for the maximization of profit over development. Perhaps the clearest example of this policy is the collection of the Third World's foreign debt. The debt is the primary tool with which Third World development is suppressed. The structural adjustment policies that are part and parcel of that debt insure that the debtor country will be unable to develop in a manner that would allow it to achieve a favorable insertion into the world market. In this way, Hinkelammert argues, the West has found a method of shedding blood that easily allows it to wash any stain off its hands.[12]

What conclusions does Hinkelammert draw in the face of savage capitalism's triumph? There are no visible, viable alternatives to the current vicious order. We are, as he suggests in the title of another article, stuck in a moment of uncertainty, "¿Capitalismo sin Alternativas?"[13] We remain in the grip of a "mysticism of death," a madness, a culture that in its destruction of people and nature amounts to a celebration of collective suicide.[14]

A savage capitalism, repressive states, excluded populations, madness, sacrifice, and the absence of alternatives. These are matters that will occupy our attention for much of the remainder of this work. But first we must ask, how did we arrive in this condition? How has capitalism accomplished this victory? For the beginning of an answer we turn to Gilles Deleuze and his history of desire and capitalism.

Capitalism and desire

Gilles Deleuze is frequently characterized as a postmodern philosopher; about such philosophers there is a debate over the extent to which they are or are not political.[15] In the case of Deleuze, there can be little dispute. His philosophy is political through and through.[16] This is perhaps nowhere more apparent than in his account of capitalism and desire. In the wake of the failed revolution of 1968 in France, Deleuze turned his attention to rethinking revolutionary politics.[17] Perceiving the bankruptcy of both social democracy and Soviet state socialism as forms of resistance to and liberation from the advancing capitalist order, he began an effort to think otherwise, to explore new ways of conceiving human relations and revolutionary practice. The result of this effort was a history of capitalism and desire, a history that suggests contemporary capitalism's dominion is not merely an economic affair – concerning modes of production, the efficient manipulation of labor, and the creation of wealth – but is ontological. Capitalism's victory hinges on its successful capture and discipline of the constitutive human power, desire.

Politics and ontology

The philosophical point of departure for Deleuze's history of capitalism and desire is the claim that "politics precedes being."[18] This enigmatic statement serves as a fitting introduction to his history insofar as it provides a glimpse of the politics and ontology that underpin it. Politically, the claim that "politics precedes being" is a critique of would-be revolutionaries whose vision of resistance to the capitalist order is circumscribed and hence crippled by the "social unconscious":[19] that ensemble of ideas, institutions, and social arrangements erected and propagated by state, party, class, etc. but attributed a certain fixed, unquestioned status as a "given." In particular, Deleuze's account of capitalism and desire is meant to challenge the unquestioned assumption of would-be revolutionaries that politics and therefore revolutionary struggle are a matter of statecraft. The modern vision of "politics as statecraft" was given its classic articulation by Max Weber when he defined politics as "the leadership, or the influencing of the leadership, of a *political* association, hence today, of a *state*."[20] "Politics as statecraft" is the conception of politics that emerged with the Enlightenment and reached its pinnacle in Hegel that holds that the realm where persons come together in a polity, in a politics, is rightly overseen by and finds its highest expression in the state; it is the investiture of the state with sovereign authority over the socius and, consequently, privileging the state as the fulcrum of social and political change. The assertion that "politics precedes being" calls this into question by suggesting that the arrangement of social space is not in fact attended by a metaphysical fixity that would bestow upon a particular arrangement the status of an unchanging and unchangeable "given." More specifically, the organization of social space with the state at its summit does not precede the multitude of contingent relations that constitute social space. In other words, this arrangement of social space, with the sovereign state at its center, is a particular arrangement of social space, an arrangement that can (and, as we shall see, must) be otherwise.

As a critique of the politics of statecraft, "politics precedes being" is the instantiation of what Deleuze calls a "micropolitics of desire."[21] As he describes it, a micropolitics of desire is concerned with the multiplicity of becomings, the fluidity of forces that interact in every moment to produce life.[22] Here we arrive at the ontology proper undergirding his account of capitalism and desire. Reaching back to the medieval theologian, Duns Scotus, Deleuze develops an ontology of difference anchored in the univocity of being. Simply put, the proposition that being is univocal means that "being" has only one sense and is said in one and the same sense of everything of which it is said.[23] For medievals such as Scotus, this meant that God is deemed "to be" in the same univocal manner as creatures.[24] At first, this would appear to be a rather odd way to establish an ontology of difference that celebrates multiplicity, becoming, and flux. If being is univocal, then what could the difference between beings be? Deleuze answers, again echoing Scotus, that difference is a matter of degrees of power, or, rather, degrees of desire.[25] Everything is desire, flows of desire. What distinguishes desire, what renders desire distinct, singular, is a matter of degree. Univocal being, desire, is differentiated by degrees of intensity. "Between a table, a little boy, a little girl, a locomotive, a cow, a god, the difference is solely one of degree of power in the realization of one and the same being."[26]

Coupled with the claim that desire is univocal is the further claim that desire is productive. Production constitutes the immanent principle of desire. Accordingly, desire cannot be mistaken for a lack, deficiency, or absence.[27] Desire is not a desire for something; it is not a matter of acquiring or grasping an object. It is not about possession. Nor is it a matter of meeting needs or seeking pleasure; this, too, would be a lack. Rather, desire produces; it gives. It works. It creates.[28] Desire is a positive force, an aleatory movement that neither destroys nor consumes but endlessly creates new connections with others, embraces difference, and fosters a proliferation of relations between fluxes of desire.

The world, then, is constituted by flows of intensities of desire. The movement of desire, however, is not anarchic. By means of various machines (social machines and their formations of power, semiotic machines and their regimes of signs), desire is always already organized or assembled. For example, society is an assemblage of desire. A given society or social formation is nothing other than productive desire under determinate conditions: "the social field is immediately invested by desire, . . . it is the historically determined product of desire."[29] Society, in other words, is the effect of the assembly of desire in a particular way by a host of social formations and semiotic codes. The subject, likewise, is an assemblage of desire. No less than society, human subjectivity is the product of desire under determinate conditions. The subject is an assemblage of intensities of desire; it is the result of the capture of desire by a particular regime of subjectification.

If desire is always already assembled, however, it is not necessarily assembled in one particular way (one privileged form of society, one privileged subjectivity). This returns us to where we began, with the statement, "politics precedes being." This means that any and every assembly or organization of desire is inherently unstable, that resistance and revolution are always possible. This is the case because in Deleuze's ontology desire is de-finalized; it is shorn of any teleology. Desire resists any and every end, any and every assembly and organization. Simply by virtue of its being the intrinsically productive, creative, anarchic force that it is, desire is antagonistic to every attempt to capture and assemble it. Desire is intrinsically antagonistic to every organization and hence at any moment may find a line of flight, a crack in that order and explode it. As a consequence, every organization, every social formation, every subjectivity is a contingent, unstable assemblage of desire, whose duration is uncertain – lasting a day, a season, a year, a life – and order is nothing but a temporary checking of disorder; stability nothing but variation within tenuous limits.[30]

Desire, capitalism, and the state-form

In light of the proposition "politics precedes being," then, we can surmise that the advent of savage capitalism is not cast by Deleuze as the "end of history" whereby desire has attained its true repose. To the contrary, capitalism's victory is a matter of the contingent capture and disciplining of desire. However, the relation of capitalism to desire is not as immediate as this might suggest, for capitalism's victory is subsequent to the work of social formations, such as the state-form. Capitalism depends on social machines for the organization of the social basis of production. This is to say, capitalism acts on desire that has already been assembled, made receptive, by means of the social machine that is the state-form.[31] Thus, according to Deleuze, the history of capitalism and desire is the history of the struggle between desire and three manifestations of the state-form that have sought to capture desire.

The first of these is the archaic imperial state, which acted upon primitive agricultural communities. These communities organized or assembled desire according to lineal-territorial codes. The flows of goods, people, and privileges were coded according to kinship (filiation) and marriage (alliance). With the arrival of the archaic state, these primitive territorial codes are now deterritorialized by being subjected to the despotic overcoding of the emperor. The imperial state's overcoding simultaneously effects a reterritorialization of the primitive codes of people, labor, and gift/debt whereby a particular kind of property, money, and labor are formed. The emperor becomes the sole public-property owner, the master of the surplus or stock, the organizer of large-scale works, and the cornerstone of all public functions.[32] Humans are subjected to enslavement to the extent that they become constituent pieces of a machine that is under the control of a higher unity. The primitive codes are forced into a bottleneck: a new inscription is established that makes all desire the property of the sovereign.[33] In other words, the primitive codes cease to be self-regulating and come under the jurisdiction of a transcendent agency, the state.

Recalling the preceding discussion of Deleuze's ontology, however, we know that the state's jurisdiction is always uncertain, unstable, contested. The law of the state, Deleuze writes, is not the law of all or nothing.[34] The arrival of the state is not the arrival of a power that imprisons the entire social field of desire. The state exercises sovereignty, but it reigns only over what it successfully captures or interiorizes, and while it may succeed in capturing and disciplining some flows of desire, it does not capture all. Hence, the state's control is always tenuous, contingent. The sovereignty enjoyed by the state is contingent upon the state's ability to continuously exert control that fixes relations of desire on part of the social field.

State sovereignty always being tenuous and contested, it is unsurprising that the archaic state's effort at overcoding the primitive society is not entirely successful. In the process of overcoding, the archaic state frees large quantities of decoded flows of desire that elude capture:

> The State does not create large-scale works without a flow of independent labor escaping from its bureaucracy (notably in the mines and metal-lurgy). It does not create the monetary form of the tax without flows of money escaping, nourishing or bringing into being other powers (notably in commerce and banking). And above all, it does not create a system of public property without a flow of private appropriation growing up *beside* it, then beginning to pass beyond its grasp.[35]

Flows escape its overcoding, and in an effort to capture them, the archaic state undergoes a mutation. Extremely diverse states – evolved empires, autonomous cities, feudal systems, monarchies – now appear. These states no longer operate on the basis of overcoding or the enslavement of primitive codes, rather they function to organize conjunctions of decoded flows of desire. They proceed not by enslave-ment but by subjectification and subjection. Flows of labor, money, and property are no longer captured and put at the service of the public sovereign. Instead the state becomes a machine that regulates deterritorialized flows, that coordinates and integrates relations of flows it can no longer contain. Hence, according to this regime, the human being is no longer enslaved by or a component of the machine but becomes a worker or user who is subjected to the machine.

This mutation constitutes a subtle shift in the topography of the social field. Whereas the archaic state attempts (always unsuccessfully) to circumscribe the social field through overcoding, the diverse state is itself positioned on the social field traversed by decoded flows. The archaic state functioned as the transcendent unity of the social field; the new state-form has become immanent to the field of social forces. Its ability to capture flows of desire being overwhelmed, this state no longer attempts to prevent the decoded flows from flowing and ceaselessly engen-dering new flows; instead, the best this new state can achieve is the regulation of decoded flows; that is, it manages to fix or limit the relations between persons and things, between labor and capital. In a sense it is able to tie a knot in the flows at certain points: decoded flows are still bound by concrete forms and personal rela-tions of dependence. Private property is still associated with particular, concrete land, people, and things. Labor is still tied to individual workers' relations of dependence on particular owners. The decoded flows are still inhibited or con-strained.

Yet flows of desire escape even these limited restraints, and they continue to escape until the diverse state-form is overwhelmed. This happens as the flow of labor escapes determination as slavery or serfdom (concrete relations of personal dependency) and becomes naked, free labor and as wealth is no longer merchant's or landed wealth (wealth tied to concrete land, people, things) but becomes pure homogeneous capital, a filiative capital where money begets money and value begets surplus value.[36] History is now on the brink of capitalism. Capitalism is born when decoded flows of desire overwhelm the state's ability to perform topi-cal conjunctions (tying labor and capital to specific, concrete people, land, or things), and flows of unqualified labor encounter flows of unqualified capital.

Thus, the advent of capitalism is the crossing of a new threshold of deterritorialization. Capitalism mobilizes forces of deterritorialization that infinitely surpass those of the state.[37] The various state-forms deterritorialized desire – freeing it from the previous social formation's coding and overcoding – but their deterritorialization was always relative; they always reattached desire (in the form of labor and capital) to the earth, to the concrete territories under the state's relative control. Capitalism, however, is not at all territorial.[38] Its object is the abstract, generalized flow of labor and capital. For this reason, Deleuze identifies capitalism as a general axiomatic of decoded flows. It is an axiomatic, dealing "directly with purely functional elements and relations whose nature is not specified, and which are immediately realized in highly varied domains simultaneously," as opposed to dealing in codes, which "are relative to those domains and express specific relations between qualified elements."[39] Hence, capitalism oversees an "enormous, so-called stateless, monetary mass that circulates through foreign exchange and across borders, eluding control by the States, forming a multinational ecumenical organization, constituting a *de facto* supranational power untouched by governmental decisions."[40] Savage capitalism exemplifies this superior deterritorializing force with particular clarity as capital assumes the form of the transnational corporation, the division of labor is internationalized, flexible manufacturing systems are advanced, a standardized market/global culture and consumption patterns expand, the informal sector of the economy grows, complex systems of credit and exchange are introduced, and so forth.[41] Each of these developments reflects capitalism's abstract, deterritorializing nature: capitalism is not constrained by any territory or tied to any organizing center.

With the advent of capitalism, with its infinitely superior forces of deterritorialization, the usefulness of the state-form, with its limited deterritorializing power, is called into question. What, if any, role does the state have in this new context or has it been rendered obsolete? Obviously, the state-form is still with us; the birth of capitalism has not rendered it superfluous. Quite the contrary, with the rise of capitalism the state-form undergoes another mutation. This time the modern nation-state emerges as the pinnacle of the becoming-immanent of the state-form. The modern nation-state is the state-form completely subsumed by the capitalist axiomatic. Capitalism is "an independent, worldwide axiomatic that is like a single City, megapolis, or 'megamachine' of which the States are parts or neighborhoods."[42] In this setting, instead of functioning as a transcendent paradigm of overcoding, the state operates as a model of realization for the worldwide capitalist axiomatic. "Never before," writes Deleuze, "has a State lost so much of its power in order to enter with so much force into the service of the signs of economic power."[43] States serve capitalism by organizing and combining the various domains in which capital is realized. They organize the social basis of production and prepare it for insertion into the worldwide capitalist machine (think of recent governmental efforts on behalf of NAFTA and GATT).

This holds true for all states. All states serve capitalism. The capitalist axiomatic is like a megapolis of which all the nations constitute neighborhoods. And these neighborhoods need not look alike. As an international ecumenical organization, capitalism neither proceeds from an imperial center that imposes itself on and homogenizes an exterior nor is it reducible to a relation between similar formations.[44] The neighborhoods need not be homogeneous, for the capitalist axiomatic is capable of traversing diverse social formations simultaneously. It is not wedded to any single mode of production or logic of accumulation but instead effects an "isomorphy" between formations – be they states or modes of production. In other words, capitalism as an axiomatic can effect surplus value from a diversity of formations. As Deleuze writes:

> To the extent that capitalism constitutes an axiomatic (production for the market), all States and all social formations tend to become *isomorphic* in their capacity as models of realization: there is but one centered world market, the capitalist one, in which even the so-called socialist countries participate . . . [I]somorphy allows, and even incites, a great heterogeneity among States (democratic, totalitarian, and especially, "socialist" States are not facades).[45]

The recent history of New Labour's rule in Britain, of socialist France, or of García's Peru bear this out.

The unity or consistency of the capitalist axiomatic consists in the relation of production for the market. How production for the market is effected is flexible, as long as desire produces for the market. There is a relative independence of the capitalist axioms. They can be added, as was the case following the World Wars – axioms for the working class, employment, union organization, social institutions, the environment, the role of the state, domestic and foreign markets, and so forth – or they can be subtracted, as was the case in Chile under Pinochet, NAFTA and GATT, and as characterizes savage capitalism generally. Capitalism is flexible: whatever it takes to ensure production for the market.

This flexibility insures the isomorphy of the models of realization and consequently the integration of non-capitalist sectors and modes into the market. Take the example of the Third World. The neoconservatives are not wrong when they point out that much of Latin America is not "capitalist" in the classic sense associated with the presence of capitalist modes of production. Where they err is (among other things) in their failure to appreciate the flexibility of contemporary capitalism. Hence, capital acts as the relation of production even in the non-capitalist modes that predominate in the Third World. Thus, the underdeveloped sectors do not constitute a separate world but rather are integral components of the worldwide capitalist megapolis. It is as though capitalism has put a new twist on Augustine's famous dictum, "Love and do as you please." Now it is, "Produce for the market and do as you please." This flexibility accounts for the productive topography of domains like Brazil or North Carolina.[46] In Brazil there is a broad spectrum of modes of production, from the Stone Age production of the indigenous peoples of the Amazon basin to the advanced computer technology of São

Paolo. These very different modes of production co-exist within the same national space and produce for the same market. Amazonian artifacts appear on the tourist markets of downtown São Paolo beside laptop computers and video cameras.[47] A similar situation, although perhaps not as pronounced in its extremes, exists in North Carolina, where the Research Triangle Park engages the most technologically advanced production, while virtually in its shadow, migrants harvest tobacco in conditions resembling those of slavery.

As capitalism has enveloped the globe, all states function as models of realization for capital. In the era of savage capitalism, the principal way this function is carried out is negative. States find their *raison d'être* in reterritorializing the flows of desire that capitalism unleashes. When capitalism advances, it deterritorializes desire, releasing it from its captivity to prior social formations and codes. The modern state, functioning as an apparatus of capture, reterritorializes this desire so that it is available to capital. As is painfully clear to the countless Latin Americans who have felt the state's wrath in response to their resisting capitalism's advance, and as is becoming increasingly clear to North Americans (in Seattle, for example), the "small-state, strong-state" of savage capitalism exists to neutralize and crush resistance, to block the flow of desire that it might not escape altogether and recover its original aleatory movement.

At this point, we arrive at the place where Foucault's account of governmentality proves illuminating. Deleuze's account of capitalism and desire suggests that capitalism disciplines desire and that it does so by means of a sort of pincer movement. The capitalist machine deterritorializes desire: it overruns all previous social formations and releases the flows of desire that these formations had organized and regulated. The capitalist machine also reterritorializes desire: it subjects desire to the axiomatic of production for the market. In this process capitalism relies on the state-form to prepare desire for participation in the capitalist order. This is where Foucault is helpful.

Governmentality and technologies of the self

Deleuze displays capitalism as a discipline of desire and suggests that the state is not an emancipatory agent but a repressive instrument of the capitalist order. Supplementing Deleuze's account with Michel Foucault's work on governmentality is useful because Foucault illumines the ways in which capitalist dominion is extended by means much more insidious than the state. In other words, Foucault reminds us that the state-form of which Deleuze wrote is much more than the ensemble of institutions called "the state." Rather, it is a project that includes a whole host of what Foucault called "technologies of the self."

Beheading the king: power beyond the state

In response to criticism that he neglected larger social and political systems (like "the state"), towards the end of his life Foucault shifted his attention from analyses of discursive formations and apparatuses of power, for which he was well known, to what he called "governmentality." If the turn to governmentality, however, is in part a response to those who pressed Foucault to develop a more explicit analysis of political entities like the state, then it is undoubtedly not the response for which they were hoping, for Foucault's account of governmentality does not propound a theory of the state as such. To the contrary, what Foucault says about govern-mentality may be read as a repudiation of any attempt to put forward a theory of the state. It is as if Foucault responded to his critics with an attack on every account of political power that concentrates such power in institutions of the state, that attempts to anchor government in essential properties and propensities of the state. Foucault argued on several occasions that "We need to cut off the King's head"[48] and by this he meant that there was a need to move political theory (and revolutionary practice) beyond its obsession with the state. Models of thought and practice that continued to conceive of power as something essentially negative and as the sole possession of the state are bankrupt. Such models effect-ively conceal the many ways – positive as well as negative – in which power is actually exercised. They overlook "all the mechanisms and effects of power which don't pass directly via the State apparatus, yet often sustain the State more effect-ively than its own institutions, enlarging and maximizing its effectiveness."[49] Foucault explains:

> I don't want to say that the State isn't important; what I want to say is that relations of power, and hence the analysis that must be made of them, necessarily extend beyond the limits of the State. In two senses: first of all because the State, for all the omnipotence of its apparatuses, is far from being able to occupy the whole field of actual power relations, and further because the State can only operate on the basis of other, already existing power relations. The State is superstructural in relation to a whole series of power networks that invest the body, sexuality, the family, kinship, knowledge, technology and so forth.[50]

Neither the source nor the sole proprietor of power, the state exists on a field that is always already crossed by power, by relations of power. Thus, those who would resist the deprivations of the current order need to look beyond the state; they need to attend to the whole series of power networks that invest the socius.

Implicit in this move beyond the state is an ontology with close parallels to that of Deleuze. Just as Deleuze held that reality consists of omnipresent productive power, Foucault holds that reality is constituted by a positive power that is dis-persed, present everywhere, with no singular or unique source.[51] Therefore, when the state exercises power, it does so only to the extent that it manages successfully to harness or capture some of those always already existing forces. It is the recog-nition that the state is not the sole proprietor of power that prompts consideration of what Foucault calls "governmentality."

Technologies of power

Governmentality is quite simply the art of government. In the light of the pre-ceding discussion of the need to "behead the king," Foucault clearly does not mean by "the art of government" what is commonly meant by that term today, namely the machinations and deceits of the agents and institutions of modern political life. Rather, Foucault refers to government in the broadest of senses, as the "conduct of conduct." Governmentality, he says, concerns, "[h]ow to govern one-self, how to be governed, how to govern others, by whom the people will accept being governed, how to become the best possible governor."[52] A broad definition indeed. Governmentality concerns the conduct of oneself and the conduct of others at the micro and macro political levels. At the macro level, governmentality engages power in terms of political sovereignty – the state and society. At the micro level, it engages power in terms of individual conduct. This distinction between the two dimensions of governmentality is further clarified when Foucault distinguishes between four technologies of power:

> (1) technologies of production, which permit us to produce, transform, or manipulate things; (2) technologies of sign systems, which permit us to use signs, meanings, symbols, or signification; (3) technologies of power, which determine the conduct of individuals and submit them to certain ends or domination, an objectivizing of the subject; (4) technologies of the self, which permit individuals to effect by their own means or with the help of others a certain number of operations on their own bodies and souls, thoughts, conduct, and way of being, so as to transform themselves in order to attain a certain state of happiness, purity, wisdom, perfection, or immortality.[53]

Technologies, according to Foucault, are ensembles of knowledges, instruments, persons, systems of judgment, buildings, and spaces bound together by certain pre-suppositions and objectives.[54] Governmentality, he says, concerns the convergence of the last two technologies, technologies of domination and technologies of the self, totalizing power and individualizing power.[55] Governmentality encompasses the relation between the totalizing power that the state exercises as a framework for unity and the individualizing power that Foucault calls "pastoral," a power that aims at ensuring, sustaining, and improving the lives of each and every individual.[56]

Pastoral power

At this point, Foucault's account of governmentality takes the form of a genealogy, which commences with the emergence of pastoral power in ancient Oriental soci-eties, particularly the Hebrews, prior to its adaptation by the early Christians. The term "pastoral power" is derived from the shepherd's practice of watching over sheep. The idea of a deity or king functioning as a shepherd flourished among

Oriental societies, especially the Hebrews, where God and eventually the monarch was cast as the shepherd of the people.[57] This is in contrast with the ancient Greeks, to whom this particular style of power was foreign.[58] Whereas the Greeks cast their God as possessing the land, which mediated the relation between the people and the deity, the pastoral image casts the deity as directly owning the people. Whereas the Greek idea of a good lawgiver is of one who establishes a strong system that is able to function without the lawgiver's presence, the pastoral model assumes the immediate, direct, and sustained involvement of the shepherd in the maintenance of the flock. Whereas the Greek deity saves the community as a community, the shepherd saves the whole flock by means of constant, individualized kindness. Finally, whereas the Greeks cast the wielding of power as a duty of sorts, the shepherd exercises power as a devotion. The shepherd watches over and attends to the needs of each one of the flock; power is more personal.[59]

According to Foucault, Christianity appropriated and intensified this individualizing pastoral power and it did so primarily through techniques developed to aid in the discovery and formulation of the truth about oneself, namely, the practices of examination of conscience and confession. Of course, Christianity did not develop these practices *ex nihilo* but appropriated them from the ancient Greeks and Romans. Ancient Greco-Roman philosophy had encouraged self-examination and "knowing thyself" as part of a tradition of practices known as "the care of the self." Foucault emphasizes two aspects of this ancient tradition that are significant with regard to Christianity's adaptation of the tradition. First, the ancient tradition is administrative rather than juridical. That is, the point of self-knowledge is not to judge or condemn the self but to aid the self in establishing itself, in attaining the truth. Second, the focus of the examination is not thoughts and intentions, but activity. The Ancients concerned themselves with what they did; they did not interrogate their thoughts with the goal of uncovering an elusive desire that lurked just beyond awareness.[60]

As early Christianity developed a pastoral power, it intensified that power by radically transforming the Greco-Roman practice of "the care of the self." According to Foucault, this occurred as the practice of confession and penance developed. The earliest form of confession and penance developed a technology of self-disclosure known as *exomologesis*. Several facets of this practice bear directly on the intensification of pastoral power. First, whereas the Greco-Roman tradition was essentially private, Christian practice involved *public* confession. This amounted to an intensification of pastoral power insofar as public confession coupled to an elaborate and complex system of sin and merit meant that the shepherd now acquired intimate knowledge of every detail of the sheep's life. Second, while the medical and juridical models prevalent in the earlier tradition were not absent, by far the most prominent model used to explain *exomologesis* was the model of death or torture or martyrdom. Penance was a ritual martyrdom. It marked a rupture of the self with the self, the past, and the world. Hence, Christian care of the self was oriented not so much towards the acquisition of truth and the establishment of a self as it was towards the renunciation and sacrifice of the self. "In the ostentatious gestures of maceration," Foucault observes, "self-revelation in *exomologesis* is, at the same time, self-destruction."[61]

Foucault then takes up *exagoreusis*, the form of confession and penance that developed in the monastic traditions of the fourth century and that marks a further modification and intensification of the ancient tradition in two important ways. First, obedience became a permanent and comprehensive relation that was an end in itself.[62] In the ancient tradition, the obedience of a disciple to a master was of limited duration and a means to the good life. Second, as a result of the elevation of contemplation, self-examination became much more concerned with thoughts than with actions, with present thoughts rather than past actions.[63] Whereas according to the classic technology, examination was for the sake of making adjustments to acts, thereby reducing the gap between what one did and what one ought to have done, the Christian technology was geared towards excavating guilt. Furthermore, this excavation could occur only by means of verbalization: confession to another. Both of these alterations – concerning obedience and verbalization of thought – reflect *exagoreusis* as a further refinement of a technology of self-disclosure geared towards the renunciation and sacrifice of the self.

Reason of state

From the Christian expansion of pastoral power Foucault's narrative jumps to the fifteenth and sixteenth centuries, for it is here, with the rise of the modern state, that individualizing pastoral power is coupled with the totalizing power of the state. This occurred as the doctrine of "reason of state" and its accompanying "science of police" developed.

The Italian jurist Giovanni Botero, in his 1589 treatise entitled *The Reason of State*, defined reason of state as a "perfect knowledge of the means through which states form, strengthen themselves, endure, and grow."[64] This definition brings to the fore several distinctives of this emergent doctrine. First, it is regarded as an art, as a technique that conforms to certain rules. These rules, moreover, are not matters of custom or tradition but rather they pertain to a certain rational knowledge. Second, the rationale for this art of government is the state itself.

The novelty of this rationale is brought into high relief when considered against the double foil of Christianity and Machiavelli. The medieval Christian tradition subordinated temporal government to supernatural ends; that is, just government was government in accord with a hierarchy of human, natural, and divine laws. Reason of state, in contrast, operates on a much more mundane logic. Crowning a trend begun at least as early as the eleventh century, reason of state asserted that temporal government was not accountable to any transcendent law or principle. Instead, it held, the principles of government are immanent in the state itself. This logic also clashed with the tradition of princely sovereignty, of which Machiavelli's *The Prince* (1513) is the most famous example. Machiavelli gives an account of public power that is personal and charismatic and that is located in the person of the prince. Hence, when Machiavelli refers to "the state," he does so in accord with what was at that time the commonplace meaning, namely, he is refer-ring to the general condition of the ruler.[65] The doctrine of reason of state, however, marks a departure from that tradition. Reason of state was concerned neither with the wisdom of God nor with the strategies of princes; rather its con-cern was the viability and durability of the state irrespective of the security of the particular ruler.[66] With the emergence of reason of state, political power is no longer located in the person of the prince but is equated with an ensemble of insti-tutions and means of coercion distinct from both the people and the prince. Maintaining the state no longer means assuring the sovereign's personal ascen-dancy over the realm; rather it now concerns the apparatuses of government that the ruler is obliged to maintain. In other words, the state emerges in its own right and the aim of government is to strengthen the state.[67]

The attainment of this end presupposed a certain kind of knowledge, which is the third distinctive feature of reason of state. Whereas the Christian tradition asserted that the ruler must be virtuous, reason of state marks the advent of the politician, the ruler for whom not virtue but a specific political competence and knowledge are paramount. Government of the state, now understood as an ensem-ble of institutions that organize and preserve order within a particular domain, is only possible if the state's capabilities and limitations are firmly grasped. Government is henceforth bound to knowledge. The state's ability to act depends on a concrete, precise, measured knowledge of the state's strength. Consequently, the art of governing characteristic of reason of state was closely associated with the development of what was then called political statistics or political arithmetic and the concept of "population." The subjects of government were now assembled on a grid that could be observed, measured, and recorded (birth and mortality rates, geographic distribution, and so on).

Finally, reason of state entails a new, pastoral kind of relationship between the state and the individual. Under the old regimes of sovereignty, the sovereign's relation with his or her subjects was relatively loose and impersonal. The sovereign essentially taxed and ruled on death. With the emergence of reason of state, how-ever, the state is no longer content just to tax; now it must organize productive activity. It is no longer satisfied with ruling on death; now it administers life. This pastoral relationship is a consequence of the state's changing rationale. Reason of state is concerned first and foremost with strengthening and perpetuating the state, but it realizes that its strength and prosperity lie in the strength and prosperity of its population. The state, therefore, takes an abiding interest in the individual details of its subjects' lives.[68] Each individual is now addressed (measured by the new political statistics) in terms of how that individual's life may contribute to or detract from the state's strength.

The science of police and the disciplines

As reason of state flourished, with its distinctive rationale (the state) and knowledge (statistics, population), it was given concrete form by a technique or practice of power that developed in seventeenth-century Europe under the name the "science of police." The term "police" is not used here in the essentially negative, contemporary sense of an institution for the maintenance of order and prevention of harm. Rather, this early science of police was an administrative science with an exceptionally broad reach. In essence, police science included everything – all persons and things – that provided the state with resilience and splendor. As feudalism dissolved, theorists of police science saw the social terrain as a vast open space traversed by people and things that needed regulation and order. The science of police was about the task of forming the social body, shaping the newly conceived "population" into an efficient and productive body. The extent of the regulation they proposed to accomplish this feat went far beyond anything that had previously been enacted. Governing power reached into all sorts of areas of life by means of specific and detailed regulation.[69] In sum, police science underwrites political governance by the extension of an individualizing, pastoral power. It is government as the exercise of a specific, permanent, and positive intervention in the behavior of individuals.[70]

Here Foucault's account of the emergence of governmentality coincides with the history narrated in his earlier work, *Discipline and Punish*. There Foucault displayed the ways in which the body is directly involved in a political field by means of technologies of domination. He unmasked how power relations have an immediate hold upon the body as "they invest it, mark it, train it, torture it, force it to carry out tasks, to perform ceremonies, to emit signs."[71] That display was remarkable for its bringing to light the ways in which governing apparatuses may capture the body in a system of subjection without resorting to instruments of violence and ideology. Governing apparatuses hold the body in a particular regime of subjectification by weaving an intricate web of micropolitical forces, a "heterogeneous ensemble consisting of discourses, institutions, architectural forms, regulatory decisions, laws, administrative measures, scientific statements, philosophical, moral and philanthropic propositions."[72] This is to say that disciplinary power should not be identified simply with a single institution or cluster of institutions, nor with overt violence. The paradigmatic example of this disciplinary power is Jeremy Bentham's Panopticon, which Foucault describes at length:

> We know the principle on which it was based: at the periphery, an annular building; at the centre, a tower; this tower is pierced with wide windows that open onto the inner side of the ring; the peripheric building is divided into cells, each of which extends the whole width of the building; they have two windows, one on the inside, corresponding to the windows of the tower; the other, on the outside, allows the light to cross the cell from one end to the other. All that is needed, then, is to place a supervisor in a central tower and to shut up in each cell a madman, a patient, a condemned man, a worker or a schoolboy. By the effect of backlighting, one can observe from the tower, standing out precisely against the light, the small captive shadows in the cells of the periphery. They are like so many cages, so many small theatres, in which each actor

is alone, perfectly individualized and constantly visible. . . . Each individual, in his place, is securely confined to a cell from which he is seen from the front by a supervisor; but the side walls prevent him from coming into contact with his companions. He is seen, but he does not see; he is the object of information, never a subject in communication."[73]

To perfect the Panopticon, Bentham suggested that the windows of the central tower be fitted with blinds, thereby concealing the presence or absence of the guard. In this situation, unable to verify the occupancy of the tower, it was asserted that inmates would internalize the surveillance and in effect become their own guards. Inducing in its object a state of consciousness that insures the automatic functioning of power is what renders the Panopticon such a compelling example of the disciplinary power that subtended the emergent art of government in the seventeenth and eighteenth centuries. The Panopticon is the model of a governing power that creates subjects who, in the absence of direct force, nevertheless police themselves.[74] Beyond this, however, it is the diagram of a mechanism of power, a generalizable model of functioning, a metaphor of sorts for a host of power relations – those operative not only in prisons, but in all sorts of enclosures, like hospitals, schools, armies, and factories, indeed, in the human sciences as a whole – with their constituent forms of observation, surveillance, and judgment enforcing and reinforcing the normative gaze.

The resonance between the police of state reason and Foucault's account of the disciplines is unmistakable. What we see happening in the police science of reason of state is the convergence of technologies of domination (the disciplines) with technologies of the self (sciences of population), with the result that the modern art of government, governmentality, was born.

Economic government and the rise of liberalism

At this time, however, governmentality was young and immature. Indeed, Foucault argues, reason of state inhibited the development of a full-blown art of government, even as it took steps in that direction, to the extent that it remained under the yoke of sovereignty. Governmental rationality under the sign of reason of state remained subordinate to the theoretical and institutional structures of state sovereignty.[75] Everything passed through the bottleneck of the state. As the seventeenth and eighteenth centuries unfolded, however, this model of government became increasingly problematic. Faced with a series of political and economic crises and the rapid growth of peoples and commerce, people began to lose confidence in the sovereign state touted by the theorists of state reason. Whereas the state had been called upon to organize commerce and regulate society in its minutest detail, now that same state was viewed with suspicion. Indeed, the state was deemed to have pernicious political and economic effects.[76] It was engaged in endless warfare and harmful protectionist economic practices that interfered with the changing economic climate.

Foucault argues that the nascent governmentality of state reason collapsed as the economy escaped its grasp. This escape is linked to the problem of population. Although the concept of population was essential to the rise of state reason, as it continued to develop it contributed to state reason's collapse. Whereas statistics had initially undergirded the regulatory apparatuses of the sovereign state, it gradually revealed that the population was subject to movements and forces (epidemics, mortality rates, spirals of labor and wealth, changing customs and activities etc.) that were not amenable to and hence did not correspond to the sovereignty model.[77] The ebb and flow of the life of populations constantly exceeded the regulation of the state. Hence, before long the sovereign state lost its position as the container of the population and instead became but a segment of the population.

The perspective of population also undermined state reason's rationale. The individualizing, pastoral power exercised by police science on the population encouraged the fragmentation of what had been the end of the state. As knowledge of the population expanded, the state increasingly had a difficult time correlating the diverse ends and processes and interests of the population with the end of the state. As populations and commerce expanded, the state found itself unable to guide those currents through the bottleneck of the state. Ironically, the subject that this state created by targeting individuals with the pastoral power of police science was more than this state could contain.

Faced with an expanding population of interested individuals engaged in a flourishing commerce, the Physiocrats pressed the case against reason of state, arguing that far from constituting a chaotic swamp that needs the state to order it, society and its economy generate their own order and prosperity. Individual interests do not need the state's control; rather, they naturally and spontaneously converge in the public interest. Thus was born the doctrine of *laissez-faire*, which held that society was a self-regulating mechanism that only suffered under the weight of the excessive and detailed regulation of the sovereign state's police science. Adam Smith's famous "invisible hand," bringing good out of individuals' self-interested pursuits, is part of this development.[78] Indeed, the invisibility of Smith's hand is of particular importance, for it marks the total dissolution of the state's economic sovereignty. The invisible hand functions precisely because it is invisible. The state cannot know how the individual pursuit of interests will conspire towards the public interest; the processes of the economy are opaque. They are not transparent to the state.[79] The economy escapes the state. Not only does it escape the state, but it returns to capture its former master. Now the state finds itself immersed in a field that it had previously sought to contain and control.

With the economy's escape from the sovereign state, governmentality undergoes a mutation. Liberalism emerges and severs the link between maximal governmental effectiveness and maximal government itself.[80] Whereas reason of state identified government and state apparatuses, liberalism extends or diffuses government beyond the state apparatuses across the entire social field. With the arrival of liberalism, governmental reason is no longer identified with the totalizing reason of the state but is reformulated in terms of civil society.

The early modern theorists of civil society, such as Hobbes, Locke, and Rousseau, developed the concept of civil society against the foil of nature. Civil society is synonymous with rational, orderly political society and it is set over against the disorder of an irrational nature. Hobbes, for example, in the famous passage in *Leviathan*, contrasts political society with the state of nature, where life is a war of all against all.[81] By the latter half of the eighteenth century, however, the meaning of the terms had shifted and civil society was no longer being equated with political society and contrasted with nature. Rather, the early liberals like Adam Ferguson began to *distinguish* civil society *from* political society and the state. Moreover, they argued that civil society is a natural society that had its own laws and patterns. It is in a sense self-organizing or self-governing, and political society – the state – must recognize and respect these natural patterns. The state must govern in accord with these naturally occurring relations. In other words, the state's exercise of governmental power must be integrated into the power relations immanent in society.

The recognition of civil society, with its naturally self-regulating processes and non-totalizable multiplicity of economic subjects of interest, prompted a redefinition of the function of the state. According to reason of state, the prosperity of the population was only a means to bolster the state and, as a consequence, its mercantilist logic channeled all wealth to the economically sovereign state. According to the *laissez-faire* logic of the liberal state, flows of wealth and prosperity dry up when the state attempts to contain them, therefore the state must become immanent to the economic processes; that is, it must forego the direct acquisition of wealth and instead support the pursuit of individual interests. Hence, the liberal state is the state of liberty and freedom, with liberty and freedom understood in terms of *laissez-faire*. That is, when the early liberals speak of government as a "system of natural liberty,"[82] they are advocating a system that bolsters the *laissez-faire* operation of the natural economic processes. The objective of liberal government is the securing of the optimal conditions for the autonomous functioning of the economic processes within society.[83] The liberal state is responsible for the controlled insertion of bodies into the machinery of production, for the adaptation of the population to the economic processes.[84]

The liberal state's concern for the controlled insertion of bodies into the machinery of production returns us to the intersection of technologies of domination and technologies of the self. Under the liberal regime, the technologies of power continue to occupy a prominent role in the art of government, but they undergo subtle alteration. Recall that liberalism severs the link between maximal governmental effectiveness and maximal government itself, between government and state apparatuses. In this new situation, technologies of power that constitute the art of government are dispersed. They take up new positions as components in a much broader web of governmentality, a web that extends beyond the state apparatuses. Further explanation of this requires taking up the liberal understanding of civil society in more detail.

Civil society and government through freedom

Since at least the time of the Physiocrats, it was argued that society apart from the state was governed by natural processes. The early liberals insisted that the state coordinate its governing activities with those forces already at play within society. Civil society, then, is not a space that is fundamentally antagonistic to government. On the contrary, Foucault insists, the early liberal conception of civil society is rightly understood as the correlate of a particular art of government: recall that in response to a crisis in state reason's art of government, civil society was put forward as that space deemed capable of governing the non-totalizable multitude of economic subjects of interest. Even as it restrains the state and champions civil society, then, liberalism cannot be rightly understood as opposed to government. Liberalism does not juxtapose government and freedom. Rather, liberal government is government *through* freedom. More specifically, liberalism is economic government, in a dual sense. First, it is government that is particularly attuned to the precepts of political economy. Second, it is government that advocates efficient, economical government. It recognizes that some government is more effective and efficient when left in private hands. This illumines the state/civil society distinction as well as the public/private split that emerged with liberalism. Such distinctions do not establish boundaries between government and freedom; rather, they demarcate modes of government. They mark the interface of different techniques of power that together constitute governmentality.

In this regard it may be helpful to think of various privately led campaigns of moralization/normalization often associated with health, education, philanthropy, or religion that flourish in civil society; these private campaigns participate in the art of government as they promote specific techniques of the self. By encouraging practices of saving or the acquisition of insurance or particular parenting roles or the habits of cleanliness, sobriety, fidelity, self-improvement, responsibility and so on, they exert a pastoral power, essential to government, that insures that individual freedom is exercised in ways appropriate to the optimal functioning of the economy.[85] Civil society and the realm of the "private" designate areas of the social field where, in the name of efficiency, government is the responsibility of apparatuses other than the state. By establishing civil society, liberalism does not dismantle government; it only ends the narrow identification of government with the state.

Recognizing the liberal state and its civil society as a matter of government through freedom positions us to appreciate the changes wrought in the technologies of power under this new regime of governmentality. In the era of reason of state, technologies of power flourished but remained within the sphere of state sovereignty. They constituted a network of power that rendered each individual malleable to the ends of the sovereign state. Under the liberal state, however, the technologies of power are de-centralized. Once again, Bentham's Panopticon is illuminating. Recall that the Panopticon was designed to function with the central tower unoccupied. Thus, when fully functional, disciplinary power does not emanate from a center but is a mobile network of power that radiates like a thousand points of light across the social field. Furthermore, it is not insignificant that Bentham offered to build and operate the Panopticon himself. Liberalism takes a broad approach to governmentality, perceiving it to extend beyond the state to encompass civil society as well. Indeed, one of the hallmarks of liberalism is its belief that many if not most aspects of government are best – that is, most economically – left to private mechanisms. Hence, the push for the privatization of technologies of power, of which Bentham's offer is but one example. Others abound. For example, during this time legislation was enacted that conceded national mineral rights to private mining companies on the condition that they ensure the "good order and security" of the population, or that essentially handed the regulation of labor over to those who ran the factories, on the grounds that, "since it is futile to claim ability to provide for every detail of production with regulations emanating from public authority . . . taking account of the variety of occupations, the best course is to authorise those responsible for directing work to regulate everything relating to it."[86] In a similar manner, the science of police became the human sciences and was dispersed broadly in independent fields like medicine, psychiatry, psychology, criminology, pedagogy, and so forth. More contemporary examples could easily and endlessly be culled from the pages of any newspaper. Under liberalism, disciplinary power extends beyond the state, permeating civil society.

Societies of control

In the years just prior to his death, Foucault suggested that the disciplinary society was entering into a crisis, prompting yet another mutation in the art of government:

> In the last few years society has changed and individuals have changed too; they are more and more diverse, different, independent. There are ever more categories of people who are not compelled by discipline (qui ne sont pas astreints à la discipline), so that we are obliged to imagine the development of society without discipline. The ruling class is still impregnated with the old technique. But it is clear that in the future we must separate ourselves from the society of discipline of today.[87]

Foucault's remarks remained largely undeveloped until Deleuze expanded upon them in terms of what he called "societies of control."

Picking up from where Foucault left off, Deleuze notes that the disciplinary society associated with liberalism consisted largely of vast spaces of enclosure, such as the school, hospital, prison, and factory. Criss-crossing civil society like the tunnels of a mole, these enclosures ordered social space by manipulating the timing and spacing of human activity.[88] The force employed by disciplinary mechanisms to accomplish this was, according to Foucault, "heavy, ponderous, meticulous and constant."[89] By the 1960s, however, it was clear that such cumbersome forms of power were no longer efficient and effective. Just as the subject of interest formed by police science eventually escaped, prompting the development of the liberal state, by the mid-twentieth century the subject of discipline was mounting effective resistance. Whether in the school, the factory, or the family, the disciplined subject was showing itself less compelled by discipline.

Consequently, liberal governmentality underwent a mutation in the late 1960s and early 1970s and in the wake of disciplinary society emerged a society of control, a neoliberal intensification of governmentality. Whereas early liberalism was characterized by what might be called a passive *laissez-faire* attitude, with government striving to minimize intervention in and interference with the naturally occurring patterns and processes of the economy, neoliberal governmentality displays a much more active attitude. Neoliberal government aggressively encourages and advocates the extension of economic reason into every fiber and cell of human life. Economic or market rationale controls all conduct. Capitalism has enveloped society, absorbing all the conditions of production and reproduction. It is as if the walls of the factory had come crumbling down and the logics that previously functioned in that enclosure had been generalized across the entire time-space continuum.[90] With the crossing of this threshold, a new era has dawned, as Hinkelammert suggested. It is the golden age of capitalism, a time when capitalism can set aside its ill-fitting human mask. "It is the coming out of capital," Brian Massumi writes, "a new golden age of greed that dares to say its name. Without a wince. Capitalism no longer has to justify itself. It no longer has to hide behind fascist-paranoid quasicauses and argue that it serves the common good."[91] Capitalism has prevailed. It has subsumed society; it has become social. No longer is it sufficient for modern economic individuals to accept their place beside their machines, in their cubicles, in the lines at the malls as producers and consumers; now they must submit every aspect of their lives to the logic of the economy; they must be entrepreneurs of themselves. Accordingly, the previous era's welfare state is dismantled in the name of reform, and bodies – even children's, who until recently were thought to inhabit a sphere at least nominally sheltered from the economy[92] – are delivered to the logic of the market. Churches are now run like businesses, with ministers proclaiming themselves "CEOs" and corporations offering contributions in exchange for advertising space. Schools are corporate-sponsored training camps for producers and consumers. Athletic events are saturated with corporate logos and viewed by the participants as merely a means to financial gain in the form of endorsements. Public media and public libraries face extinction. Capitalism has taken control.

This control, this art of governmentality, however, is exercised in a manner quite different from that which distinguished disciplinary societies. According to Deleuze, the time-frame of the closed disciplinary system is collapsing and we are increasingly subjected to ultrarapid forms of free-floating control.[93] At the heart of disciplinary society was the closed space, the enclosure. The disciplined, docile body was formed by being channeled through a series of enclosures – school, hospital, factory, army, prison – where it was molded in accord with a norm. Currently these enclosures are in crisis. The hospital is giving way to neighborhood clinics, HMOs, hospice, and day care. The factory is giving way to the flexible productions of the corporation, which more closely resembles a gas or a spirit in its penetration of society.[94] The penal system is experimenting with electronic collars. Even school is being replaced by perpetual training. In societies of control, the body is rendered pliable not by careful containment and conformity to a norm, but by a flexible, variable, modulation that is ubiquitous. If disciplinary societies resembled the work of a mole, societies of control imitate the serpent. Instead of stumbling over the tunnels of the mole, we are caught in the infinite undulations of the snake.[95] The corporation, homework, the internet, cell-phones, and ATMs: structured passages are receding before the spread of a web or net (or market) of control. "The disciplinary man was a discontinuous producer of energy, but the man of control is undulatory, in orbit, in a continuous network."[96] The human being is no longer enclosed but in debt and unlike the enclosure, debt goes everywhere, all the time. The credit card has surpassed the time card as the dominant mechanism of insertion into the economy.[97] In all these ways and more, pastoral power has become virtually omnipresent, exerting control over persons, delivering desire into the maw of savage capitalism.

With the arrival of societies of control, we have reached the conclusion of Foucault's genealogy of governmentality, of the conjunction of technologies of domination with the pastoral power of technologies of the self. What is most important for our purposes is his display of the generalization or dispersal of governmentality under liberal government through freedom, and the further intensification of that dispersal under neoliberal societies of control. From this account we see humanity delivered to the capitalist order by means of a vast matrix of technologies of power that extend across the social field and are not identical with the state apparatuses. Governmentality highlights how what Deleuze calls the state-form is rightly understood as an ensemble of technologies of desire[98] that are not centered in the state but dispersed across the socius. Desire is captured by capitalism and enslaved to the axiomatic of production for the market not merely by the repressive capacity of the state but also through the exercise of a pastoral power operative in a multitude of technologies of desire promoted in various spaces of enclosure (prison, factory, school, home), human sciences, civic programs, practices, and organizations, and so forth.

Beyond madness?

When faced with the madness that is savage capitalism, the temptation is to despair, to answer "yes" to Hinkelammert's query, ¿Capitalismo sin Alternativas? It is possible to come away from the preceding analysis with the sense that capitalist discipline is so pervasive that resistance is futile, that we are rendered powerless before the web of technologies that constitute governmentality.

Such a reaction, although perhaps understandable, contravenes the expectations of both Deleuze and Foucault, who saw their work as a contribution to revisioning revolutionary practice. That politics precedes being, that power is ubiquitous and hence not the sole possession of the state and its (para)military, is reason for hope. Desire is restless. As the anarchic, creative force that it is, it resists every capture, it eludes every end. And this applies to all desire, not to some specifically "revolutionary" desire or privileged subject (generals, workers, academics, the poor). "Desire" writes Deleuze, "is revolutionary in its own right . . . by wanting what it wants."[99] With every mutation of the state-form, with every intensification of governmentality, flows of desire nevertheless eluded capture. And desire continues to resist even now, even in the grips of savage capitalism, unexpectedly finding cracks in the system and creating lines of flight. Deep in the Lacandon forest, suddenly on the Plaza de Mayo, slowly on a dormant farm in Brasilia, regularly on the streets of Quito, San Salvador, Caracas, Lima, sporadically on a dusty path in Cochabamba, flows of desire strain against the capitalist discipline and sometimes escape.

Hence, revolution, as Deleuze envisions it, is a matter nurturing these flows of desire.[100] Escape from capitalism is not a matter of destruction but of creation, addition, intensification. It is a matter of overwhelming capitalism's ability to adapt desire to the axiomatic of production for the market. The path beyond capitalism is not one that destroys capitalism but rather exceeds it. Revolution, in other words, is a matter of achieving absolute deterritorialization. Previously it was pointed out that capitalism's power of deterritorialization, its ability to release desire from social formations and codes, infinitely surpasses that of the state. But, according to Deleuze, capitalism does not achieve absolute deterritorialization because even as it deterritorializes desire, it reterritorializes desire, disciplining it in accord with the axiomatic of production for the market. Hence, desire never attains genuine freedom: the anarchic, creative, experimental movement that Deleuze labels "schizophrenia."

Capitalism, observes Deleuze, in its voracious deterritorializing, is a form a madness, and as a way beyond this madness he proposes intensifying the madness, continuing the process of deterritorialization until desire is free of all order – schizoid desire, pure autopoesis.[101] We are compelled, however, to ask, is madness the way beyond madness? Or does madness intensified finally collapse in the black hole of nihilism, where life becomes death and an absolute violence is unleashed? Perhaps madness is simply madness, schizoid desire nothing but the far side of the madness that is savage capitalism, which makes it that much more savage.

Deleuze's revolution of madness beyond madness is anchored in the ontological claim "politics precedes being," which is to say that it begins with an ontological rupture, a certain "capture of being."[102] Specifically, it is rooted in the univocity of being, which is a rupture with the Thomistic *analogia entis* or "analogy of being," and is a capture of being in the sense that it renders being knowable, calculable, an "object." The appeal of the univocity of being for Deleuze is that it abolishes transcendence[103] and it secures difference (as degree, intensity), and the interplay of difference that he characterizes as love, joy, playing, and dancing.[104]

Yet, Deleuze cannot get to where he wants to go, starting from where he starts, and as a consequence his madness is distinguishable only as a difference of degree from the madness that is savage capitalism. It is as if Deleuze has forgotten his own insight, that capitalism's victory is ontological. Hence, by beginning with the univocity of being, he has already suffered ontological defeat. He has already conceded the crucial capture, the capture of being, that leaves desire vulnerable to the ravages of capitalism.

This is the case because relations of desire in the univocal mode can finally only degenerate into the violence of conflict and conquest.[105] In rejecting the analogy of being that preserves ontological difference while nevertheless permitting participation of one in another, Deleuze is left with discrete singularities for whom relations are always external and never constitutive of identity.[106] As a consequence, these singularities can only relate to one another through the formal mechanism of contract (between producer and consumer, between victor and vanquished). Once captured in the univocal code, singularities become "objects" and relations between objects are a matter of capture and possession. This follows from the fact that the discrete individuals Deleuze celebrates, precisely as discrete individuals, are intrinsically unrelated on account of the absolute and unbridgeable difference (of degree or intensity) that distinguishes them. Hence, they can only form relations either by forcing themselves on others (by piercing the sacrosanct veil of analogically unmediable difference and seizing the other), or by entering into a contract with the other (which as a purely external or formal relation rooted in the aleatory coincidence of the calculi of discrete individuals' wills, remains a kind of possession).

The inescapable violence of Deleuze's vision rooted in univocity is perhaps easier to ascertain when approached from the angle of desire's being shorn of any teleology. The development of the univocity of being sundered notions of the good, of love, of justice from the active power of being.[107] Thus it is no surprise when Deleuze de-finalizes desire, casting it as an experimental, anarchic force that defies every *telos* and resists every organization. The question is on what grounds does he assert that when this self-creating, self-asserting desire is released from every organization, the flows of liberated desire will enter into joyful, harmonious relations? From whence cometh the confidence that the flows of desire, deprived of any shared end and barred from analogous participation in the other (which entails desire be understood not merely as assertive or creative, but also as receptive), will not simply collide in absolute war? As was perhaps most famously pointed out by Thomas Hobbes, the sort of nominalist-voluntarist account of desire that Deleuze advocates requires a teleology (whether divinely given or imposed by a secular state) to avoid a state of *bellum omnis contra omnem*. Lacking a shared end and ontologically incapable of entering into non-possessive relations, liberated univocal desire does indeed resemble a "war-machine" (to mimic one of Deleuze's own descriptions). And Deleuze's assertion otherwise becomes a plea for the miraculous,[108] which remains eternally unanswered because, transcendence having been banished, the heavens are empty. Thus, Deleuze's championing of assertive, creative desire looks more

34

like the advancement of arbitrariness, and portends not the proliferation of joy and harmony but the endless spilling of blood and shedding of tears.

Having embraced the univocity of being, Deleuze is delivered to an account of desire that in the name of securing difference insures that relations of desire will be conflictual. In this way, Deleuze does not escape capitalist discipline, for capitalism has so construed the market that it too mediates all relations of desire agonistically. Capitalist discipline distorts desire into a competitive force: competing for resources, for market share, for a living wage, for the time for friendship and family, for inclusion in the market, and so forth. Of course, Deleuze's capitulation to savage capitalism comes as no surprise, given that, as his analysis masterfully shows, capitalism is erected on the same ontology of univocal desire shorn of any particular telos.

In the end, then, Deleuze's vision does not dismantle capitalist discipline. But this was never really his goal; his objective was to envision a way beyond capitalism and there is a sense in which he has accomplished this. The revolution of schizoid desire, of absolute deterritorialization, promises to surpass capitalism in the sense that were it to succeed, we would be delivered to a world that exceeds even the savagery of savage capitalism. *Bellum omnis contra omnem.* Absolute war. After all, there is some truth to the long-standing claim that capitalism has a pacifying effect. Deleuze's revolution would leave us without even this and, as terrifying as capitalism is, this is a truly hideous prospect.

Is there a way beyond both the madness of capitalism and schizoid desire? Is there a balm for the sickness of capitalism that does not leave us sicker yet? Is there a path beyond madness to health? A therapy that will heal desire of the distortions and deformities inflicted by capitalist discipline?

In the next chapter, I will begin to consider this possibility by taking up one particularly prominent account of Christian resistance to capitalism. Since the 1960s, Latin American liberationists have been among a handful of thinkers who have boldly proclaimed that Jesus Christ, and the body of Christ that is the Church of the poor, is about the work of liberating desire from the clutches of capitalism.

Notes

1 Francis Fukuyama, "The End of History?" *National Interest* 16 (Summer 1989), 15.
2 This article is found in Franz J. Hinkelammert, *Cultura de la Esperanza y Sociedad sin Exclusión* (San José: DEI, 1995), 25–38. While I use this article to frame the discussion that follows, I draw from the entire book to unpack the theses. All translations are mine.
3 Ibid., 27–28.
4 Ibid., 92.
5 Ibid., 17.
6 While this phrase accurately portrays Hinkelammert's analysis, I actually take it from Alfred Stepan, "State Power and the Strength of Civil Society in the Southern Cone of Latin America," in *Bringing the State Back In*, eds. Peter B. Evans, Dietrich Rueschemeyer, and Theda Skocpol (Cambridge: Cambridge University Press, 1985), 324.

7 Hinkelammert, *Cultura de la Esperanza*, 29.

8 Ibid., 319.

9 The reference to foraging in garbage dumps and feeding one's children newspaper is drawn from Susan George's *A Fate Worse Than Debt* (New York: Grove Press, 1988), 137. She recounts the story of a social worker in the Brazilian town of Porto Alegro who, upon approaching a hut near the River Guaibe, was greeted by five young children whose parents were out foraging in the garbage heaps. In response to the social worker's queries about when they had last eaten, one of the children answers that they had eaten the day before when their mother had kneaded little cakes for them out of wet newspaper.

10 Hinkelammert, *Cultura de la Esperanza*, 32.

11 Ibid., 133.

12 Ibid., 39. He also suggests that the collection of the debt amounts to a "genocide without comparison in history" (13).

13 "Capitalism without alternatives?" See Franz J. Hinkelammert, "¿Capitalismo sin Alternativas? Sobre la sociedad que sostiene que no hay alternativa para ella," *Pasos* 37 (1991): 11–24.

14 Hinkelammert, *Cultura de la Esperanza*, 127, 195, 303.

15 Ronald Bogue, "Gilles Deleuze: Postmodern Philosopher?," *Criticism* 23 (1990): 401–418.

16 See Paul Patton, "Conceptual Politics and the War-Machine in *Mille Plateaux*," *SubStance* 44/45 (1984): 61.

17 In the course of this study I will refer to several works in which Deleuze collaborated with another author, the most notable example being his work with Félix Guattari. I do not attempt the futile task of sorting out the voices; instead I will simply refer to the texts as being Deleuze's. For Deleuze's remarks on his collaborative efforts, see Gilles Deleuze and Claire Parnet, *Dialogues*, trans. Hugh Tomlinson and Barbara Habberjam (New York: Columbia University Press, 1987), 16–19; and Gilles Deleuze and Félix Guattari, *A Thousand Plateaus: Capitalism and Schizophrenia*, trans. Brian Massumi (Minneapolis: University of Minnesota Press, 1987), 3.

18 Deleuze, *Dialogues*, 17; Deleuze, *A Thousand Plateaus*, 203.

19 The phrase "social unconscious" comes from Philip Goodchild, *Deleuze and Guattari: An Introduction to the Politics of Desire* (Thousand Oaks, CA: Sage Publications, 1996), 3 and *passim*.

20 Max Weber, "Politics As a Vocation," in *From Max Weber: Essays in Sociology*, eds. and trans. H. H. Gerth and C. Wright Mills (New York: Oxford University Press, 1946), 77 (italics in original).

21 Deleuze, *Dialogues*, 17; Deleuze, *A Thousand Plateaus*, 203.

22 This micropolitics does not rule out macropolitical struggle against the capitalist order, since "every politics is simultaneously a *macropolitics* and a *micropolitics*," but, as we shall see, it does dramatically change how one goes about such struggle (Deleuze, *A Thousand Plateaus*, 213).

23 Gilles Deleuze, "Seminar Session on Scholasticism and Spinoza," trans. Timothy S. Murphy [On-line] Available from http://www.imaginet.fr/TXT/ENG/140174.html [6 August 1999].

24 For a fuller account of Scotus' theology and its consequences see Catherine Pickstock, *After Writing: On the Liturgical Consummation of Philosophy* (Malden, MA: Blackwell Publishers, 1998), 121-166. For Deleuze's treatment of Scotus and the emergence of the univocity of being along the trajectory of Scotus, Spinoza, and Nietzsche, see Gilles Deleuze, *Difference and Repetition*, trans. Paul Patton (New York: Columbia University Press, 1994), 35–42. For a helpful narrative of Deleuze's philosophical development in this regard, which unfortunately does little with Scotus, see Michael

Hardt, *Gilles Deleuze: An Apprenticeship in Philosophy* (Minneapolis: University of Minnesota Press, 1993).

25 Deleuze, "Seminar Session on Scholasticism and Spinoza," 4.

26 Ibid.

27 Deleuze, *Dialogues*, 91; see also Deleuze, *A Thousand Plateaus*, 154.

28 By positing the ontological primacy of productive desire, Deleuze runs the risk of sounding like a vulgar Marxist who reduces everything to the economic forces of production and their shadows. Indeed, the emphasis on production resonates with the traditional Marxist focus on the modes of production, a focus renewed in Marxist circles in the 1960s and 1970s. However, Deleuze's account of productive desire does not equate, in any uncomplicated way, productive desire with the modes of production. Rather, desire produces the modes of production. Productive desire is what makes the modes possible. Drawing the facile equation "productive desire equals modes of production" overlooks the way in which Deleuze's ontology of desire collapses any distinction between a productive base and a nonproductive superstructure. Everything is desire, hence everything is productive: productions of productions, productions of consumptions. The economy produces, but so too does culture, and religion, and the family, and so forth. See Gilles Deleuze and Félix Guattari, *Anti-Oedipus: Capitalism and Schizophrenia*, trans. Robert Hurley, Mark Seem, and Helen R. Lane (Minneapolis: University of Minnesota Press, 1983), 4.

29 Deleuze, *Anti-Oedipus*, 29.

30 Brian Massumi, *A User's Guide to Capitalism and Schizophrenia* (Cambridge: MIT Press, 1992), 58–59.

31 Deleuze, *A Thousand Plateaus*, 434.

32 Ibid., 428.

33 Deleuze, *Anti-Oedipus*, 199.

34 Deleuze, *A Thousand Plateaus*, 360.

35 Ibid., 449.

36 Ibid., 452–453; see also Deleuze, *Anti-Oedipus*, 231.

37 Ibid., 453 (italics added).

38 Ibid., 454.

39 Ibid., 454.

40 Ibid., 453.

41 Kenneth Surin, "On Producing the Concept of a Global Culture," *The South Atlantic Quarterly* 94 (1995): 1185.

42 Deleuze, *A Thousand Plateaus*, 434–435.

43 Deleuze, *Anti-Oedipus*, 252.

44 Deleuze, *A Thousand Plateaus*, 435.

45 Ibid., 436.

46 For a succinct account of the arguments concerning feudalism and capitalism in Latin America, see Ernest Laclau, *Politics and Ideology in Marxist Theory* (London: New Left Books, 1977), 15–50.

47 I owe this example to Surin, "Concept of a Global Culture," 1191.

48 Foucault, *Power/Knowledge: Selected Interviews and Other Writings 1972–1977*, ed. Colin Gordon (New York: Pantheon Books, 1980), 121; Michel Foucault, *The History of Sexuality, Volume 1: An Introduction*, trans. Robert Hurley (New York: Vintage Books, 1990), 88–89.

49 Foucault, *Power/Knowledge*, 73.

50 Ibid., 122.

51 Michel Foucault, *The History of Sexuality*, 93.

52 Michel Foucault, "Governmentality," trans. Rosi Braidotti, rev. by Colin Gordon in *The Foucault Effect: Studies in Governmentality*, eds. Graham Burchell, Colin Gordon, and Peter Miller (Chicago: University of Chicago Press, 1991), 87.

53 Michel Foucault, "Technologies of the Self," in *Technologies of the Self: A Seminar with Michel Foucault*, eds. Luther H. Martin, Huck Gutman, Patrick H. Hutton (Amherst, MA: University of Massachusetts Press, 1988), 18; see also Michel Foucault, "About the Beginning of the Hermeneutics of the Self: Two Lectures at Dartmouth," *Political Theory* 21 (1993): 203.

54 Nikolas Rose, "Identity, Genealogy, History," in *Questions of Cultural Identity*, eds. Stuart Hall and Paul DuGay (London: Sage Publications, 1996), 132.

55 Ibid., 132; see also Michel Foucault, *Power/Knowledge*, 144; Gilles Deleuze, "What is a *dispositif?*" in *Michel Foucault: Philosopher*, ed. and trans. Timothy J. Armstrong (New York: Routledge, 1992), 159–166. Michel Foucault, "The Subject and Power," *Critical Inquiry* 8 (1982): 782.

56 Michel Foucault, *Politics, Philosophy, and Culture: Interviews and Other Writings 1977–1984*, ed. Lawrence D. Kritzman (New York: Routledge, 1988), 67.

57 Foucault emphasizes that this was a pervasive idea or theme and does not necessarily mean that this is the way power was in fact exercised. See his *Politics, Philosophy, and Culture*, 63.

58 Foucault admits that shepherd imagery does occasionally appear among the ancient Greeks and Romans, but it does not mark an individualizing power. See his *Politics, Philosophy, and Culture*, 63–67.

59 Foucault, *Politics, Philosophy, and Culture*, 61–63.

60 Foucault, "Technologies of the Self," 19–39.

61 Foucault, "About the Beginning of the Hermeneutics of the Self," 215.

62 Foucault, "Technologies of the Self," 44.

63 Foucault, "About the Beginning of the Hermeneutics of the Self," 217.

64 Cited by Foucault in *Politics, Philosophy, and Culture*, 74.

65 Occasionally, particularly in *The Discourses*, Machiavelli does use the term *lo stato* in ambiguous ways that hint at future usages. For this reason, Quentin Skinner casts Machiavelli as a transitional figure of sorts. For more on this and the debate concerning how to read Machiavelli, see Quentin Skinner, "The state," in *Political Innovation and Conceptual Change*, eds. Terence Ball, James Farr, and Russell Hansen (Cambridge: Cambridge University Press, 1989), 91–131; and Quentin Skinner, *The Foundations of Modern Political Thought* 2 vols. (Cambridge: Cambridge University Press, 1978), in particular 1: 128–138 and 2: 349–358.

66 Skinner suggests that the theorists of the absolute state or reason of state were influenced by Renaissance republicanism, which critiqued traditional personalist conceptions of political power on the grounds that such power is inevitably corrupt. The sovereign will not serve the common good. Skinner furthermore suggests that the republican tradition is distinguished from absolutism insofar as it did not distinguish between the state and the citizenry. Reason of state and the theorists of the absolute state, such as Bodin, Grotius, Suarez, and Hobbes, distinguish between not only the prince and the state, but also between the people and the state. See Skinner, "The state," 104–121.

67 Michel Foucault, "The Political Technology of Individuals", in *Technologies of the Self: A Seminar with Michel Foucault*, eds. Luther H. Martin, Huck Gutman, Patrick H. Hutton (Amherst, MA: University of Massachusetts Press, 1988), 149–150; Foucault, *Politics, Philosophy, Culture*, 74–76. Shifting the rationale from the person of the prince to the state creates a space for a plurality of forms of government. One early work cited by Foucault states that "governor can signify monarch, emperor, king, prince, lord, magistrate, prelate, judge and the like." See Foucault, "Governmentality," 90.

68 Foucault notes that the reverse side of this "biopolitics" is a "thanatopolitics." Just at that point in history where states evidence the most concern for their populations, they also embark on the greatest slaughter of those populations. This is understandable: "Since the population is nothing more than what the state takes care of for its own

sake, of course, the state is entitled to slaughter it, if necessary." See Foucault, "The Political Technology of Individuals," 160.

69 Two examples of the extent of this new "science of police." First, a German treatise summarizing the police regulations of Nuremberg in the late Middle Ages is organized according to the following headings: 1. Of security 2. Of customs 3. Of commerce 4. Of trades 5. Of foodstuffs 6. Of health and cleanliness 7. Of building 8. Of fire 9. Of forests and hunting 10. Of beggars 11. Of Jews. The second example comes from a 1757 work entitled *Code of Police*, by the Frenchman M. Duchesne. He begins by stating that "police has as its general object the public interest." The table of contents in this volume conveys just how general that object is: 1. Of religion 2. Of customs 3. Of health 4. Of foodstuffs 5. Of highways 6. Of tranquillity and public order 7. Of sciences and liberal arts 8. Of commerce 9. Of manufactures and mechanical arts 10. Of servants, domestics, and nurses 11. Of the police of the poor. See Pasquale Pasquino, "Theatrum politicum: The genealogy of capital–police and the state of prosperity," in *The Foucault Effect: Studies in Governmentality*, eds. Graham Burchell, Colin Gordon, and Peter Miller (Chicago: University of Chicago Press, 1991), 109–110.

70 Foucault, "The Political Technology of Individuals," 159.

71 Michel Foucault, *Discipline and Punish*, trans. Alan Sheridan (New York: Vintage Books, 1979), 25.

72 Foucault, *Power/Knowledge*, 194; See also Deleuze, "What is a *dispositif?*, 159–166.

73 Foucault, *Discipline and Punish*, 200.

74 Ibid., 202–203.

75 Graham Burchell, "Peculiar interests: civil society and governing 'the system of natural liberty'," in *The Foucault Effect: Studies in Governmentality*, eds. Graham Burchell, Colin Gordon, and Peter Miller (Chicago: University of Chicago Press, 1991), 124.

76 Denis Meuret, "A political genealogy of political economy," trans. Graham Burchell *Economy and Society* 17 (1988): 231, 235.

77 Foucault, "Governmentality," 99.

78 Adam Smith, *An Inquiry into the Nature and Causes of the Wealth of Nations*, ed. Edwin Cannan (Chicago: University of Chicago Press, 1976), 477.

79 Smith, *The Wealth of Nations*, 208.

80 Michel Foucault, "Naissance de la biopolitique," in *Résumé des cours*. Cited in Burchell, "Peculiar interests," 138.

81 Thomas Hobbes, *Leviathan* (New York: Penguin Books, 1968), 186.

82 Smith, *The Wealth of Nations*, 208.

83 Burchell, "Peculiar interests," 139.

84 Foucault, *History of Sexuality*, 141.

85 I owe these examples to Graham Burchell, "Liberal government and techniques of the self," *Economy and Society* 22 (1993): 272.

86 Colin Gordon, "Governmental Rationality: An Introduction," in *The Foucault Effect: Studies in Governmentality*, eds. Graham Burchell, Colin Gordon, and Peter Miller (Chicago: University of Chicago Press, 1991), 26–27; Jacques Donzelot, "The promotion of the social," *Economy and Society* 17 (1988): 407.

87 Foucault quoted in Michael Hardt, "The Withering of Civil Society," *Social Text* 14 (1995): 41.

88 The mole metaphor is taken from Gilles Deleuze, "Postscript on the Societies of Control," *October* 59 (1992): 5.

89 Foucault, *Power/Knowledge*, 58.

90 Hardt, "The Withering of Civil Society," 35.

91 Massumi, *A User's Guide*, 131.

92 I have in mind here the recent changes to Aid to Families with Dependent Children. While these changes are recent, their theorization is not. Milton Friedman discusses

children as consumer goods in his classic, *Capitalism and Freedom* (Chicago: University of Chicago Press, 1982), 33.

93 Deleuze, "Postscript," 4.

94 Ibid., 4.

95 The image of the snake comes from Deleuze, "Postscript," 5. The phrase "infinite undulations of the snake" I owe to Hardt, "The Withering of Civil Society," 34.

96 Ibid., 5–6.

97 Granted not everyone has a credit card, or a time card, and while some of us surf the net, others do not have access to electricity. Hence Deleuze and Foucault both caution against thinking simplistically in terms of sovereignty being replaced by the disciplines which are in turn replaced by control. Old formations may not be abolished so much as modified in accord with the dictates of a new logic. Furthermore, the logic of societies of control may only be visible at the most developed coordinates of the global capitalist order. Again, the capitalist axiomatic is quite adept at using and integrating heterogeneous formations. While societies of control may be emerging in a few centers, disciplinary societies may continue to effect models for capital's realization in peripheral regions.

98 An astute reader will note that I have conflated Foucault's work on technologies and power with Deleuze's ontology of desire to arrive at "technologies of desire." It should be noted that although Deleuze and Foucault were close friends, at least until the final years of Foucault's life, and deeply admired each other's work, there were differences between them. For the purposes of my project, however, the substance of these differences and the ways in which Foucault might object to his being assimilated into Deleuze's ontology of desire are not important. For a concise account of their relationship and the compatibility of their work, see Goodchild, *Deleuze and Guattari*, 131–135, as well as the conversation between Deleuze and Foucault, published as "Intellectuals and Power" in *Language, Counter-Memory, Practice*, ed. Donald Bouchard (Ithaca, NY: Cornell University Press, 1977), 205–217. For an example of how Deleuze used Foucault, see his work, *Foucault*, trans. Seán Hand (Minneapolis: University of Minnesota Press, 1988). See also the essay by Deleuze, "Desire and Pleasure", in *Foucault and His Interlocutors*, ed. Arnold I. Davidson (Chicago: University of Chicago Press, 1997), 183–192.

99 Deleuze, *Anti-Oedipus*, 116.

100 See Deleuze, *Anti-Oedipus*, 246 and *passim*.

101 Ibid., 373 and *passim*.

102 The claim that "politics precedes being" is an instantiation of the univocity of being because it implies a distinction similar to Scotus' "formal distinction," marking a virtual reality between essence and existence, a possible that is not yet actual, a possible that through an act of the will (politics) becomes actual (being). See Deleuze's discussion of Scotus in *Difference and Repetition*, 39ff. I owe the phrase "capture of being" to Éric Alliez, *Capital Times*, trans. Georges Van Den Abbeele (Minneapolis: University of Minnesota Press, 1996), 197.

103 It abolishes transcendence, first capturing it by subordinating it to being (God is in the same sense as humanity), then banishing it by attributing to it an infinite intensity of being that exceeds any measure. See Catherine Pickstock, *After Writing: On the Liturgical Consummation of Philosophy* (Malden, MA: Blackwell Publishers, 1998), 122–123.

104 Deleuze, *Anti-Oedipus*, 347; Gilles Deleuze, *Nietzsche and Philosophy*, trans. Hugh Tomlinson (New York: Columbia University Press, 1983), 194; Gilles Deleuze, *Expressionism in Philosophy: Spinoza*, trans. Martin Joughin (New York: Zone Books, 1992), 246; Gilles Deleuze, *Spinoza: Practical Philosophy*, trans. Robert Hurley (San Francisco: City Light Books, 1988), 126.

105 My understanding of the impact of Scotus and the univocity of being relies heavily upon the treatments of Alliez, *Capital Times*; Pickstock, *After Writing*; and Kenneth

Schmitz, "Is Liberalism Good Enough?" in *Liberalism and the Good*, eds. R. Bruce Douglass, Gerald M. Mara, and Henry S. Richardson (New York: Routledge, 1990), 86–104.

106 The proliferation of relations in Deleuze would appear to be more accurately described as a proliferation of "expressions." Desire enters into relations as it expresses itself. The other in this situation resembles a canvas upon which desire expresses itself. Furthermore, the extent to which univocal desire can be genuinely creative is questionable, since new relations are only the old with more added. The already given is simply rearranged.

107 Alliez, *Capital Times*, 211–212; Pickstock, *After Writing*, 157.

108 Pickstock, *After Writing*, 132.

2

THE CHURCH OF THE POOR
IN THE WAKE OF
CAPITALISM'S TRIUMPH

Neoconservatives gloat that we are all capitalists now and State Department pundits tout the triumph of capitalism as the end of history. But is capitalism really the master of us all or can desire be freed from its servitude to the capitalist market? Over the course of the past several decades, Latin American liberationists have emerged among the most prominent and compelling voices to defy the capitalist orthodoxy. Contending that the God of Jesus Christ is actively involved in history struggling against the capitalist order that consigns much of the world's population to misery and premature death, liberationists have boldly sought to quicken Christian resistance to the capitalist order.

This chapter takes up their account of that resistance. Beginning with the Latin American liberationists' own recognition that their vision is in crisis, I argue that their vision is insufficiently radical. Although commendable in many respects, when their understanding of Christian resistance to capitalism is read against the backdrop of Deleuze and Foucault's account of capitalist discipline, it is clear that their revolutionary vision remains circumscribed by the very capitalist order they hope to overcome. As a result, the revolutionary movement they hoped to nurture has not succeeded in escaping the capitalist order, but with the arrival of the "end of history" has been overrun by it.

On the surface, this might appear to be just another in a long line of criticisms of liberationist social theory. From its inception, liberationist thought has come under steady fire from both the right and the left for its social theory. Critics argue that Latin American liberationists' insightful claims about the Church's "preferential option for the poor" are hampered by a deficient social theory, usually spelled out in terms of a failure to appreciate the merits of "democratic capitalism" or of an undue reliance on Marxist analysis or even of an insufficient commitment to Marxist theory.[1] In contrast with the commonplace criticisms, however, I locate both the cause and potential solution to the crisis in liberationists' understanding of the Church. In this chapter's critical moment I argue that in an age scarred by a capitalism that achieves dominion by disciplining desire, the ecclesiological innovations inaugurated by the Latin American liberationists for the sake of surmounting the flaws of the New Christendom ecclesiology dominant in the 1960s are insufficient. Liberationist ecclesiology has been disciplined by the capitalist order and, as a result, the Church of the poor is cast as indirectly political (its commitment remains at the level of an abstract value or "preferential option") while the state is endowed with revolutionary expectations. Against the backdrop of Deleuze and Foucault's analyses, it is clear that such a vision of politics as statecraft delivers the liberationists to the capitalist order because its hope is misplaced (in the state) and possible resources for the struggle (specifically, the technologies of desire enacted in Christian community) are displaced – stripped of immediate socio-political import as the Church is rendered apolitical.

In this chapter's constructive moment, I begin to develop an alternative vision of Christianity, one that builds upon the insights of the liberationists while striving to evade capitalist discipline. Specifically, I argue that refusing politics as statecraft and reclaiming the Church as a fully social, political, economic reality in its own right may establish it as a genuine site of resistance to capitalist discipline. Indeed, there are signs that some base communities are, in the words of Leonardo Boff, "reinventing the church," rejecting statecraft and living Christianity as a way of life that is directly and immediately political. These communities may be enacting the true politics, creating spaces where desire is healed of the madness that is capitalism.

The crisis in Latin American liberationist thought

What has happened to the "irruption of the poor" so enthusiastically announced in the 1970s by Latin American liberationists? Whence cometh the revolution of the impoverished and oppressed majorities so eagerly awaited and vociferously proclaimed? Perhaps what critics say about liberationist thought and the revolution it envisions is true. It is a fad that is quickly fading, its hopes misplaced in a discredited theory; its dreams displaced by the death of socialism; its vision replaced by neoliberal economics riding the wave of what has been celebrated as the "capitalist revolution."[2]

Latin American liberationist thought is in crisis; it has run up against the end of history, the triumph of savage capitalism. It has become entangled in the infinite undulations of the ascendant capitalist order. Latin American liberationists do not deny this unpleasant reality. On the contrary, a sense of crisis pervades recent liberationist thought. Leonardo Boff writes about "the general crisis in left-wing thought" brought on by the collapse of socialism and Jon Sobrino observes that we are witnessing the closing of a period that was shot through with the hope and praxis of historical liberation.[3] Pablo Richard recognizes a complete collapse of hope that renders the current situation "worse than it was at the outset of the conquest."[4] Franz Hinkelammert speaks of "capitalism without alternatives" and Javier Iguíñiz laments the fading of the irruption of the poor and the weakening of the liberating process.[5]

Liberationist thought is in crisis. This crisis need not be fatal, however, for the wound that precipitated it is self-inflicted and its remedy may be at hand. Liberationist thought is in crisis, not because the capitalist juggernaut really is irresistible, as Fukuyama would have us believe, but because the liberationists have succumbed to the capitalist order by accepting that order's discipline. In particular, they have embraced the modern vision of politics as statecraft. They have acquiesced to the separation of religion from the socio-political-economic spheres of life, which entails depriving the Church of a forthright political presence, and have turned to the state as the principal agent of resistance to the capitalist order. In other words, liberationist thought is in crisis because it does not grasp that capitalism, as Deleuze and Foucault have shown, is not simply an economic system that has escaped its proper domain and can be reined back in by the state. By advocating an apolitical Church and endorsing politics as statecraft, the liberationists reflect a failure to perceive that the state is but one component in a system of governmentality that functions to deliver desire to the capitalist order. More importantly, however, by advocating an apolitical Church and hitching the revolution to the state, the liberationists reflect a failure to perceive the true nature of both the struggle and the resources God may have provided for waging it, namely that the conflict between capitalism and Christianity is between competing technologies of desire. Capitalism is a discipline of desire; Christianity is a therapy of desire.

At first glance, the claim that the liberationists' vision is circumscribed by the capitalist order insofar as it embraces the modern disciplining of the Church, which deprives it of an immediate political presence in favor of politics as statecraft, may seem counter-intuitive. After all, are not the liberationists known for their political activism? Are not liberationists denounced or lauded precisely for politicizing the Church? Certainly one of the celebrated hallmarks of liberationist thought is their persistent demand that the chasm between faith and politics not remain unbridged, that Christianity not remain above the fray of human misery. So how can liberationists be accused of adhering to a vision of the Church that is apolitical, that leaves politics to the state?

If liberationists were the thinly veiled Marxists or the overly politicized priests that their critics envision and consequently had written a great deal about the Church and state and politics, this claim could be either verified or dismissed in short order. However, given that the liberationists are people of faith and devote most of their energy to examining the great spiritual themes of the Christian life in light of the Latin American reality, they say relatively little about the relation between the Church and state and politics. A thorough consideration of this claim, therefore, requires an indirect and circuitous approach, one that begins with the New Christendom ecclesiology, that model of the Church against which the liberationists consciously developed their vision of the Church of the poor. By setting the liberationists' revolutionary vision in its proper context – developments in Catholic ecclesiology in twentieth-century Latin America – what the liberationists say is amplified and the submerged outline of a full-blown account of the Church and state and politics is clearly discernible.

Before the revolution: New Christendom in Latin America

Beginning with the New Christendom model, however, is not without its difficulties, for Latin American liberationist thought is often heralded as a completely new way of doing theology. It is credited with theorizing a new way of being the Church; it is accorded the status of a veritable "paradigm shift" in theology.[6] While it makes little sense to deny or minimize the novelty and significance of liberationist thought, such claims may lend themselves to concealing the ways in which liberationist thought shares a great deal with what preceded it. The commitment to an apolitical Church and politics as statecraft is a case in point. As I will show, the New Christendom model of the Church, which dominated Latin America during the first half of the twentieth century, envisioned the Church as an apolitical custodian of moral values and conceded politics to the state. Furthermore, as the New Christendom model entered into crisis in the 1960s and the liberationists initiated ecclesiological innovations to overcome what they perceived to be its weaknesses, they did not reformulate the Church's role in political life in such a way as to challenge the political primacy of the state; on the contrary, they continued to assume that the state was the pinnacle of political life and the fulcrum of social change.[7]

The origins of New Christendom in Latin America

The rise of New Christendom in Latin America is a direct consequence of the challenges faced by the Latin American Church at the end of the nineteenth and early twentieth centuries. As it entered the twentieth century, the Church was struggling to come to terms with the precipitous decline of its influence since the independence movements a century earlier led to the rise of liberal states, states that proved hostile to the Church and its interests. Following the Vatican's lead in the latter half of the nineteenth century, the Latin American Church had staunchly resisted the advance of liberalism by actively involving itself in politics by means of open, and sometimes official, endorsement of conservative parties and politics.[8]

This changed, however, with the election in 1922, of Pope Pius XI. Pius initiated a new era in the Church's approach to politics when he propagated what came to be known as "social Catholicism" or the "New Christendom" ecclesiology. Having lost confidence in the ability of confessional political parties to advance the Church's mission, he shifted the Church's energies to its social rather than political witness. Henceforth, the Church would approach politics *indirectly*. The centerpiece of this new model was the formation of voluntary associations that would contribute to re-Catholicizing society by creating a critical mass of Catholic laity active in society, who were formed in the principles and values of which the Church is the custodian.[9] Chief among these groups was Catholic Action, a lay organization that under the guidance of Pius XI became a bridge between the spiritual and the temporal, between religion and politics, by forming Christians who would enter the world of politics prepared to put Christian values and principles (such as those articulated in the growing collection of "social encyclicals") into action.

New Christendom first took hold in Latin America in the late 1920s through the spread of Catholic Action groups. These groups gradually spread throughout Latin America, becoming a major factor in the life of the Church as they nurtured a whole generation of Catholic leaders who would rise to positions of national political and intellectual leadership.[10] By means of a pedagogical method that stressed evaluating social issues in light of the Gospel (and the social encyclicals) and acting on the basis of that evaluation, Catholic Action produced laity and clergy who were committed to social change. Moreover, as a result of this strategy's deliberate distancing of the Church from conservative political parties, by mid-century the New Christendom model had created a space for reformist and progressive voices in the Church. It ushered in an era of cooperation between the Church and the state, whereby the Church, assuming an apolitical position, encouraged the state and urged Catholics to cooperate with national and international development efforts. Consequently, the Church threw its weight behind cultural, economic, and social development initiatives, such as literacy and mass education programs, radio schools, agrarian reform (particularly of Church land), cooperatives, and centers for the study of social issues.

This indirect approach to politics and its coupling with a developmentalist program also found support in various papal encyclicals and the work of the second Vatican Council, but the most significant influence on the development of the New Christendom model in Latin America, and the clearest display of its commitment to an apolitical Church and politics as statecraft, was found in the work of the French Catholic lay philosopher, Jacques Maritain.[11] As Tristán de Athaide, an admirer of Maritain's, said in 1948, "The Thomist renovation in America as well as the Christian solution of the social problems of the New World, owe to Maritain more than to any other modern thinker the vitality of its current expansion."[12] Maritain's neo-Thomism impacted Latin American Catholicism through several venues. Latin American intellectual leaders taught and propagated Maritain's neo-Thomism to generations of Latin American students.[13] Maritain's ideas were embraced by the leaders of both the Catholic Action movement and the Christian Democratic Party, and young cadres of Catholic Action were exposed to his work through participation in international conferences. His works, particularly *Integral Humanism* and *The Rights of Man and Natural Law*, circulated widely and had an extensive readership in Latin America.[14] Finally, Maritain himself traveled to Latin America in the late 1930s, expounding his vision of an integral humanism that undergirded the New Christendom model of the Church's relation to politics.[15]

Distinguishing the spiritual and the temporal

The cornerstone of this vision is what came to be known as the "distinction of planes," a distinction between the spiritual and the temporal orders of existence.

"Each of us," writes Maritain, "belongs to two States – a terrestrial State whose end is the common temporal good, and the universal State of the Church whose end is eternal life."[16] This distinction between the spiritual realm proper to the Church and the temporal realm precludes any confusion between religion and temporal realities such as nation, race, or culture. "For the Christian, the true religion is essentially supernatural and, because it is supernatural, it is not of man, nor of the world, nor of a race, nor of a nation, nor of a civilization, nor of a culture – it is of the intimate life of God."[17]

This distinction, however, is not a divorce. The two realms, although distinct, are related. Specifically, a hierarchical relation exists between them. As Maritain says, the two distinct powers are not on the same plane; rather, one is above the other. Specifically, the temporal is subordinated to the spiritual:

> The State being the most perfect natural community . . . which mankind can form in this world, it is of supreme importance to draw the distinction and define the relations of subordination between politics, which are ordered to the whole of the terrestrial State as to their proximate and specific end, and ethics which are ordered to the divine transcendent whole. The subordination of politics to ethics is absolute and even infinite, being based on the subordination of ends; for the good of the State is not God Himself, and remains far, far inferior to the supreme beatitude of man.[18]

Politics is subordinate to ethics. No prince of the nations of this world can know anything of the spiritual Kingdom of God. The temporal authorities are incompetent in matters spiritual. Such secrets reside with Christ and his priesthood.

This subordination of the temporal to the spiritual, however, does not signal a return to an earlier age when the spiritual dominated the temporal realm. New Christendom is new precisely in that it is a vision adapted to a new age, one in which the temporal order has "come of age."[19] New Christendom is new insofar as it refuses the theocratic temptation – the temptation to conceive of the spiritual as immediately and directly relevant to the temporal – and recognizes that Christ did not come to change the kingdoms of the earth or to accomplish a temporal revolution.[20] Far from a nostalgic longing for a faded grandeur, New Christendom understands Christianity as a transcendent, spiritual reality that is above all particular, concrete, temporal institutions.[21] It recognizes the genius of Christianity in effecting the interiorization of the moral life. With the appearance of New Christendom, writes Maritain, Christianity has succeeded in escaping the claims of the "Judaeo-Christian particularism" that tainted its early years and has attained a spiritual universality based on "interiorizing in the heart of man – in the secret of the invisible relations between the divine personality and the human personality – the moral life and the life of sanctity."[22]

Hence, New Christendom recognizes and respects the integrity of the temporal in a manner inconceivable to Christendom. Christendom, according to Maritain, viewed the temporal realm instrumentally; that is, it conceived of the temporal merely as a means to the singularly important eternal end. In contrast, New Christendom acknowledges that in the modern world, the temporal realm has attained a proper integrity and autonomy and therefore can no longer be trampled upon in pursuit of the ends of the higher, spiritual plane. Thus, the New Christendom model accords the temporal end a legitimacy or validity that precludes its instrumental use. In other words, the ends of the temporal order, namely the earthly and perishable goods of our life here below, are no longer simply to be dismissed out of hand by the spiritual.

The vision of New Christendom, then, is one in which the secular is no longer starkly opposed to the sacred as the impure to the pure. Instead there is a vital unity, whereby the sacred vivifies and superelevates the temporal while the temporal in turn serves the sacred by facilitating the attainment of the supernatural end.[23] Concretely, this means that the Church is no longer mistaken for a temporal institution or power. Indeed, because its end is eternal and above all temporal matters, the Church is incompetent in the realm of temporal affairs.[24] Rather the Church, as a distinctly spiritual entity, exerts an indirect influence on the temporal realm in the form of suprapolitical counsels and directions. The Church, declares Maritain, is the custodian of a "doctrinal firmament of principles and truths" that animate or vivify the human personality and conscience.[25] The Church is a moral and spiritual force that works at the level of the human heart, not at the level of politics. In this way, as a custodian of universal spiritual values, it functions as a sort of "leaven" of the temporal realm.[26]

Politics and the state

Prior to the Second World War, Maritain envisioned this New Christendom as a novel form of civilization, one whose emergence was imminent. The war, however, shook Maritain and chastened his hopes for a new civilization.[27] As a consequence, in the years after the war the foil for Maritain's vision of a New Christendom was not so much a novel society as it was liberal democracy.[28] This is not to say that Maritain simply embraced liberalism. Rather, he adopted much of the liberal agenda – pluralism, democracy, separation of powers, rights – minus its bourgeois roots, striving instead to articulate such a vision within the context of his Thomistic philosophy.

This subtle shift in Maritain's focus brings into sharp relief the way in which the New Christendom model, with its distinction of the spiritual and temporal, embraced a conception of politics as statecraft. The vision of New Christendom sketched thus far clearly advocated the withdrawal of the Church from the temporal realm of politics. The Church is an apolitical entity – the trans-cultural, mystical body of Christ – that only indirectly relates to the social, political world. This evacuation of the temporal realm by the Church creates a vacuum. Although with occasional comments like "the authority of the State is supreme in its own order",[29] his pre-war writings suggest the state's political primacy, it is in his post-war writings that the state's sovereignty over the temporal becomes explicit.

Ironically, that politics is fundamentally a matter of statecraft becomes clear as Maritain mounts an argument *limiting* the reach of the state. The crux of this argument concerns not the spiritual and the temporal, but the person and society. Persons, according to Maritain, by reason of their spiritual endowments, are not merely part of the temporal realm.[30] While not reducible to the temporal, however, they nevertheless do participate in that order. In particular, they enter into and are subject to society. And this is no mere accident; persons are intrinsically social. Indeed, they crave society.[31]

On the basis of the human person's intrinsic sociality, however, the state cannot set itself up as the pinnacle of human life. Because society is not simply an aggregate of individuals, but instead consists of human persons who derive their vitality from a spiritual font, society's end exceeds the claim of the state. The state's sovereignty is checked by the fact that the value of the person is not exhausted by the state, that the human is both in and outside the state:

> Man is a *part* of the political community and is inferior to the latter, by reason of the things which, in him and of him, depend as to their very essence on the political community, and which, as a result, can be called upon to serve as means for the temporal good of this community . . . . On the other hand man *transcends* the political community by reason of the things which, in him and of him, deriving from the ordering of the personality as such to the absolute, depend as to their very essence on something higher than the political community and properly have to do with the supra-temporal fulfillment of the person as a person.[32]

The human being as a person, as one with a spiritual endowment, transcends the claims of the state; the state's sovereignty is always constrained by the supernatural inviolability of the person. For this reason, Maritain suggests that the concept of "sovereignty" should be discarded altogether.[33]

While he seeks to dismantle the idea of sovereignty, however, Maritain does not desire the state's abolition. Although he recognizes that the idea of sovereignty emerged hand in hand with the modern state, he nevertheless makes a crucial distinction between the two developments. The emergence of the state was a good thing that unfortunately was intertwined with the emergence of the idea of sovereignty: "According to a historical pattern unfortunately most recurrent, both the normal development of the State – which was in itself a sound and genuine progress – and the development of the spurious–absolutist–juridical and philosophical conception of the State took place at the same time."[34] The point is not to dismantle the state. On the contrary, says Maritain, in modern civilization the state is more and more necessary to human persons in their political, social, moral, and intellectual progress.[35]

> I should like to point out that the people have a special need of the State, precisely because the State is a particular agency specializing in the care

of the whole, and thus has normally to defend and protect the people, their rights and the improvement of their lives against the selfishness and particularism of privileged groups and classes.[36]

The point of the critique of sovereignty is not to condemn the state but to restore it to its true nature.

The state's true nature is recovered when the state takes its place, not separate and above, but at the top of the pyramid that is the body politic. The body politic consists of the society of persons interacting with themselves and various autonomous groups and institutions. The state, as the greatest temporal authority, sits atop of this whole. It functions as the central agent of the body politic, specializing in the interests of the whole. The state is charged with looking after the common welfare and, by means of its monopoly over the legitimate use of force, securing public order. In other words, the state is not an end in itself but exists for the sake of the common good. It is an instrument of the body politic for the common good. The state is neither absolute nor sovereign. Only God can claim that.[37]

What is noticeably absent from Maritain's cartography of the body politic is the Church. Crossing the body politic are persons, various and sundry autonomous groups, and the state. The Church is not included among those autonomous groups and associations that constitute civil society. This is because the Church is supra-temporal. Although its members are a part of and its institutions occupy temporal space in the body politic, the Church in her essence is above the body politic: "While being *in* the body politic – in every body politic – through a given number of her members and her institutions, the Church as such, the Church in her essence, is not a part but a whole; she is an absolute universal realm stretching all over the world – *above* the body politic and every body politic."[38] The recognition of the Church's pre-eminent position above the temporal realm of politics is one of the achievements of the modern age. Nothing less than the outworking of a Gospel imperative, the Church's abdication of temporal rule and the concomitant recognition of the "complete differentiation" and "full autonomy" of temporal society, have liberated the Church from dangerous political entanglements and cleared a space for the recovery of its legitimate ministry as the bearer of absolute, immutable, and supra-temporal principles.[39] In other words, the Church is above the body politic because it is a supra-temporal body – a mystical body – that traffics in universal values and principles.

Such a position and such a ministry, however, do not mean that the Church and the body politic pass like two ships in the night, neither recognizing the other. On the contrary, the spiritual and the temporal cooperate. Temporal society has need of the Church insofar as it depends on a kind of faith to hold society together in pursuit of the common good. In particular, says Maritain, the well-ordered temporal society requires a democratic secular faith and it is the Church, through the application of its absolute principles to concrete historical reality, that underwrites just such a faith.[40] The Church contributes to temporal society as it carries out its supreme task of the moral enlightenment and moral guidance of persons, inspiring them and shaping their consciences in accord with the standards and principles that should undergird the social and political order.[41]

From reform to revolution: the rise of liberation theology

New Christendom was the ecclesiology that rose to a position of prominence in Latin American Catholicism during the first half of the twentieth century. It was a reformist, developmentalist vision of the Church espoused by the Vatican, theorized by Maritain, and lived by a dedicated group of bishops, priests, and laity across the Latin American continent. At the heart of this vision was the desire to sever the ties between the Church and the status quo by withdrawing the Church from direct involvement in the political realm. As a consequence of the Church's evacuation of the temporal realm in favor of an indirect, moral influence, the state was left as the uncontested overseer of the political realm. Politics was a matter of statecraft.

As our attention now turns to Latin American liberation theology our concern remains its revolutionary vision. Is it fundamentally a vision of politics as statecraft? Is the Church deprived of an immediate political presence in favor of a sovereign state? In the remainder of this chapter I will show that the liberationists are in fact committed to such a revolutionary vision, one that in light of the work of Deleuze and Foucault is clearly inadequate to the task of liberating humanity from capitalist discipline. The case for this claim, to reiterate a point made earlier, proceeds by juxtaposing the liberationists' vision with that of the New Christendom model. Hence, now that we have an outline of the basic precepts of the New Christendom model before us, as we take up Latin American liberation theology the question becomes, "As the liberationists move beyond the New Christendom model, do they jettison that model's vision of an apolitical Church and politics as statecraft?"

The crisis of New Christendom

Because Latin American liberation theology is often put forward as a radically new way of doing theology, it is worthwhile to briefly consider the years just prior to the publication of Gustavo Gutiérrez's landmark work, *A Theology of Liberation*, in 1971. An overview of this period both begins to provide a sense of what the problems with the New Christendom model were perceived to be and nuances claims for liberation theology's novelty by showing its emergence *out of* and not simply *in opposition to* the problematics of New Christendom.

Discontent with New Christendom's approach to the Church's engagement with the world was precipitated by an number of overlapping factors, beginning with the failure of its reformist and developmentalist program on the economic and political levels. In fact, economic conditions actually deteriorated as the developmentalist program of import-substitution and national industrialization

51

championed by New Christendom's adherents was overrun by mutations in the international capitalist order, including the transnationalization of production, capital, and finance, and the restructuring of the international market in such a way that underdeveloped regions on the periphery were encouraged to export their resources to the developed centers.[42] Politically, by the mid-1960s, populist and reformist governments were giving way to more authoritarian and repressive regimes and, perhaps most significantly, the crown jewel of New Christendom's political success – the Christian Democrats' ascendancy to power in Chile – was unraveling. The New Christendom era of the Church cooperating with the state for the sake of the social development was coming to a very harsh end and the era of "national security" and "low-intensity warfare" was dawning. The space for reform was quickly being filled in an outpouring of violence.

Another factor in the eclipse of New Christendom was the dissatisfaction born of a new awareness among students and priests of the plight of the poorest sectors of society. In the wake of student chaplain-turned-guerrilla Camilio Torres' challenge to students to "ascend to the people" and take up the revolutionary cause,[43] many students exposed themselves to the plight of the poor and were radicalized as a result. This experience in turn led to their questioning the relevance of the New Christendom's reformist and developmentalist approach to social and political issues.

As the students were radicalized, they prompted the chaplains who worked with them to rethink their own approach to the social question. Gustavo Gutiérrez is a case in point. As a student himself, he had been involved in Catholic Action and credits that group with introducing him to "the social side of the Christian message."[44] When he decided to become a priest he was sent to study in Europe, where he became acquainted with those theological currents that would triumph at Vatican II and that would surpass New Christendom's fading star.[45] However, it was not until Gutiérrez returned to Peru and took up his priestly work as the chaplain/director of the National Union of Catholic Students in 1960 that the vision that would flourish in time as "liberation theology" began to take shape. Prior to this experience, Gutiérrez's theological horizon consisted of New Christendom and his progressive European mentors.[46] As the director of the UNEC, Gutiérrez encouraged students to analyze their role in society and to engage in service projects among the poorest sectors of society. The students concluded that developmentalist programs did little to alleviate the misery of the poor and they began to question the validity of the New Christendom model of Christian social involvement. Confronted with their questions and fearing that they might abandon the Church – a Church that was deeply embedded in a social order they deemed oppressive and whose doctrine constrained their involvement in social and political causes[47] – Gutiérrez was forced to re-examine his understanding of both the Church and the Christian's role in the revolutionary currents that were then being felt across Latin America.[48]

Gutiérrez was not alone. Across the continent priests were going to the people, immersing themselves in the life and struggles of the poor masses, and as a result challenging the reformist orientation of New Christendom.[49] One group of radicalized priests, for example, issued a statement that declared:

> As human beings, Christians, and priests of that Christ who came to liberate the people from all bondage and bade His Church to carry on His work, we feel ourselves one with the Third World . . . [T]his inescapably obliges us to join in the revolutionary process for *urgent, radical change* of existing structures and to reject formally the capitalistic system we see around us and every kind of economic, political and cultural imperialism. We shall go forward in search of a Latin American brand of socialism that will hasten the coming of the New Man . . . [This] will necessarily mean a socialization of the means of production, of economic and political power, and of culture.[50]

A similar shift of vision is evident in the statements issued by other priest groups. Clearly many were beginning to look for a more radical model of social change than that advanced by New Christendom and for new ways Christians could be involved in promoting such change.

Finally, the search for an alternative to New Christendom drew support from both the Second Vatican Council and the Second General Conference of Latin American Bishops. Even as proponents of the New Christendom model appealed to Vatican II for support, those radicalized persons who found themselves increasingly dissatisfied with New Christendom saw in the Council's *aggiornamento* several new emphases that encouraged them in their search for a more revolutionary Christian commitment. Among these were the affirmation of the "pilgrim" status of the Church in the world. This was interpreted as a renunciation of the ecclesiastical triumphalism of a New Christendom that sought to Christianize the social order, that saw the Church's task as that of bringing the temporal order into accord with a Christian blueprint. Instead, Vatican II was seen as initiating a new respect for the integrity and autonomy of the temporal. In a similar vein, the Council's effort to attend to the "signs of the times" was interpreted as a move beyond New Christendom's deductive approach of applying Christian principles to the world in favor of a more inductive approach that begins with careful analysis of the situation, then turns to Scripture and theological analysis, before finally making pastoral application.[51] Finally, the Council created a space for cooperation and dialogue with Marxists by suggesting that all persons – believers and unbelievers alike – ought to work for the betterment of the world, and that such work cannot be realized apart from "sincere and prudent dialogue."[52] This was an opening of which the radical segment of the Church was to take full advantage.

Perhaps the single most significant event to give impetus to the rise of liberation theology was the Second General Conference of Latin American Bishops that met in August of 1968 in Medellín, Colombia. This meeting has been called the "Magna Carta" of liberation theology and about it Enrique Dussel has written,

". . . Medellín was of imponderable importance for Latin America. It was not only the moment of the 'application' of the Second Vatican Council but also of the discovery of the real Latin America and the transition to a clear commitment to liberation."[53]

At Medellín, the work of Vatican II was reinterpreted in light of the Latin American situation and, as suggested above, the impact of that reinterpretation is hard to overstate. The Medellín documents, however, are by no means uniform in their embrace of a radical liberationist vision. To the contrary, they are rather mixed, containing elements of both the New Christendom perspective and a more radical liberationist perspective.[54] Indeed, of the sixteen sections of the *Conclusions*, only three – those on justice, peace, and poverty – made a strong impact.

In the years following the conference these three documents were appropriated by the liberationists, who pointed to them as the institutional legitimation of the new directions they were pursuing.[55] A sense of these new directions comes through clearly in the opening paragraphs of the document on poverty, where the bishops write:

> The Latin American bishops cannot remain indifferent in the face of the tremendous social injustices existent in Latin America, which keep the majority of our peoples in dismal poverty, which in many cases becomes inhuman wretchedness. A deafening cry pours from the throats of millions of men, asking their pastors for a liberation that reaches them from nowhere else.[56]

As they move from an examination of the historical situation through doctrinal analysis to pastoral application, all three of these documents place the Church firmly on the side of "integral human development and liberation." According to these documents,[57] the situation in Latin America is characterized by "institutionalized violence," "unjust structures," "internal colonialism" and "external neocolonialism." Together these amount to a "sinful situation" that leaves the Latin American countries dependent on the economic centers of power. In light of this situation, the bishops call for "all-embracing, courageous, urgent, and profoundly renovating transformations." In particular, the Church is called to respond to this situation by avoiding the "dualism which separates temporal tasks from the work of sanctification" and by recognizing that "to create a just social order . . . is an eminently Christian task." The bishops commit the Church to a program of radical social change oriented toward "authentic liberation" and the construction of "a new society" in which the human person is "an agent of his own history." The Church is encouraged to carry Christ's message of liberation to the poor by becoming a poor Church, by being in solidarity with the poor and giving "preference to the poorest and most needy sectors." This will require the task of "conscientization," of encouraging and educating the consciences of believers to help them perceive the responsibilities of their faith in both their personal and social life.

The language employed by these documents, although rather restrained in comparison with that which liberation theologians would use in years to come, is a sharp departure from both the traditional conservative and careful reformist rhetoric that had characterized the institutional Church in Latin America to date.

A theology of liberation

All of these factors began to congeal in the late 1960s, and a new, more militant model of the Church, identified simply as the "the Church of the poor," emerged. This new model, the fruit of the labor of countless persons over the course of the decade, found its programmatic statement in Gustavo Gutiérrez's 1971 book, *A Theology of Liberation*, which some thirty years later remains the classic statement of the ecclesiological issues at stake in the rise of liberation theology.[58] Thus, as we consider the liberationists' early revolutionary vision and its relation to New Christendom's vision of an apolitical Church and politics as statecraft, we turn to Gutiérrez's work.

Gutiérrez begins by addressing the issue, why speak of liberation instead of development? His answer begins with the assertion that a "broad and deep aspiration for liberation inflames the history of humankind in our day, liberation from all that limits or keeps human beings from self-fulfillment, liberation from all impediments to the exercise of freedom."[59] This process is rightly called liberation because the programs that underwrote the favored terms to date, development and developmentalism, have proven ineffective and even counterproductive. The failure of reformist efforts has cleared the way for a new awareness:

> [T]here can be authentic development for Latin America only if there is liberation from the domination exercised by the great capitalist countries, and especially by the most powerful, the United States of America . . . It is becoming more evident that the Latin American peoples will not emerge from their present status except by means of a profound transformation, *a social revolution*, which will radically and qualitatively change the conditions in which they now live.[60]

"Liberation" is more appropriate because only it expresses the inescapable moment of a radical break with the status quo. Only liberation points to "a profound transformation of the private property system, access to power of the exploited class, and a social revolution that would break [Latin America's] dependence [and] allow for a change to a new society, a socialist society."[61]

The term "liberation" reflects better than "development" the radical social and political transformation that is necessary, but it would be a mistake to think that liberation was only a matter of social and political transformation. The liberation about which Gutiérrez writes is an "integral liberation," a holistic liberation that recognizes the multi-dimensionality of life and seeks to transform each level. In response to critics who erroneously charged that liberationists were guilty of reducing Christianity to a political ideology – in effect attending to this world while ignoring more "spiritual" concerns proper to the world to come – Gutiérrez writes in an essay published after *A Theology of Liberation*:

> One of the oldest themes in the theology of liberation is the totality and complexity of the liberation process. This theology conceives total liberation as a single process, within which it is necessary to distinguish different dimensions or levels: economic liberation, social liberation, political liberation, liberation of the human being from all manner of servitude, liberation from sin, communion with God as the ultimate basis of a human community of brothers and sisters.[62]

Specifically, Gutiérrez discerns three distinct but interrelated levels of liberation: what broadly might be called the "social," the "personal," and the "theological." The first level, that of the social, concerns liberation from concrete, historical situations of oppression, exploitation, and marginalization. It addresses the dismal poverty and inhuman wretchedness in which so many Latin American poor struggle to survive and accordingly encompasses what is usually identified as the political, social, and economic. The second level, the personal, consists of a "profound inner freedom."[63] It is an expression of the inner longing of persons to be the artisans of their own destiny; it marks humankind's assumption of conscious responsibility for its own future.[64] This denotes the realm commonly referred to as the personal, private, or perhaps even the psychological.[65] The third level, the theological, looks toward communion with Christ and freedom from sin. It manifests itself in the value or principle of love – in a turning away from a selfish gaze on oneself and a turning towards God and neighbor – and is commonly identified as the religious or spiritual dimension of life.

The first move of the liberationist vision, precisely as a vision of *liberation* instead of *development*, is a forthright rejection of the political and economic agenda that the progressive adherents of the New Christendom model had supported as the way forward for Latin America: revolution instead of reform, socialism instead of capitalism. Does this critique of New Christendom's progressive politics extend as far as a rejection of the de-politicizing of the Church in favor of politics as statecraft? For an answer, we turn to Gutiérrez's account of the relation of salvation and liberation.

The autonomy of the temporal

Having unpacked, at least initially, the concept of liberation, Gutiérrez turns his attention to what he identifies as the fundamental problem of a theology of liberation: what is the relation between salvation and the historical process of liberation? In more traditional terms, this is the issue of the relationship between the Church and society or the Church and the world. The answer Gutiérrez proposes to this traditional quandary emerges in the midst of a narrative construal of the temporal realm's slow struggle to escape oppressive ecclesiastical supervision. This narrative begins with Christendom, the model that dominated the Church's approach to the world for most of its 2,000-year existence. According to the Christendom approach, the Church understood itself as the exclusive depository of salvation. Because of this exclusiveness, it deemed itself a powerful force in relation to the world, a force that inevitably and rightly expressed itself in the political arena. Furthermore, the Christendom model asserted that temporal activity ought to be oriented toward the interest of the Church. "Under these circumstances," says Gutiérrez, "participation in temporal tasks has a very precise meaning for the Christian: to work for the direct and immediate benefit of the Church."[66] Gutiérrez offers not so much a critique of this position as a forthright dismissal.[67] The Christendom approach is dismissed as dysfunctional, given that the close unity between faith and social life that it requires no longer exists, although Gutiérrez does acknowledge that this mentality continues to linger in some sectors of the Church, where it engenders pastoral attitudes out of touch with reality and conservative political positions.

The Enlightenment essentially broke the back of Christendom and instigated the formulation of Maritain's "New Christendom." This position represents a genuine advance beyond Christendom. Specifically, Gutiérrez credits this approach with recognizing the autonomy of the temporal realm insofar as the temporal was freed from direct interference by the ecclesiastical hierarchy. "Much more clearly than in the past," he says, "the world emerged as autonomous, distinct from the Church and having its own ends."[68] The temporal realm was no longer understood as directly and immediately subordinate to the Church. The temporal realm was freed from both ecclesiastical authority and the Church's mission. In other words, the Church was no longer responsible either for ruling or for constructing the world; its influence became strictly moral, limited to the mediation of the conscience of the individual Christian. Gutiérrez also appreciates the way in which the New Christendom approach "led many Christians to commit themselves authentically and generously to the construction of a just society."[69] It embraced the search for a society based on justice, respect for the rights of others, and human fellowship, which, given the long tradition of the Latin American Church's strong ties to the existing social order, was no small accomplishment.

Nevertheless, the New Christendom model is not adequate. It has shown itself unable to adapt to the signs of the times, to the radical process of liberation that is under way in Latin America. At the theological level, it did not go far enough in recognizing the autonomy of the temporal. The Church remains the sole repository of salvation. "The view of the Church as a power in relation to the world has been profoundly modified. But it continues to be, in a certain way, at the center of the work of salvation. A certain ecclesiastical narcissism is still evident."[70] Based on the world's assertion of its secularity, however, contemporary theological reflection has reason to challenge such narcissism. Gutiérrez acknowledges that secularization is most commonly understood as a desacralization of the world, as a dismissal of the theological dimension of life, and he is clear that this must be resisted.[71] However, he asserts, there is a more positive side to the temporal realm throwing off its ecclesiastical yoke, one that is perfectly consistent with a Christian vision of life. This is secularization understood as the transformation of human self-understanding from a cosmological to an anthropological vision. It is secularization as the recognition by humanity that it is the agent of its own history, responsible for its own destiny. Stemming from the growth of modern science, which enabled humanity to manipulate nature, from Descartes and Kant, who unmasked the creativity of human subjectivity, from Hegel and Marx, who each in their own way revealed human history to be the unfolding of freedom, secularization in this sense "is a process which not only coincides perfectly with a Christian vision of human nature, of history, and of the cosmos; it also favors a more complete fulfillment of the Christian life insofar as it offers human beings the possibility of being more fully human."[72]

Secularization so understood may pose a serious challenge to traditional models of Christianity, but it poses no threat to the faith as such. It is no threat because secularization in the positive sense is built upon a new understanding of grace. The old temporal-spiritual, nature-supernature dichotomies were underwritten by a doctrine of *pure nature* that completely separated the two orders. Recent theological reflection, however, has affirmed that there is no such thing as pure nature, as nature that has not already been acted upon by divine grace. "In reality," says Gutiérrez, "there is no pure nature and there never has been; there is no one who is not invited to communion with the Lord, no one who is not affected by grace."[73] The old understanding of pure nature mistakenly conceived of grace and of God's presence as something that was localized, particularized, external. Grace was viewed as something that was the exclusive possession of the Church and the Christian faith. Such an understanding, however, goes against the grain of the Incarnation. With the advent of Christ, a two-fold process of universalization and internalization of grace was initiated, as Gutiérrez explains at length:

> What we have here, therefore, is a twofold process. On one hand, there is a universalization of the presence of God: from being localized and linked to a particular people, it gradually extends to all the peoples of the earth. . . . On the other hand, there is an internalization, or rather, an integration of this presence: from dwelling in places of worship, this presence is transferred to the heart of human history; it is a presence which embraces the whole person. Christ is the point of convergence of both processes. In him, in his personal uniqueness, the particular is transcended and the universal becomes concrete. In him, in his Incarnation, what is personal and internal becomes visible. Henceforth, this will be true, in one way or another, of every human being . . . Since the Incarnation, humanity, every human being, history, is the living temple of God. The "pro-fane," that which is located outside the temple, no longer exists.[74]

In other words, the positive sense of secularization goes hand in hand with the recognition that grace is present and available beyond the confines of the Church.

Secularization can be embraced because the Church has been "uncentered," because it is no longer viewed as the center and sole locus of salvation. Secularization can proceed without threatening Christianity because in a world that is always already graced, secularization does not have to entail a rejection of the spiritual.

In this situation New Christendom is rendered obsolete because the world is no longer defined by the spiritual realm, the world is no longer viewed from the perspective of the Church. On the contrary, in an entirely worldly world, in a world that has asserted its full autonomy and secularity, religion is redefined by the profane; the Church is seen in terms of the world. Indeed, says Gutiérrez, the Church must turn to the world and allow itself to be inhabited and evangelized by the world.[75] In the final analysis, then, at the theological level New Christendom falters because the frontiers between the life of faith and temporal works, between the Church and the world, are more fluid than it realizes and can accommodate.[76]

But the theological breakdown of New Christendom is not its only shortcoming. New Christendom also fails at the level of pastoral action. At this level, the commitment it fostered to the struggle for a just society degenerated into timid and rather vague invitations to defend "the dignity of the human person."[77] Whereas initially New Christendom was a rallying point for the progressive vanguard and was rejected as subversive by the prevailing system, by the 1960s it had been absorbed by the social order it had intended to modify, even "to the point of becoming, in certain countries, a political mainstay of the most conservative and reactionary elements of all."[78] Its socio-economic analysis was insufficiently scientific and rigorous, with the result that it ignored the in-depth causes of the prevailing problems and the concrete conditions necessary for the construction of a just society.[79] Moreover, the New Christendom model constrained the political activity of the lay apostolic movements that were its mainstay, by subjecting them to the same restrictions on political engagement to which the clergy were subject, namely they could "inspire" but not intervene directly.[80]

At this point, it is clear that the liberationists reject the New Christendom model because it is in several ways too confining: its political and economic vision is limited to ineffective reformist palliatives; its appreciation for the autonomy of the temporal is insufficient; and the various qualifications it places on Christian engagement in the social and political realm undermine commitment to the struggle under way for liberation. The liberationists' vision of the Church of the poor, in contrast, is a model of the Church moving out of its privileged enclave or ghetto and taking a firm stance in solidarity with the poor against injustice. It is a model of the Church fully immersed in the process of liberation. Language of the Church being immersed in the liberation process evokes images of a politically engaged Church; indeed it suggests a return of sorts to a Christendom model of Christian social and political engagement (a model, at least in some forms, at odds with "politics as statecraft"), which prompts us to take up the question of salvation and politics.

Salvation and politics

The Church of the poor is immersed in the liberation struggle. Even so it is not a revival of the earlier Christendom model, this time from the left. Not only is the Church of the poor the product of Christians' radical commitment to the libera-tion process, it is also a response to the world's assertion of its autonomy. The Church of the poor embodies the commitment of Christians to the struggle for jus-tice within the parameters set by a world come of age, that is, by a world that has gained its rightful independence from ecclesiastical control even as it is infused by grace. In other words, the Church of the poor is committed to the revolution, but in a manner that respects the autonomy of the temporal. A fuller explanation of the nature of this commitment necessitates a reconsideration of "integral libera-tion" and the multi-dimensionality of life.

On one hand, the concept of integral liberation arises from the recognition by the Church that salvation is not something purely otherworldly and spiritual. "Salvation – the communion of human beings with God and among themselves – is something which embraces all human reality, transforms it, and leads it to its full-ness in Christ."[81] The salvation that Christ brings is a radical liberation from all misery, despoliation, and alienation. Christ's salvation embraces all of human real-ity, the personal and social dimensions as well as the religious dimension. Hence, liberating historical events are part of the growth of the Kingdom; they are salvific events, even if they are neither the culmination of the Kingdom nor all of salva-tion.[82]

On the other hand, the concept of integral liberation is founded on the recog-nition of the multi-dimensionality of life. Integral liberation encompasses every dimension of life, but the distinctions between the dimensions are not thereby dis-solved. Central to Gutiérrez's account of the multi-dimensionality of life is his insistence that the independence and autonomy of each of the realms or dimen-sions be respected. Each realm must respect the integrity and autonomy of the others. Each realm has its own demands and its own laws, which the other realms must respect. For example, going against the grain of the long and bloody history of Latin America during which the theological realm unduly and inappropriately infringed upon the political realm, Gutiérrez insists that the theological and polit-ical realms are distinct and autonomous.

The autonomy of the realms means that there is no *direct* relation between the theological and the political. In other words, the Gospel or Christian faith cannot be read as embodying a particular political program or option:

> To assert that there is a direct, immediate relationship between faith and political action encourages one to seek from faith norms and criteria for particular political options . . . Thus confusions are created which can result in a dangerous politico-religious messianism which does not suffi-ciently respect either the autonomy of the political arena or that which belongs to an authentic faith.[83]

Faith – the content of the theological realm of life – simply cannot provide a concrete social or political plan and it should not even try, lest it lapse into a dangerous and misguided politico-religious messianism. The Church, restricted to its proper, theological domain is unable to make political recommendations. "It is not possible," Gutiérrez writes, "to deduce political programs from the gospel or from reflection on the gospel. It is not possible, nor should we attempt it; the political sphere is something entirely different."[84]

The severing of any direct relation between the theological and the political realms of life, however, does not leave the realms unrelated, thereby repeating the errors of idealist or spiritualist theologies. The wall between the realms is bridged by means of what Gutiérrez calls a "social appropriation of the gospel," which amounts to a correlation of faith and history, a translation of faith into political activity.[85] Gutiérrez's well-known statement that theology is "critical reflection on praxis" introduces theology as the first of two mediating moments between the theological and the political.[86] Theology deduces from the practice of the faith (theological practice – prayer and commitment to God[87]) certain values or principles (namely, love) that then must be instantiated in the realm of the political.[88] The social sciences embody the second mediating moment as they correlate the value received from theology with the fruits of their own analysis of the social-political-historical situation. The whole process goes something like this: from the Christian practice of faith, which is essentially prayer and commitment to God, theology derives values which it then correlates with the social scientific analysis of reality to come up with a plan for political action.[89]

The Church of the poor respects the autonomy of the temporal realm. It does not pretend to have any competence in socio-political matters. Its perspective is strictly ethical.[90] In other words, the Church of the poor is not a political Church; it remains an apolitical entity. The appearance of the Church of the poor is not the beginning of a struggle for a revolutionary Christendom where the Church pursues political power on behalf of the poor and oppressed. On the contrary, in light of the abuses of the past and the secular world's rightful autonomy, the Church of the poor refrains from political engagement in any direct sense. Only in an indirect or general sense may it be considered a political agent. Hence Gutiérrez distinguishes between two meanings of "political:" a broader, more inclusive sense and a more specific sense. The former refers to a general level of values and principles that have political consequences. The latter refers to the level of specific, concrete, political plans and options. The Church cannot help but be political in the first, indirect sense of the term, but it is not political in the second, more concrete sense. Gutiérrez clarifies this point at length in an interview:

[W]hat does it mean that the church "ought to be political?" That is difficult to say. If it means that proclaiming the gospel necessarily and inescapably has political consequences, then I am in agreement. If that means that the church should conduct itself like a political party, then I do not agree . . . I think that the work of proclaiming the gospel necessarily has historical consequences. But it is not directly political work. There is a classic distinction between politics as a global matter, as a search for a common good, and politics in a stricter, more technical sense, more partisan, also legitimate, but that does not correspond to the church. No one, not even the church, is saved from the first consequence. The church says something and it has political consequences.[91]

The Church of the poor is political only in the indirect sense that its denunciation of injustice and its annunciation that the values of the Gospel have political consequences.

Beyond New Christendom and statecraft, or not?

Such is the liberationists' vision of the Church of the poor as it emerged in the late 1960s. Embracing the process of liberation, entering into solidarity with the impoverished masses, denouncing capitalism and the dependency it fosters, going to the people instead of continuing to cooperate with the dominant classes, this vision of the Church unquestionably marks a radical departure from the New Christendom model that preceded it. Yet for the many and important ways in which the liberationists' vision of the Church of the poor represents an unequivocal break with the prevailing reformist and developmentalist model of the Church, the liberationist vision does not amount to a wholesale rejection of the theological infrastructure of New Christendom. As I have shown, the liberationists were nurtured in the bosom of New Christendom, and as they were immersed in the life of the poor they began to challenge and ultimately reject that model based on its endorsement of developmentalism, which stemmed from inadequate social analysis, and its restraint of the political options of Christians, which stemmed from the refusal to recognize the grace-full autonomy of the world. Said differently, although liberationists reject New Christendom, it remains the backdrop of their thought. Raised as they were in New Christendom, their rejection of it amounts to a rejection of key components; significant continuities remain.

Even as they embraced the process of liberation, the liberationists did not reject New Christendom's attempt to depoliticize the Church. On the contrary, the early liberationists sought to complete this depoliticization. They endorsed the modern Church's evacuation of the political realm. As Pablo Richard notes, the Church of the poor wants to be genuinely apolitical.[92] In other words, when it came to the Church's involvement in politics, liberationists maintained the long-standing distinction between the spiritual and temporal planes, indeed, Gutiérrez celebrates the emergence of the temporal in terms that echo quite clearly his New Christendom heritage. Again, Pablo Richard is illuminating in this regard when he asserts that the theological vision that underwrites the Church of the poor amounts to a reworking of the theological "distinction of planes" from within a commitment to the popular classes.[93]

At first glance this claim flies in the face of Gutiérrez's assertion that the liberationist model of the Church actually weakens and blurs the lines between the Church and the world. This discrepancy vanishes, however, when it is recalled that this claim is advanced in the midst of a discussion of grace. From the perspective of recent theological developments that have discarded the notion of a pure nature in favor of a universalized and interiorized grace, the distinction between the Church and the world has indeed dissolved, or rather, the Church has become indistinguishable from the world insofar as the world is gracefully oriented towards a future promised by the Lord.[94] However, it is precisely because the world is already infused with grace that the liberationists feel free to maintain the autonomy of the political realm and bar the Church from direct intervention in that realm. Put another way, the universal reality of an interiorized grace *allows* the political realm to assert its independence from ecclesiastical oversight without thereby losing its orientation towards God, while the historical record of the oppressive results of direct ecclesiastical intervention in the political realm *demands* that the Church refrain from such intervention.

The result of the liberationists' maintaining the distinction of planes and endorsing the Church's retreat to the apolitical space created by such a distinction is that the state assumes control of the temporal realm. With the endorsement – one might even say "strengthening," given the way in which the world is cast as grace-endowed and hence not intrinsically in need of the Church's inspiration as was the case under New Christendom – of New Christendom's distinction of planes comes New Christendom's conception of politics. The state surfaces as the principal agent of social and political order. Politics becomes a matter of statecraft. Admittedly, this is not immediately self-evident; liberationists say little explicitly about the temporal primacy of the state. More often they give the impression of attacking the state. They denounce the dominant institutions and classes that perpetrate and perpetuate injustice, and the state is unquestionably one of these institutions. Such denunciations, however, are perfectly compatible with a conception of politics as statecraft. They are compatible insofar as such denunciations are not a condemnation of the state as such, but of the misuse of the state apparatus by the powers and classes that exercise hegemonic control. In other words, such condemnations arise out of an instrumentalist vision of the state, a vision of the state as a neutral ensemble of institutions that may be used for good or for ill, depending on who is at the helm and to what purposes they direct those institutions. This is the vision of both politics and the state behind the liberationists' occasional reference to the popular movement's "taking power" and establishing a new society.[95]

That the liberationists continue to think within the boundaries of the conceptual inheritance of New Christendom with regard to the construal of an apolitical Church and politics as statecraft is suggested in several other facets of their vision as well, including their positive appraisal of the Enlightenment, their early advocacy of socialism and embrace of dependency theory. Previously it was suggested that politics became a matter of statecraft with the birth of the modern era and it was shown how liberationists celebrate the birth of the modern era as the pinnacle of the human aspiration for liberation. Given liberationists' valorization of the Enlightenment in general,[96] it is not a large step to conclude that liberationists accept the Enlightenment's construction of politics as statecraft. This is a reasonable conclusion despite the fact that the liberationists do not embrace the Enlightenment project uncritically and without reservation. Gutiérrez is a case in point. On the grounds that the promises and benefits of the Enlightenment were not fully realized and shared by everyone, Gutiérrez does distance himself to some degree from the Enlightenment and the quest for the modern freedoms:

> Today we see clearly that what was a movement for liberty in some parts of the world, when seen from the other side of the world, from beneath, from the popular classes, only meant new and more refined forms of exploitation of the very poorest – of the wretched of the earth. For them, the attainment of freedom can only be the result of a process of liberation from the spoliation and oppression being carried on in the name of "modern liberties and democracy."[97]

Noting the oppression that has gone hand in hand with the quest for the modern freedoms, Gutiérrez tempers his approbation of the Enlightenment:

> The movement of liberation that proceeds from the "underside of history" is not purely and simply a continuation of the movement for modern freedoms. Far from it! The discontinuities and oppositions between the two have theoretical significance and therefore very extensive practical consequences.[98]

This critique raises the possibility that Gutiérrez, even as he praises the Enlightenment's quest for freedom and embraces its differentiation of life, nevertheless distances himself from the way the Enlightenment typically wanted to see this liberation accomplished, namely, through the activity of the state as it oversees civil society. However, as Gutiérrez's account of the shortcomings of the Enlightenment continues, it becomes clear that politics as statecraft is not what is deemed problematic.

According to Gutiérrez, the cause of the "unsatisfied Enlightenment"[99] is a radical individualism that emerged with the rise of the capitalist class: the bourgeoisie with their belief in the right of private ownership. Gutiérrez puts forward the French Revolution – an event he holds up as exemplary of both the best and worst of the Enlightenment – as a prime example. A radical individualism sidetracked the French Revolution. On the one hand, the French Revolution proclaimed the right of all human beings to participate in the society to which they belonged. Thus it embodied the human desire for a truly democratic society, which is rightly celebrated as an achievement of modernity. On the other hand, such proclamations remained largely ambiguous and formal, given that they were not necessarily tied to just economic conditions.[100] According to Gutiérrez, it was the emergence of a radical individualism that blocked the full working out of the logic of the Enlightenment, a logic that would have made the connections between the modern freedoms and the economic conditions of their possibility.

Gutiérrez's account of the Enlightenment and its flaws contains nothing to suggest that he in any way distances himself from the received idea of politics as statecraft. This commitment is further reinforced by what liberationists see as the completion of the Enlightenment project: socialism. Socialism brings to economics what democratic forms of participation brought to politics.[101] Thus, particularly in their earlier works, Gutiérrez and the other liberationists referred not infrequently to socialism as the path to social-political-economic liberation, and it is clear that this socialism is directed at the attainment of state power for the purpose of establishing the social ownership of the means of production.[102] Furthermore, the liberationists, although they emphasize, following Mariátegui, the need for Latin America to develop indigenous forms of socialism, clearly locate themselves within the tradition of Marxist socialism, a tradition that in its various manifestations has understood politics as statecraft.[103]

Finally, in addition to their positive appraisal of the Enlightenment and socialism, liberationists' embrace of dependency theory entails a commitment to politics as statecraft. In its various forms, dependency theory was firmly statist in its orientation. The state was presented as the main lever of power, the dominant political agent, the key to social change. Liberationists took up this theory, both its analysis and its proposed solutions (socialism and autonomy from external dominion), without any hint that the statist conception of politics was problematic. As they decried the "development of underdevelopment" whereby nations at the "center" prospered because nations on the "periphery" suffered, they remained convinced that the state, "*el Leviathan criollo*,"[104] was the proper overseer of the political realm as well as the principal engine of social and political change.[105] The state was cast as the agent of change, as that force which can and should initiate moves to break the cycle of dependency and underdevelopment and strengthen the national economy.

At this point, it is clear that at least at this early point in their development, the liberationists' break with New Christendom did not include a rejection of New Christendom's vision of an apolitical (indirectly political) Church and politics as statecraft. Although little is said about the state *per se*, the liberationist vision, as displayed by Gutiérrez, remains firmly ensconced within the New Christendom problematic of the relation of the Church and world.

From revolution to civil society: liberationists at the end of history

Liberationist thought, however, did not remain at a standstill with the passing of that initial period. Indeed, the sense that Latin America was on the brink of a revolution led by the recently mobilized poor who would shake off the forces of neocolonialism and dependency, seize the state, and create a new socialist society did not last long. The heady revolutionary fervor of the late 1960s and early 1970s that filled liberationists with utopian expectation has evolved over the course of the last few decades into a more temperate enthusiasm for an emergent civil society. How did we get from the "irruption of the poor" to the birth of civil society, from revolution to democracy? What is the substance of these conceptual shifts in liberationist thought and what are the continuities? And how do these shifts and continuities pertain to the issue at hand, namely, the problematic commitment to an apolitical Church and politics as statecraft?

It makes little sense to deny that the move from revolutionary to more democratic impulses represents a significant transition in the development of liberationist thought. However, while there is a general consensus that this is a significant shift, what it signifies remains contested. More conservative observers tend to see this long overdue development as a hopeful and welcome sign that wild-eyed leftists are (finally!) coming to their senses and recognizing the superiority of the capitalist order underwritten by liberal polities. Liberationists tend to cast the development as a move quite consistent with their own realism, with their long-standing recognition of and adjustment to the signs and limitations of the times. Between the two poles lies the rest of us, who attempt to discern the meaning of what appears to be at times a tempering of the previous years' powerful social and political analysis. Is this a retreat or withdrawal? Is it a tactical move designed to evade the Vatican's censure? Or is it merely the pursuit of other interests that have lain dormant since the earliest days of liberationist thought?

A sketch of the relevant developments in Latin America over the last few decades suggests that it is the poles and not the center that are closer to the truth. The conceptual shift from the revolution of the wretched of the earth to popular participation in civil society is, as liberationists claim, a mark of certain continuities in their thought, and it is also, as their critics claim, a capitulation to the regnant capitalist order. More specifically, the shift of the last thirty years, for all of its significance, embodies a consistent and abiding commitment to politics as statecraft.[106] And as Deleuze and Foucault have shown, it is precisely this commitment that, in the age of savage capitalism, delivers liberationists to the capitalist order.

From liberation to captivity to crisis . . .

Beginning midway through the 1960s, even as the liberationists were declaring their support for the social revolution, a wave of repressive violence swept across the land, brutally crushing anyone who dared challenge the status quo. A reign of terror was initiated as military coups in Brazil (1964), Peru (1968), Bolivia (1971), Chile (1973), Uruguay (1973), and Argentina (1976) established bureaucratic-authoritarian regimes that soon became synonymous with systematic violence and brutally repressive order.[107] This experience, as well as the sting of a conservative backlash within the Catholic hierarchy,[108] prompted liberationists to speak more circumspectly of the coming revolution. This new sobriety and prudent patience are reflected in Leonardo Boff's suggestion that the defining mark of the age was not liberation but captivity:

> In all likelihood our generation will not witness the liberation of our continent from hunger and alienation nor the emergence of a more humane, open, and fraternal society. We must work liberatively within a pervasive system of captivity. . . . We today live in a situation of captivity. To believe and hope and work for liberation in such a situation, when we are fairly sure that we will not live to see the fruits of our work, is to incarnate in our own day the cross of Christ. We must establish a solid mystique of hope that goes beyond what is immediately verifiable.[109]

This experience led in the early eighties to a revision and revaluation of things like dependency theory and popular culture. Of particular significance was the revaluation of both the state and democratic processes.[110] Living under the heel of brutal authoritarian states prompted leftists of all stripes to question statist conceptions of politics. Should so much hope be invested in the state? Can it be trusted to use power benevolently? These questions in turn led to a reconsideration of what had previously been viewed with suspicion, namely, democratic processes.[111] Perhaps formal democratic processes and procedures, insufficient though they may be by themselves, should not be dismissed out of hand as illusory and manipulative, as mere tools of the ruling elites? This conceptual shift in the direction of democracy and popular protagonism was further encouraged by challenges to the cruder uses of dependency theory.[112] Certainly the transnational forces of international capitalism did not unilaterally impose themselves on the dependent nations and peoples? Certainly there was cooperation and even, at times, active support *internally* for the policies and practices of the capitalist world order?

The arrival of the "end of history," the defeat of the Sandinistas and the collapse of socialism as a viable alternative to capitalism in the late 1980s, brought this questioning to a head. Several expressions of this sense of crisis have been mentioned previously. Others abound. Xabier Gorostiaga recognizes in history's end a "crisis of paradigms" and Javier Iguiñiz, a "programmatic vacuum."[113] Gutiérrez observes that the period that gave birth to liberation theology was "coming to an end."[114] Elsa Tamez decries the fading of solidarity in the midst of a "messianic drought."[115] Perhaps the strongest and most profound expression of this sense of crisis belongs to Franz Hinkelammert:

> The world which now appears and announces itself is a world where there is only "one lord" and "master," where there is only one system . . . [T]here is no place of asylum . . . The empire is everywhere. It has total power and it knows it . . . [T]he consciousness of an alternative is lost. It seems there are no longer any alternatives. . . .[116]

. . . *to civil society*

Few liberationists have been willing to concede that there are no alternatives. Instead, they have turned to the rise of popular protagonism, to the increased presence of popular sectors in society, and they have identified this with the emergence of civil society in Latin America. Out of the rubble of the Latin American bureaucratic authoritarian regimes of the 1970s have arisen increased civic participation, a new commitment to the electoral process, and the withdrawal of military leaders from formal office and concomitant replacement by civilian presidents in the 1980s.[117] Taking their cue from these developments, liberationists have begun to articulate a vision of what comes after the end of history. The hopes borne by the socialist state having been dashed, liberationists are increasingly finding their political center in the concept of civil society. The opening of the Latin American political scene is being promulgated as the emergence of civil society, a reality that will democratize the state and humanize the economic order. Pablo Richard provides a good example of this "turn to civil society" when he writes at length:

> Today there is a degree of consensus that alternatives to the free market system are arising from civil society. Popular movements, grass roots or alternative movements, constitute the distinguishing feature of that civil society. From an economic standpoint the 1980s were a lost decade, but they were fruitful in generating new social movements, such as the indigenous and Afro-American movements; women's liberation movements; movements of young people and children; ecological movements; movements for alternative agriculture, for people's marketing, for appropriate technology; popular economy movements based on solidarity; movements of shanty town dwellers or of neighborhoods; human rights and solidarity movements (groups of relatives of the disappeared, and so forth); alternative or traditional health movements; movements of popular education, artistic or cultural movements; religious and Christian movements, and so forth. All these movements are building a new civil society with new social actors appearing on the scene.[118]

Even as they recognized the passing of the revolutionary moment, the liberationists welcomed the opening of civic spaces that allowed greater popular participation and influence in government. By the start of the 1990s, civil society had become many liberationists' rejoinder to Hinkelammert's pessimistic query, "¿Capitalismo sin alternativas?"

While the acceptance of the concept of civil society is approaching something of a consensus in Latin America, it would be a mistake to suggest that a similar consensus of opinion surrounds how the concept of civil society is understood. Helio Gallardo, for example, suggests that there are at least three different theories of civil society circulating simultaneously.[119] One model, that of neoliberalism, identifies civil society with the free market and places it over against the state. A second model associates civil society with the emergence of a "new historic sub-ject," which is identified with the various flourishing popular groups. According to this model, these movements will unite in a revolutionary front, seize the state, and establish a socialist order (at which time the state will dissolve into civil society). Gallardo rightly notes that this model offers little more than unreconstructed, traditional leftist politics. The third model casts civil society as a tributary of polit-ical society or the state. Civil society constitutes the realm of citizenship in which popular social movements participate in order to influence and inform politics and the state.

Latin American liberationists are best identified with the third model of civil society. Having felt the repressive weight of an all-powerful state, they have embraced civil society as a means whereby the state can be democratized. By "democratized" liberationists mean that the state is de-bureaucratized and de-militarized; it is opened up, made responsive and accountable to the poor majorities.[120] In the words of Pablo Richard:

> A new space for solidarity is *civil society*. In this space it is not a matter of seizing power, but rather of constructing a new power, from the social movements, with a logic distinct from that of the market. From civil soci-ety we can fight to reconstruct the state, a democratic state at the service of the common good, at the service of the life of all, especially the excluded and nature.[121]

The democratized state is a sort of friendly or domesticated Leviathan that, under the influence of popular pressure, is committed to defending the life of the mar-ginalized and oppressed. It no longer exists simply to service the marketed desires of the industrialized countries of the North and the Latin American elite who serve them; instead it seeks to nurture more egalitarian social relations. The state is cast as one component in a broad effort to build up the common good. The democra-tized state embodies a new, open form of popular participation in the project of government, which is labeled "social democracy" or "participatory politics."[122]

Thus, in stark contrast to neoliberal theories that advocate a minimalist state, liberationists' vision of civil society maintains a vital role for the state. The col-lapse of traditional socialist models of revolution has opened the eyes of liberationists to the need for new, democratic forms of struggle; it has not blinded them to the continued importance of the state in regulating and constraining the capitalist market. This continued commitment to a substantial supervisory role for the state is abundantly clear in the papers presented at a 1992 conference on liberation and development, convened for liberationists at Gutiérrez's Instituto Bartolomé de las Casas. Luiz Eduardo Wanderley accurately conveys the senti-ment of liberationists at this conference when, while discussing the primacy given to the state in Latin America, he suggests that whereas neoconservatives preach the dismantling of the state and the privatization of the Latin American economies, those who struggle for democracy for the majorities seek to eliminate the state's excesses and inefficiencies while securing the state's continued functioning in important sectors and in directing development and social planning.[123] Indeed, while the specifics may differ concerning such matters as the extent of state regulation and planning or the nature of state-business cooperation, the prominent plans put forward by liberationists for confronting the capitalist world order all call for the state's exercising a prominent role in that struggle.[124] The Creole Leviathan, itself tamed by a popular protagonism expressed through the democratic mechanism of civil society, is used to tame the capitalist economy.

The novel directions taken and the revaluations engaged in by liberationists over the course of the past several decades should be neither downplayed nor dismissed. Such moves represent valuable contributions to the work of those who would struggle against the capitalist order. The shift from revolution to civil society is certainly one of the most striking changes in Latin American liberationist thought and it too must not be taken lightly. Yet, running through this tapestry of three decades, with its changing colors and shifting shapes, is a common thread. Liberationists remain committed to an apolitical Church and a vision of politics as statecraft. While their vision of politics in recent years has been nuanced in important ways, it remains a vision of statecraft. The state remains the great hope for countering the depredations of the capitalist order.

Unfortunately, Latin American liberationists are mistaken. As Deleuze and Foucault have shown, the hope liberationists place in civil society must prove illusory. While they rightly celebrate the new opportunities for popular participation that have arisen in the wake of the collapse of authoritarian regimes, liberationists fail to appreciate how savage capitalism, through the neoliberal art of governmentality, renders even the "free space" of civil society a form of discipline and control. In this era of global capitalism, when Coca-Cola and Nike find their way into every nook and cranny of the earth well ahead of clean water, roads, and life-sustaining diets, far from furthering the cause of liberation and life, civil society can only be a means of discipline, an instrument of the regnant capitalist order for overcoming resistance and forming desire in its own image. Indeed, by opting for civil society, Latin American liberationists reflect a commitment to the same insufficiently radical vision that led them to the point of crisis at "the end of history" in the first place, namely, a vision of a Church that traffics in abstract values and apolitical options while the state is granted sovereignty over the social, political, economic field.

The Church of the poor after the end of history

Liberationists would have us believe that the state can be the ally of those who struggle against the capitalist order and that civil society is the means by which the state can be guided in that struggle. Such illusions, however, collapse under the force of Deleuze and Foucault's analyses of savage capitalism. Both the state and civil society are unmasked as servants of the regnant capitalist order, extending its hegemonic rule either by incorporating or crushing resistance. Politics as statecraft is futile. The state is not the friend of those who would be truly free of the madness that is savage capitalism. So where does this leave liberationists? Clearly their vision of the Church of the poor is inadequate; it cannot fund the resistance that they had hoped. Does this mean that the end of history is indeed the end of liberationist thought? Is savage capitalism the master of us all?

In the previous chapter the way in which capitalism functions as a technology of desire was unpacked. Capitalism manipulates human desire so that it is amenable to the demands of production for the market. In so doing, Foucault's account of governmentality reminds us, capitalism neither recognizes nor respects the autonomy of the various dimensions of life. The modern differentiation of life into autonomous realms is a ruse. Such differentiation does not delimit distinct spheres of liberty but, rather, defines thresholds of discipline. As a result, the differentiation of life is nothing other than the construction of a prison, of spaces of control. Each dimension functions as a cell block containing a particular knowledge; with each dimension safely cordoned off from the others, only the capitalist, as warden, freely circulates among all the cells. Hence, if desire is to find safe haven, if there is to be asylum from capitalist discipline, it must be constructed according to a different architectonics.

If Christians are to resist capitalism, if Christianity is to heal desire, the modern differentiation of life, with its separation of politics and religion, must be refused. Christians must recognize that the desacralization of politics that accompanied the birth of the modern nation state was not part of the irresistible march of freedom but, rather, is a crucial moment in the containment of the Church, the stripping of Christianity of its social and political presence, the deprivation of the faith of resources for the struggle.

To some extent Latin American liberationists recognize this. As we have seen, they are critical of secularization when that process leads to the absolute separation of the theological from the political. They are sensitive to the risk that the secularization process they celebrate may proceed too far. Hence, one of the celebrated hallmarks of liberationist thought is the persistent demand that the chasm between theology and politics not remain unbridged, that theology not remain above the fray of human misery. This demand is the driving force behind the ecclesiological innovations that liberationists have championed, such as prodding the Church out of its spiritualist ghetto, where it remained comfortably complicitous with the powerful, while ignoring the cries of those whom Ignacio Ellacuría has poignantly called "the crucified of history."[125]

Yet, even as liberationists are to be commended for encouraging the Church to become, in Jon Sobrino's words, "the true Church of the poor,"[126] their efforts remain insufficient. While the liberationists are busy building a bridge over the chasm between the theological and the political by means of a socio-analytic mediation, the capitalist order has effectively filled in the chasm and is sending its minions (fed on fast food, dressed in some retro pastiche, brandishing corporate logos) swarming across a divide that is no more and never was. In other words, for all that is praiseworthy in their ecclesiological efforts, liberationists continue to define the Church within the limits of the secular order. Even as they insist that the theological and the political be correlated, they maintain the division between the two realms: the Church is not an immediately political agent, the Christian faith does not present a directly political option. At best the Church inspires or motivates Christians under the force of the value of love or the preferential option for the poor to move into the real world of social conflict. In the era of savage capitalism, this will not suffice. Such a vision does not nourish resistance; it only leads to the sense of crisis that currently afflicts the liberationists. This is because in the era of savage capitalism, resistance – no less than defeat – hinges not on getting one's signs and values and religious options right, but on authorities, practices, apparatuses, on techniques of desire. That is to say, where capitalism constitutes a veritable way of life that exercises dominion by capturing and distorting desire, resistance must take the form of an alternative way of life that counters capitalism by liberating and healing desire.

Therefore only a more substantive ecclesiology, one that begins by collapsing the distinction between the theological and the social, between religion and politics, stands a chance of resisting capitalist discipline. This ecclesiology must reclaim the theological as a material, that is, as a fully social, political, economic reality.[127] This ecclesiology will recognize the practice of faith as intrinsically – instead of deriv- atively – social, political, economic. It will begin by conceiving of Christianity not as the apolitical custodian of abstract moral values like "love" that have to be trans- lated into politics but, rather, as a social, political, economic formation (an ensemble of technologies of desire) vying with other formations (technologies of desire) on a single field of lived experience.[128] It will start with the recognition that the Christian *mythos* finds its political correlate, not in the state – even one ordered toward the common good – but in the Church as the exemplary form of human community.[129] This is to say, it begins with the recovery of the Augustinian insight that politics as statecraft is but a secular parody of the true politics that is the fel- lowship of the saints.[130]

This ecclesiology will recognize the Church as an "uncivil society," a society that does not heed the siren call of state-power, a society that refuses the invita- tion to be another interest group in civil society, discerning in such a call and such an invitation surreptitious means of disciplining the Church, rendering the intrinsic political nature of its doctrinal and liturgical practices innocuous, incor- porating it into the capitalist order. This is to say, such an ecclesiology will avoid the privatizing, de-politicizing acids of modernity and recognize the Church, in the words of Reinhard Hütter, as a public in its own right.[131] The Church is a public, gathered and sustained by the Holy Spirit, constituted by peculiar prac- tices such as the breaking of bread, the welcoming of strangers in hospitality, and the reconciliation of sinners. As such, it defies modernity's conceptual confine- ment. It is a public that explodes the secular order's categories of "public" and "private," "religious" and "political," as it worships with the victims of AIDS, offers sanctuary to illegal immigrants, and operates soup kitchens in places not "zoned" for such activities. Likewise, its practice of baptism escapes the private realm of values as it challenges the boundaries of political loyalties, and celebrating the Eucharist directly threatens the economic order by offering and sharing sustenance. All of this is to say that the Church is a public that, short of emasculation, cannot inhabit the private, apolitical space assigned to it as a prison cell by modernity.

Escaping its apolitical solitude, however, does not mean that the Church rushes into the arms of civil society. The Church is a public, but it is not just another public alongside so many others on the illusory landscape of freedom called civil society. It is not, in the words of Ellacuría, "just another power in history, which follows the dynamics of other historical powers."[132] The Church is a public in its own right; it is a public *sui generis*. Hütter and others have cogently argued that the Church is not just another instantiation of the overarching genus *polis* but, rather, collapses the classic political antinomy of *polis* and *oikos*.[133] Construed in terms more pertinent to this essay, the Church is not just another lobbying group or nongovernmental organization. Reflecting on Ephesians 2:19, Bernd Wannenwetsch argues that Christian worship is the corporate joining into the politics of God.[134] The Church's politics is not defined by the secular order. Thus, it finds no home in civil society. The Church's politics culminates not in the centralized rule of the state and its civil society but in the Kingdom of God. The politics of the Kingdom, in turn, amounts to nothing less than participation in the divine life of the Trinity, a life that Leonardo Boff notes is characterized not by the centralized suppression of difference into sameness but by a perichoretic dance that celebrates difference.[135] Thus the Church embodies a de-centralized, participatory politics that defies the discipline of the state and its civil society.

Liberationists, however, need not look north for examples of ecclesiological reconstruction that may fund resistance to the depredations of the capitalist order. In the Latin American context, the Christian base communities have emerged alongside liberation theology as a sign of renewal and hope. Is it possible that the liberationists have in their midst communities of Christian practice that are avowedly anticapitalist while avoiding politics as statecraft?[136] Because the base communities are not monolithic, embracing as they do a broad spectrum of social and political practices, no simple answer will suffice.[137] Nevertheless, it does appear that some of the base communities are, in the words of Leonardo Boff,[138] "reinventing the Church," generating a new ecclesiology that neither heeds the modern boundaries between religion and politics nor succumbs to the allure of the state. These communities display in their life together the intrinsically social, political, economic nature of the Christian faith. As poor Christians come together in non-hierarchical, participatory gatherings to celebrate informal liturgies, as they reflect on Scripture, as they share food, visit the sick, establish a cooperative or undertake a joint work project, and occasionally engage in some form of protest or petition the ruling powers, they are clearly about politics. They are engaged in a long revolution, a struggle with the dominant order that is fought on all fronts, that recognizes no neat division of life into autonomous realms. Indeed, any doubt that these communities – this way of being the Church – embody a political alternative to the state vanishes as we recall the uncooperative and sometimes brutal response of the state to these activities.

One reason that the state rightly recognizes these communities not merely as one more interest group to be incorporated into civil society but as a threat is that many among the base communities are forsaking the politics circumscribed by the state and civil society.[139] To the dismay of those committed to politics as statecraft, many base communities are refusing the politics circumscribed by interest group and party. Among the base communities there is a growing sense of the futility of relying on the state to insure "capitalist development for all"[140] or "capitalism with a human face."[141] There is a growing awareness that democratic processes and civil society can be manipulated and controlled for very undemocratic ends.[142] Indeed, perhaps because they recognize that the future of Latin American democracy might resemble not Costa Rica but Guatemala or Peru, some now refer to the opening up of Latin American society as "low intensity democracy,"[143] that is, as a new phase in the old war against the poor. This refusal of the secular order's politics, however, may not be a symptom of apathy and resignation. Rather, it may be an instantiation of God's politics. As base community members move from worship, where they reflect on Genesis' account of God's creation of the land for the use of all, to the occupation of vacant land, they display the Church as a public in its own right. As they defy the state's order and the state's arms to gather to sing and pray and read Scripture, they display the body of Christ as a distinctive polity or politics. As they circumvent party figures and institutional hurdles and directly confront the state with claims, they present the state with the reality of a different public, a different politics, God's politics. As the state and civil society increasingly reveal their true nature as vassals of the capitalist order, the spread of these communities may well herald the emergence of a new, de-centralized politics capable of funding resistance to capitalist discipline and healing desire. In the next chapter, we look at this alternative politics, at the Christian community as a therapy of desire.

Notes

1 See Michael Novak, *Will It Liberate? Questions About Liberation Theology*, 2nd edn (Lanham, MD: Madison Books, 1991); Paul E. Sigmund, *Liberation Theology at the Crossroads: Democracy or Revolution* (Oxford: Oxford University Press, 1990); Joseph Ratzinger, "Liberation Theology," in *Liberation Theology: A Documentary History*, ed. Alfred T. Hennelly (Maryknoll, NY: Orbis Books, 1990), 367–374; Alistair Kee, *Marx and the Failure of Liberation Theology* (Philadelphia: Trinity Press International, 1990).

2 See, for example, Peter L. Berger, *The Capitalist Revolution* (New York: Basic Books, 1986); Michael Novak, "Introduction to the 1991 Edition," in *Will It Liberate? Questions About Liberation Theology*, ix–xxiv; Richard John Neuhaus, *The Catholic Moment* (New York: Harper & Row, 1987), 171–178; Amy L. Sherman, *Preferential Option* (Grand Rapids, MI: William B. Eerdmans Publishing Co., 1992).

3 Leonardo Boff, *Ecology and Liberation: A New Paradigm*, trans. John Cumming (Maryknoll, NY: Orbis Books, 1995), 93; see also Leonardo Boff, "Christian Liberation Toward the 21st Century," *LADOC* 25 (March/April 1995): 1, 3; Jon Sobrino, "Theology from amidst the Victims," in *The Future of Theology: Essays in Honor of Jürgen*

Moltmann, eds. Miroslav Volf, Carmen Krieg, and Thomas Kucharz (Grand Rapids, MI: William B. Eerdmans Publishing Co., 1996), 164.

4   Pablo Richard, "A Theology of Life: Rebuilding Hope from the Perspective of the South," in *Spirituality of the Third World*, eds. K. C. Abraham and Bernadette Mbuy-Beya (Maryknoll, NY: Orbis, 1994), 96, 92. See also his essay, "El futuro de la iglesia de los pobres: identidad y resistencia en el sistema de globalización neo-liberal," *Pasos* 65 (1996): 9–10. This sentiment is echoed by Helio Gallardo in his essay, "La crisis del socialismo histórico y América Latina," *Pasos* 39 (1992): 15.

5   Franz J. Hinkelammert, "¿Capitalismo sin Alternativas? sobre la sociedad que sostiene que no hay alternativa para ella," *Pasos* 37 (1991): 11; Javier Iguiñiz, "Desarrollo económico y liberación en América Latina," in *Liberación y Desarrollo en América Latina: Perspectivas*, eds. Catalina Romero and Ismael Muñoz (Lima: CEP, 1993), 45.

6   See, for example, Arthur F. McGovern, *Liberation Theology and its Critics* (Maryknoll, NY: Orbis Books, 1989), 23, 197; Rebecca Chopp, *The Praxis of Suffering* (Maryknoll, NY: Orbis Books, 1986), 4; Leonardo Boff, "The Originality of the Theology of Liberation," in *The Future of Liberation Theology: Essays in Honor of Gustavo Gutiérrez*, eds. Marc H. Ellis and Otto Maduro (Maryknoll, NY: Orbis Books, 1989), 38. See also Roberto Oliveros Maqueo, *Liberación y Teología: génesis y crecimiento de una reflexión (1966–1976)* (Lima: CEP, 1977).

7   In a sense my portrayal of the liberationists parallels Gutiérrez's portrayal of the New Christendom model when he observes that it arose as a reaction to Christendom and that, as is the case with every reaction, it remains dependent in a certain manner on the earlier model, a prisoner of the same problematic. See Gustavo Gutiérrez, *La Pastoral de la Iglesia en América Latina* (Montevideo: Ediciones Centro de Documentación, 1968), 36.

8   See Harry Kantor, "Catholic Political Parties and Mass Politics in Latin America," in *Religion and Political Modernization*, ed. Donald E. Smith (New Haven, CT: Yale University Press, 1974), 202–223. See also Lucy C. Behrman, "Catholic Priests and Mass Politics in Chile," in *Religion and Political Modernization*, ed. Donald E. Smith (New Haven, CT: Yale University Press, 1974), 191.

9   Ana María Bidegain, *From Catholic Action to Liberation Theology: The Historical Process of the Laity in Latin America in the Twentieth Century*, Working Paper no. 48 (Notre Dame: The Helen Kellogg Institute for International Studies, 1985), 5.

10 Edward L. Cleary, *Crisis and Change: The Church in Latin America Today* (Maryknoll, NY: Orbis Books, 1985), 4.

11 By examining the "theorization" of New Christendom in this section and of the "Church of the poor" in a later one, I do not mean to suggest either a strong distinction between "theory" and "praxis" or a causal effect of one on the other. With regard to the theory-praxis nexus, I follow John Milbank in asserting that there are neither disembodied ideas nor pre-theoretical praxis. Rather, theory originates in social praxis and praxis occurs always already embedded in a narrative. See John Milbank, *Theology and Social Theory: Beyond Secular Reason* (Cambridge: Basil Blackwell, 1990), 249–252. Note that Maritain's work is examined as one part of the narrative context of the Latin American Church's practice.

12 Tristán de Athaide, "Maritain y América Latina," *Política y Espíritu* 328 (December 1971): 40. Translation is mine.

13 Cleary, *Crisis and Change*, 66; Enrique Dussel, *A History of the Church in Latin America: Colonialism to Liberation*, trans. Alan Neely (Grand Rapids, MI: William B. Eerdmans Publishing Co., 1981), 107. Fernando Moreno, "Jacques Maritain y América Latina," *Tierra Nueva* 13 (1975): 58–61.

14 William Cavanaugh, *Torture and Eucharist* (Malden, MA: Blackwell Publishers, 1998), 172.

15 Paul E. Sigmund, "Maritain on Politics," in *Understanding Maritain: Philosopher and Friend*,

eds. Deal W. Hudson and Matthew J. Mancini (Macon, GA: Mercer University Press, 1987), 165.

16 Jacques Maritain, *The Things That Are Not Caesar's*, trans. J. F. Scanlan (New York: Charles Scribner's Sons, 1931), 5.

17 Jacques Maritain, *Integral Humanism*, trans. Joseph W. Evans (New York: Charles Scribner's Sons, 1968), 97.

18 Maritain, *The Things That Are Not Caesar's*, 2–3.

19 Maritain saw the emergence of the temporal as a real advance, a genuine achievement for Christianity. See *Integral Humanism*, 177; Maritain, *The Things That Are Not Caesar's*, x, 1. Maritain, of course, recognized that secularization was an ambiguous reality, one that could become a threat to Christianity: "The radiating dissolution of the Middle Ages and of its *sacred* forms is the engendering of a *secular* civilization – of a civilization not only secular, but which *separates itself* progressively from the Incarnation". *Integral Humanism*, 15, (italics in original).

20 Maritain, *Integral Humanism*, 105.

21 See Jacques Maritain, *Scholasticism and Politics*, trans. Mortimer J. Adler (New York: Macmillan Co., 1940), 222, 229, 235, 247.

22 Ibid., 247; see also Maritain, *Integral Humanism*, 124.

23 Maritain, *Integral Humanism*, 97–98, 133–134, 176–179; see also Maritain, *Scholasticism and Politics*, 201.

24 Maritain, *Scholasticism and Politics*, 209, 211–212.

25 Ibid., 203.

26 Ibid., 219.

27 Joseph Amato, *Mounier and Maritain: A French Catholic Understanding of the Modern World* (University, AL: University of Alabama Press, 1975), 141–154.

28 The vision of liberal democracy Maritain engaged was North American. Reflecting on his experience of America some years after the fact, Maritain wrote, "When I wrote [*Integral Humanism*], trying to outline a concrete historical ideal suitable to a new Christian civilization, my perspective was definitely European. . . . It took a rather long time for me to become aware of the kind of congeniality which existed between what is going on in this country and a number of views I had expressed in my book." See his *Reflections on America* (New York: Charles Scribner's Sons, 1958), 174–175 and *passim*. See also Jacques Maritain, *Christianity and Democracy*, trans. Doris C. Anson (New York: Charles Scribner's Sons, 1944).

29 Maritain, *Integral Humanism*, 176; see also Maritain, *The Things That Are Not Caesar's*, 2.

30 Jacques Maritain, *The Rights of Man and Natural Law*, trans. Doris C. Anson (New York: Charles Scribner's Sons, 1949), 2.

31 Ibid., 5–7.

32 Ibid., 16–17 (italics in original).

33 See Jacques Maritain, *Man and the State* (Chicago: University of Chicago Press, 1951), 14–19; 28–53.

34 Ibid., 14–15.

35 Ibid., 19.

36 Ibid., 26.

37 Ibid., 24.

38 Ibid., 152 (italics in original).

39 Ibid., 159, 108.

40 The paradigmatic example of this is the American Constitution, which Maritain calls "an outstanding lay Christian document." Maritain, *Man and the State*, 183. See also, Maritain, *Reflections on America*, 182.

41 Maritain, *Man and the State*, 109–114; 147–187.

42 Pablo Richard, *Death of Christendoms, Birth of the Church*, trans. Phillip Berryman (Maryknoll, NY: Orbis Books, 1987), 79–86.

43 See Camilio Torres Restrepo, "Message to Students," in *Latin American Radicalism: A Documentary Report on Left and Nationalist Movements*, eds. Irving Louis Horowitz, José de Castro and John Gerassi (New York: Random House, 1969), 496–498.

44 Gustavo Gutiérrez, "Gustavo Gutiérrez: Opting for the Poor," *The Other Side* 23 (November 1987): 12.

45 See Jeffrey Klaiber, "Prophets and Populists: Liberation Theology, 1968–1988," *The Americas* 46 (July 1989): 3–4; Christian Smith, *The Emergence of Liberation* (Chicago: University of Chicago Press, 1991), 86–87.

46 See Gustavo Gutiérrez, *The Truth Shall Make You Free*, trans. Matthew J. O'Connell (Maryknoll, NY: Orbis Books, 1990), 125.

47 According to the precepts of New Christendom, the mission of the lay apostolic organizations was to evangelize and inspire the temporal order without intervening directly. Catholic Action groups, such as the student organization UNEC, because they were officially affiliated with the Church and as such belonged to the spiritual plane, were not allowed to engage in any activity that was deemed political. See Gustavo Gutiérrez, *A Theology of Liberation*, rev. ed., trans. Caridad Inda and John Eagleson (Maryknoll, NY: Orbis Books, 1988), 37, 39.

48 Matthew O'Meagher, "Catholicism, Reform and Development in Latin America: 1959–67," (Ph.D. diss., Duke University, 1994), 645–650. See also "Gustavo Gutiérrez: Opting for the Poor," 12; Gustavo Gutiérrez, *The Power of the Poor in History*, trans. Robert R. Barr (Maryknoll, NY: Orbis Books, 1983), 25.

49 See Smith, *The Emergence of Liberation Theology*, 136–139.

50 Priests for the Third World, "Basic Agreements," in *LADOC Keyhole Series: Social Activist Priests: Colombia, Argentina*, 42 (italics in original).

51 Cleary, *Crisis and Change*, 60–61.

52 The Second Vatican Council, *Gaudium et spes*, §21, 43. Text is cited here as it is found in Michael Walsh and Brian Davis, eds., *Proclaiming Justice and Peace*, rev. and enl. edn (Mystic, CT: Twenty-Third Publications, 1991), 157–220.

53 Oliveros Maqueo, "Teología de la Liberación: su génesis, crecimiento y consolidación (1968–1988)," in *Teología y Liberación: perspectivas y desafíos. Ensayos en torno a la obra de Gustavo Gutiérrez* (Lima: CEP, 1989), 9; Comblin, "The Church in Latin America After Vatican II," *LADOC* 7 (January/February 1977): 8; Juan Carlos Scannone, "Liberación, Teología de la," in *Conceptos Fundamentales de Pastoral*, eds. Casiano Floristan and Juan-José Tamayo (Madrid: Ediciones Cristiandad, 1983), 563. All translations are mine. Dussel, *A History of the Church in Latin America*, 143.

54 See William T. Cavanaugh, "The Ecclesiologies of Medellín and the Lessons of the Base Communities," *Cross Currents* 44 (1994): 67–84; Mary E. Hobgood, *Catholic Social Teaching and Economic Theory: Paradigms in Conflict* (Philadelphia: Temple University Press, 1991), 156. This point is not lost on liberationists. See, for example, José Comblin, "Medellín: Problemas de Interpretación," *Pasos* (August 1973): 1–5; Gustavo Gutiérrez, *A Theology of Liberation*, 73; Smith, *The Emergence of Liberation Theology*, 160; Hugo Assmann, *Opresión-Liberación: Desafío a los Cristianos* (Montevideo: Tierra Nueva, 1971), 180.

55 Hence, it is unsurprising that Gutiérrez wrote the draft documents on Poverty, that he was one of two who wrote the drafts on Peace, and that Hélder Camara, Renato Poblete, and Samuel Ruiz García wrote the draft on Justice. Smith, *The Emergence of Liberation Theology*, 160.

56 Second General Conference of Latin American Bishops, *The Church in the Present-Day Transformation of Latin America in the Light of the Council*, "Document on the Poverty of the Church," §1–2. All references are to the text as found in *Liberation Theology: A Documentary History*, ed. Alfred T. Hennelly (Maryknoll, NY: Orbis Books, 1992), 114–119.

57 All references to the Medellín documents in the following paragraph are taken from

the final documents on "Justice," "Peace," and "Poverty of the Church" as found in *Liberation Theology: A Documentary History*, ed. Alfred T. Hennelly (Maryknoll, NY: Orbis Books, 1992), 97–119.

58 In the words of Roberto Oliveros, Gutiérrez's book "is a milestone, a qualitative leap in Latin American theology . . . [It] marks a 'before' and 'after' in Latin American theological reflection." Oliveros, "Teología de la Liberación," 92. Translation is mine.

59 Gutiérrez, *A Theology of Liberation*, 17–18.

60 Ibid., 54 (italics in original).

61 Ibid., 17.

62 Gutiérrez, *The Power of the Poor in History*, 144.

63 Gutiérrez, *A Theology of Liberation*, xxxviii.

64 Ibid., 23–24.

65 After all, according to Gutiérrez, progress on this level is to be associated with the insights of Freud. See *A Theology of Liberation*, 20.

66 Ibid., 34.

67 A lengthy critique appears in his earlier work, *La Pastoral de la Iglesia in América Latina* (Montevideo: Ediciones Centro de Documentación, 1968), 18–22, 31–35.

68 Gutiérrez, *A Theology of Liberation*, 37.

69 Ibid., 36.

70 Ibid.

71 In *The Truth Shall Make You Free* Gutiérrez contrasts the European experience of secularization, which has had a predominantly negative effect on faith, with what is occurring in Latin America, arguing that secularization does not of necessity have to play itself out in the same way everywhere: "Liberation theology is anything but the Latin American spearhead of the secularizing thrust or of a 'bourgeois Christianity.' We think rather that a clear rejection, inspired by Christian faith, of the inhuman poverty existing in Latin America will militate against the negative side of secularism and the modern spirit. We are convinced that liberation thinking starts from a social, cultural, and religious situation differing from that of Europe and that this situation offers unparalleled historical possibilities that we must explore and develop" (115; see also 26).

Donald E. Smith reinforces Gutiérrez's suggestion that secularization is not a monolithic process. However, he also suggests that at least in some instances secularization in Latin America has been unequivocally hostile to religion. See his "Patterns of Secularization in Latin America," in *Religion and Political Modernization*, ed. Donald E. Smith (New Haven: Yale University Press, 1974), 116–131.

72 Gutiérrez, *A Theology of Liberation*, 42, 17–22.

73 Ibid., 44. He links this realization with the work of Yves de Montcheuil, Henri de Lubac, and Karl Rahner. For an overview of the debate concerning nature and grace, see Henri de Lubac, *The Mystery of the Supernatural*, trans. Rosemary Sheed (New York: Herder and Herder, 1967) and Stephen J. Duffy, *The Graced Horizon: Nature and Grace in Modern Catholic Thought* (Collegeville, MN: Liturgical Press, 1992). See also Fergus Kerr, "French Theology: Yves Congar and Henri de Lubac," in *The Modern Theologians*, 2nd edn, ed. David Ford (Cambridge: Blackwell Publishers, 1997), 105–117, and Fergus Kerr, *Immortal Longings: Versions of Transcending Humanity* (London: SPCK, 1997), 162–184. For a critique of the liberationists on this point, as well as an alternative account of the relation of nature and grace that corresponds to the direction taken in this project, see Milbank, *Theology and Social Theory*, 206–255.

74 Ibid., 109.

75 Ibid., 147.

76 Ibid., 45. In 1969 he wrote, "The Church is the world itself that lives in history and is oriented towards a future that is promised by the Lord." See Gutiérrez, "Notes on

a theology of liberation," in *In Search of a Theology of Development*, ed. Sodepax (Geneva: Ecumenical Centre, 1970), 150.

77 Gutiérrez, *The Power of the Poor in History*, 47.

78 Ibid., 40; Gutiérrez, *A Theology of Liberation*, 41.

79 Ibid., 40, 47, 188.

80 Ibid., 37, 39.

81 Ibid., 85.

82 Ibid., 104.

83 Ibid.,138. See also Gutiérrez, *The Power of the Poor in History*, 69; Gutiérrez, *The Truth Shall Make You Free*, 64–66 (and page 78 for a problematic exception that threatens the clarity and coherence of the distinctions he is trying to maintain). This separation is also behind his oft repeated phrase that his theology is not one meant to justify positions already taken. See Gutiérrez, *A Theology of Liberation*, xiii; Gutiérrez, *The Truth Shall Make You Free*, 64.

84 Gutiérrez, *The Truth Shall Make You Free*, 64.

85 Gutiérrez, *The Power of the Poor in History*, 101, 93–94.

86 Gutiérrez, *A Theology of Liberation*, 5.

87 Ibid., xxxiv. See also Gutiérrez, *The Truth Shall Make You Free*, 56. Note that Christian praxis is theological practice and as such is, according to Gutiérrez's scheme, non-political.

88 Ibid., xxxiii. See also page 9 where theology is equated with reflection on basic human principles. As for theology being a matter of reflection on the abstract value, love, that must constantly be given content in the real material realm, see Gustavo Gutiérrez, *The God of Life*, trans. Matthew J. O'Connell (Maryknoll, NY: Orbis, 1991), 119, 137.

89 For the sake of completeness it should be noted that this relationship is not as static or as linear as I have cast it here. In truth Gutiérrez is well aware that we always start theological theorization in the middle, in the midst of an already engaged political practice. Thus a circle or dialectic already obtains: in one direction, theology extracts values from faith and correlates them with political action; in the other direction, theology (with the requisite aid of the social sciences) evaluates political practice to see if it correlates with values extracted from the faith. In spite of this flattening of Gutiérrez's account, I believe my description accurately shows the relationship between the two realms, particularly the priority of faith over (political) praxis. For more on the priority of faith and the Gospel over praxis see, Gutiérrez, *A Theology of Liberation*, xxxiv; Gutiérrez, *The Truth Shall Make You Free*, 101, 181n45.

90 Gustavo Gutiérrez, "La Iglesia y la Problemática Social," *Defensa Nacional: Revista del Centro de Altos Estudios Militares* 6 (1987): 128.

91 Gustavo Gutiérrez, "Liberation Theology: Its Message Examined," *Harvard Divinity Bulletin* 19 (Spring 1989): 7; see also Gutiérrez, *The Truth Shall Make You Free*, 129–130. When Gutiérrez writes of a "political dimension of the gospel," it is to the first, general meaning that he is referring. See Gutiérrez, *The Power of the Poor in History*, 67; Gutiérrez, *A Theology of Liberation*, 154.

Gutiérrez's positing of a two-fold sense of politics and his limiting the Church to the more abstract level bears a striking resemblance to the New Christendom model, particularly as this model is spelled out by the Latin American bishops at their Third General Conference in 1979, at Puebla. There, drawing on the social teaching of the Church and Pius XI's instructions concerning Catholic Action and politics, the bishops distinguish between politics in the general sense of concern for the common good and the fostering of values – which is the proper political task of the Church and her clergy – and politics in the concrete sense of parties, power, and ideologies – which is the domain of the laity, and which although inspired by the Church, cannot claim the direct support of the Church. See §521–530 of the Final Document, in *Puebla and*

Beyond, eds. John Eagleson and Philip Scharper (Maryknoll, NY: Orbis Books, 1979), 196–197.

Incidentally, in their pastoral letter condemning the Christians for Socialism movement, issued shortly after the Pinochet coup, the Chilean bishops invoke a similar distinction between "politics insofar as it underlies every social reality" and politics as "partisan activity," and limit the Church to the former. See "Christian Faith and Political Activity: Declaration of the Chilean Bishops," in *Christians and Socialism: Documentation of the Christians for Socialism Movement in Latin America*, ed. John Eagleson (Maryknoll, NY: Orbis Books, 1975), 196–197.

92   Richard, *Death of Christendoms, Birth of the Church*, 172.

93   Ibid., 173. See also Hugo Villela, "La Defensa de los Derechos Humans como 'Solidaridad' con los Oprimidos," in *Carter y la lógica del imperialismo*, ed. Hugo Assmann (San José: EDUCA, 1978), 396.

94   Gutiérrez, "Notes on a theology of liberation," 150.

95   Richard, *Death of Christendoms, Birth of the Church*, 184. Similar statements can be found in Gutiérrez, *The Power of the Poor in History*, 46; Richard Shaull, "The Church and Revolutionary Change: Contrasting Perspectives," in *The Church and Social Change in Latin America*, ed. Henry A. Landsberger (Notre Dame: University of Notre Dame Press, 1970),150.

96   In addition to Gutiérrez, see Jon Sobrino, *The True Church and the Poor*, trans. Matthew J. O'Connell (Maryknoll, NY: Orbis Books, 1984), 7–38. This leads Jürgen Moltmann to ask liberationists where Latin America is in their thought. See his "An Open Letter to José Míguez Bonino," in *Liberation Theology: A Documentary History*, ed. Alfred T. Hennelly (Maryknoll, NY: Orbis Books, 1990), 196–199.

97   Gutiérrez, *The Power of the Poor in History*, 186.

98   Gutiérrez, *The Truth Shall Make You Free*, 113.

99   Gustavo Gutiérrez, "Freedom and Salvation: A Political Problem," in *Liberation and Change*, ed. Ronald H. Stone (Atlanta: John Knox Press, 1977), 30. The phrase is Hegel's. For a compelling critique of the claim that the weakness of the Enlightenment project stems from its "incompletion" rather than from its foundational premises, see Uday S. Mehta, "Liberal Strategies of Exclusion," *Politics and Society* 18 (1990): 427–454. See also Anthony Arblaster, *The Rise and Decline of Western Liberalism* (Cambridge: Basil Blackwell, 1984).

100   Gutiérrez, *The Power of the Poor in History*, 49.

101   Gutiérrez, *A Theology of Liberation*, 20.

102   The paradigmatic examples of this early commitment to socialism are the group "Christians for Socialism" in Chile in 1971 (see John Eagleson, ed., *Christians and Socialism: Documentation of the Christians for Socialism Movement in Latin America*) and Juan Luis Segundo's "Capitalism Versus Socialism: Crux Theologica," in *Frontiers of Theology in Latin America*, ed. Rosino Gibellini (Maryknoll, NY: Orbis Books, 1979), 240–259. Gutiérrez was a member of Christians for Socialism and references to socialism occur in his early work. See Gutiérrez, *A Theology of Liberation*, 17, 20, 55–56, 65; Gutiérrez, *The Power of the Poor in History*, 37, 45, 46, 191. In his more recent works Gutiérrez does not refer to socialism. While it is possible that this silence is the result of the rejection of his earlier position, I am inclined to think that it is more likely the result both of a certain maturing of the movement – a recognition that the much anticipated revolution is not quite so imminent – and of an effort to avoid language that is unnecessarily provocative and too easily misunderstood.

For a recent account of the growth and development of liberation theology that highlights its relationship with Marxism, to the point of suggesting that liberation theology is rightly understood as the proletarian form of Christianity that functions as the ideology of the socialist mode of production in a manner that parallels bourgeois

Christianity's functioning as the ideology for capitalism, see Samuel Silva Gotay, *La Teología de la Liberación: implicaciones para la Iglesia y para el Marxismo* (Santo Domingo: CEPAE, 1985).

103 The Marxist tradition is not monolithic and exactly how the state is conceived and what role it plays in the revolution are contested. Nevertheless, for all of its diversity, the tradition has been marked by a consistent adherence to a conception of politics as statecraft. For more on the several different Marxist theories of the state, see Bob Jessop, *State Theory: Putting Capitalist States in Their Place* (University Park, PA: Pennsylvania State University Press, 1990). For an interesting discussion of Marxist socialism as an Enlightenment tradition and the counter-Enlightenment tradition of what he calls "old-style Christian socialism," see John Milbank, "On Baseless Suspicion: Christianity and the Crisis of Socialism," *New Blackfriars* 69 (1988): 4–19.

104 Marcos Kaplan, *Estado y Sociedad en América Latina* (Oaxaca: Editorial Oasis, 1984), 9.

105 I am suggesting that the commitment to the state was not something new because the state played a substantial role in the development of capitalism in Latin America, a much larger role than is generally recognized in developed capitalist countries. See Jorge Larraín, *Theories of Development: Capitalism, Colonialism, and Dependency* (Cambridge: Basil Blackwell, 1989), 206, 208. See also Guillermo O'Donnell, "Peripheral Developments: Comparative Historical Formations of the State Apparatus and Socio-economic Change in the Third World," *International Social Science Journal* 32 (1980): 717–729.

  On the statist orientation of thinking during this period, see Norbert Lechner, *Patios Interiores de la Democracia* (Santiago: FLASCO, 1988), 27; Iguiñiz, "Desarrollo económico y liberación en América Latina," 41, 47.

106 For an account of the evolution of the statist conception of politics in Latin America, see Alfred Stepan, *The State and Society: Peru in Comparative Perspective* (Princeton: Princeton University Press, 1978), 3–72; Howard J. Wiarda, "Toward a Framework for the Study of Political Change in the Iberic-Latin Tradition: The Corporative Model," *World Politics* 25 (1973): 206–235; Claudio Véliz, "Centralism and Nationalism in Latin America," in *Politics and Social Change in Latin America: Still a Distinct Tradition?* ed. Howard J. Wiarda (San Francisco: Westview Press, 1992), 111–124; Richard M. Morse, "Toward a Theory of Spanish American Government," in *Politics and Social Change in Latin America: Still a Distinct Tradition?* ed. Howard J. Wiarda (San Francisco: Westview Press, 1992), 125–145; Glen Dealy, "The Tradition of Monistic Democracy in Latin America," in *Politics and Social Change in Latin America: Still a Distinct Tradition?* ed. Howard J. Wiarda (San Francisco: Westview Press, 1992), 40–69.

107 It should be pointed out that the military regime in Peru under Velasco Alvarado did not start out as a bureaucratic-authoritarian state, although it became one when Morales Bermúdez came to power in 1975. For an account of the bureaucratic-authoritarian state, see Guillermo O'Donnell, "Reflections on the Patterns of Change in the Bureaucratic-Authoritarian State," *Latin American Research Review* 13 (1978): 3–38; Guillermo O'Donnell, "Tensions in the Bureaucratic-Authoritarian State and the Question of Democracy," in *The New Authoritarianism in Latin America*, ed. David Collier (Princeton: Princeton University, 1979), 285–318.

108 It is well known that Medellín functioned as a revitalizing call not only for the most radical sectors of the Church, but for the most conservative and reactionary as well. Alarmed by the direction in which they saw the Church headed, conservatives mobilized, and with the support of the Vatican gained control of CELAM and swiftly moved to squelch the growth and spread of liberation theology. José Comblin calls CELAM in the seventies, "a war machine directed against the theology of liberation." See Comblin, "The Church and the Defence of Human Rights," in *The Church in Latin America 1492–1992*, ed. Enrique Dussel (Maryknoll, NY: Orbis Books, 1992), 442; see

    also José Comblin, *The Church and the National Security State* (Maryknoll, NY: Orbis Books, 1979); Smith, *The Emergence of Liberation Theology*, 186, 189–198.

109 Leonardo Boff, "Christ's Liberation via Oppression: An Attempt at Theological Construction from the Standpoint of Latin America," in *Frontiers of Theology in Latin America*, ed. Rosino Gibellini (Maryknoll, NY: Orbis Books, 1979), 129–130.

110 What follows is drawn largely from Norberto Lechner, *Los Patios Interiores de la Democracia*, 25–29. See also Franz J. Hinkelammert, *Democracia y Totalitarismo* (San José: DEI, 1987), 211–228; Daniel H. Levine, "Paradigm Lost: Dependency to Democracy," *World Politics* 40 (1988): 377–394; Phillip Berryman, "Other Experiences, Other Concerns: Latin America and the Democratization of the Church," in *A Democratic Catholic Church: The Reconstruction of Roman Catholicism*, eds. Eugene C. Bianchi and Rosemary Radford Ruether (New York: Crossroad Publishing Co., 1992), 136–138.

111 While it was undoubtedly true of some leftists, it would be a mistake to think that concern for democracy was something novel for liberationists. As we have already seen from Gutiérrez's treatment of the Enlightenment, democracy was praised from the outset of the liberationist project. What was suspect was "bourgeois democracy," a democratic veneer that concealed undemocratic economic processes.

112 See Fernando H. Cardoso, "The Consumption of Dependency Theory in the United States," *Latin American Research Review* 12 (1977): 7–24; Arthur F. McGovern, "Dependency Theory, Marxist Analysis, and Liberation Theology," in *The Future of Liberation Theology: Essays in Honor of Gustavo Gutiérrez*, eds. Marc H. Ellis and Otto Maduro (Maryknoll, NY: Orbis Books, 1989), 272–286.

113 Xabier Gorostiaga, "La Mediación de las Ciencias Sociales y los Cambios Internacionales," in *Cambio Social y Pensamiento Cristiano en América Latina*, eds. José Comblin, José Ignacio González Faus, and Jon Sobrino (Madrid: Editorial Trotta, 1993), 123; Iguiñiz, "Desarrollo económico y liberación en América Latina," 46; see also João Batista Libânio, "Panorama de la teología de América Latina en los ultimos veinte años," in *Cambio Social y Pensamiento Cristiano en América Latina*, eds. José Comblin, José Ignacio González Faus, and Jon Sobrino (Madrid: Editorial Trotta, 1993), 57–58.

114 Gustavo Gutiérrez, quoted in Phillip Berryman, "Church and Revolution: Reflections on Liberation Theology," *NACLA Report on the Americas* 30 (March/April 1997): 10.

115 Elsa Tamez, "De silencios y gritos. Job y Qohélet en los noventa," *Pasos* 82 (1999): 2, 5; "When the Horizons Close Upon Themselves: A Reflection Upon the Utopian Reason of Qohélet," in *Liberation Theologies, Postmodernity, and the Americas*, eds. David Batstone, Eduardo Mendieta, Lois Ann Lorentzen, and Dwight N. Hopkins (New York: Routledge, 1997), 53.

116 Franz J. Hinkelammert, "Changes in the Relationships Between Third World Countries and First World Countries," in *Spirituality of the Third World*, eds. K. C. Abraham and Bernadette Mbuy-Beya (Maryknoll, NY: Orbis, 1994), 10–11.

117 Peter H. Smith, "Crisis and Democracy in Latin America," *World Politics* 43 (1991): 621.

118 Richard, "A Theology of Life," 98. See also Richard, "El futuro de la iglesia del los pobres," *Pasos* 65 (1996): 11–12, and Gorostiaga, "La Mediación de las Ciencias Sociales y los Cambios Internacionales," 134.

119 Helio Gallardo, "Notas sobre la sociedad civil," *Pasos* 57 (1995):16–28. For an interesting account of how the state and civil society have *functioned* in a variety of ways in recent years in Latin America, see Alfred Stepan, "State Power and the Strength of Civil Society in the Southern Cone of Latin America," in *Bringing the State Back In*, eds. Peter B. Evans, Dietrich Rueschemeyer, and Theda Skocpol (Cambridge: Cambridge University Press, 1985), 317–343.

120 Richard, "A Theology of Life," 100.

121 Pablo Richard, "Teología de la solidaridad en el contexto actual de economía neoliberal de libre mercado," *Pasos* 83 (1999): 6. See also Pablo Richard, "Las Iglesias de

América Latina y El Caribe en Búsqueda de Alternativas," *Pasos* 89 (2000): 14; Wim Dierckxsens, "Globalización, política, y ciudadanía," *Pasos* 87 (2000): 9.

122 Leonardo Boff, *Liberation and Ecology: A New Paradigm,* trans. John Cumming (Maryknoll, NY: Orbis Books, 1995), 82, 83, 127.

123 Luiz Eduardo Wanderley, "El desarrollo desde la práctica y perspectiva de los sujetos sociales," in *Liberación y Desarrollo en América Latina: Perspectivas,* eds. Catalina Romero and Ismael Muñoz (Lima: CEP, 1993), 284.

124 Catalina Romero and Ismael Muñoz, eds., *Liberación y Desarrollo en América Latina: Perspectivas* (Lima: CEP, 1993), *passim.*

125 Ignacio Ellacuría, "The Crucified People," in *Mysterium Liberationis: Fundamental Concepts of Liberation Theology,* eds. Ignacio Ellacuría and Jon Sobrino (Maryknoll, NY: Orbis Books, 1993), 580–603.

126 Jon Sobrino, *The True Church and the Poor.*

127 I suggest that this is a "reclaiming" because, as John Milbank has written, "once there was no secular." For more on this, see his *Theology and Social Theory: Beyond Secular Reason.* For one attempt to reclaim the theological as material, see Nicholas Lash, *A Matter of Hope* (Notre Dame: University of Notre Dame Press, 1981).

128 Although Christian theological convictions may preclude the assertion that Christianity is *just* one social formation among others or even that it is a social formation *like* other social formations in anything other than an analogous way. See, for example, Reinhard Hütter, "The Church as Public: Dogma, Practice, and the Holy Spirit," *Pro Ecclesia* 3 (1994): 334–361. See also his "Ecclesial Ethics, The Church's Vocation, and Paraclesis," *Pro Ecclesia* 2 (1993): 433–450.

129 I owe this way of putting things to Frederick Christian Bauerschmidt, *Julian of Norwich and the Mystical Body Politic of Christ* (Notre Dame, University of Notre Dame Press, 1999), 9. See also Milbank, *Theology and Social Theory,* 388.

130 See William T. Cavanaugh, "The City: Beyond Secular Parodies," in *Radical Orthodoxy,* eds. John Milbank, Catherine Pickstock, and Graham Ward (New York: Routledge, 1999), 185.

131 Reinhard Hütter, "The Church as Public: Dogma, Practice, and the Holy Spirit," *Pro Ecclesia* 3 (1994): 334–361.

132 Ignacio Ellacuría, "The Church of the Poor, Historical Sacrament of Liberation," in *Mysterium Liberationis,* eds. Ignacio Ellacuría and Jon Sobrino (Maryknoll, NY: Orbis Books, 1993), 548. See also Ignacio Ellacuría *Conversión de la Iglesia al reino de Dios* (San Salvador: UCA Editores, 1985), 15.

133 Hütter, "The Church as Public," 352–357; Bernd Wannenwetsch, "The Political Worship of the Church: A Critical and Empowering Practice," *Modern Theology* 12 (1996): 269–299; Milbank, *Theology and Social Theory,* 364–369.

134 Wannenwetsch, "The Political Worship of the Church," 279–280.

135 Leonardo Boff, *Trinity and Society,* trans. Paul Burns (Maryknoll, NY: Orbis, 1988), 118–119, 196.

136 At this point perhaps a word is in order about the anti-statist politics advocated in this work. Particularly in the context of the United States, where a virulent strand of anti-Federalism is currently flourishing, it may appear that my argument plays into the hands of those who wish to strip the poor of any protection and deliver them to the market. My response to this is two-fold. First, the anti-statist position I advocate is to be distinguished from the neoliberal economists and their disciples insofar as, whereas they profess to be anti-statist, in fact they only oppose a certain kind of (welfare) state. Rhetoric aside, they actually embrace what Alfred Stepan ("State Power and the Strength of Civil Society," 324) calls a "small-state, strong-state," that is, a state that is long on disciplinary power (military/police) and short on welfare. Second, the anti-statist position I put forward only leaves one naked before the forces of the market if the Spirit is not forming alternative communities capable of resisting.

137 For more on the diversity of such groups, see Phillip Berryman, "Basic Christian Communities and the Future of Latin America," *Monthly Review* 36 (1984): 27–40; John Burdick, *Looking for God in Brazil* (Berkeley: University of California Press, 1993); W. E. Hewitt, "Myths and Realities of Liberation Theology: The Case of Basic Christian Communities in Brazil," in *The Politics of Latin American Liberation Theology*, eds. Richard L. Rubenstein and John K. Roth (Washington, DC: Washington Institute Press, 1988), 135–155; Rowan Ireland, *Kingdoms Come: Religion and Politics in Brazil* (Pittsburgh: University of Pittsburgh Press, 1991); John M. Kirk, "Whither the Catholic Church in the 1990s?" in *Capital, Power, and Inequality in Latin America*, eds. Sandor Halebsky and Richard L. Harris (Boulder, CO: Westview Press, 1995), 241-244; Daniel H. Levine, *Popular Voices in Latin American Catholicism* (Princeton: Princeton University Press, 1992).

On the prospects for the emergence of anti-capitalist and non-statist politics beyond the base communities see Roger Burbach, "Socialism is Dead. Long Live Socialism," *NACLA Report on the Americas* 31 (November/December 1997): 15–20; James Petras, "Latin America: The Resurgence of the Left," *New Left Review* 223 (May/June 1997): 17–47.

138 Leonardo Boff, *Ecclesiogenesis: The Base Communities Reinvent the Church*, trans. Robert R. Barr (Maryknoll, NY: Orbis Books, 1986); see also Pedro A. Ribeiro de Oliveira, "Conflict and Change in the Brazilian Catholic Church," in *A Democratic Catholic Church: The Reconstruction of Roman Catholicism*, eds. Eugene C. Bianchi and Rosemary Radford Ruether (New York: Crossroad Publishing Co., 1992), 139–155.

139 See Berryman, "Other Experiences, Other Concerns: Latin America and the Democratization of the Church"; William T. Cavanaugh, "The Ecclesiologies of Medellín and the Lessons of the Base Communities," 78–80; Helio Gallardo, "Actores sociales, movimiento popular y sujeto histórico en la América Latina de la década de los noventa," in *América Latina: Resistir por la Vida*, ed. REDLA-CPID (San José: DEI, 1994), 80–84; Helio Gallardo, "Globalización, reforma del Estado y sector campesino," *Pasos* 63 (1996): 5; Isabel Rauber, "Actores sociales, luchas reivindicativas y política popular," *Pasos* 62 (1995): 15–31.

140 Helio Gallardo, "Notas sobre la situación mundial observada desde América Latina," *Pasos* 54 (1994): 21.

141 Juan José Tamayo, *Presente y Futuro de la Teología de la Liberación* (Madrid: San Pablo, 1994), 78. It should be noted that Tamayo does not use this label (as I am) in association with liberationist economic proposals such as those put forward at el Instituto Bartolomé de las Casas.

142 See José Comblin, "The Church and the Defence of Human Rights," 435, 453; Enrique Dussel, "From the Second Vatican Council to the Present Day," in *The Church in Latin America 1492–1992*, ed. Enrique Dussel (Maryknoll, NY: Orbis Books, 1992), 168, 178; Helio Gallardo, "Democratización y Democracia en América Latina," *Pasos* 68 (1996): 10–19; Helio Gallardo, "Elementos de antipolítica y de política in América Latina," *Pasos* 65 (1996): 21, 23; Judith Adler Hellman, "Social Movements: Revolution, Reform and Reaction," *NACLA Report on the Americas* 30 (May/June 1997): 13–18; Franz J. Hinkelammert, *Democracia y Totalitarismo*, 211–228; Jorge Nef, "Demilitarization and Democratic Transition in Latin America," in *Capital, Power, and Inequality in Latin America*, eds. Sandor Halebsky and Richard L. Harris (Boulder, CO: Westview Press, 1995), 81–107.

143 Gorostiaga, "La Mediación de las Ciencias Sociales y los Cambios Internacionales," 133. An association is obviously being made with the notorious military practice of "low intensity warfare." See Michael T. Klare and Peter Kornbluh, *Low Intensity Warfare* (New York: Pantheon Books, 1988) and Jack Nelson Pallmeyer, *War Against the Poor* (Maryknoll, NY: Orbis, 1989).

3

CHRISTIANITY, DESIRE, AND THE TERROR OF JUSTICE

In the third chapter of Genesis, according to the Christian tradition, desire is ensnared by a serpent, with horrendous consequences. Life is now sustained only by the sweat of the brow; creation does not willingly yield its fruits. Human relations become agonistic; they are tainted with dominion and violence. Desire is corrupted, captured, bent from its true course. With the arrival of savage capitalism, desire has been ensnared in the coils of yet another serpent, with consequences no less dire. The veins of the earth are torn open and drained with impunity. Much of humanity languishes while a privileged minority revels in its cancerous consumption. Desire is entangled in a vast array of technologies that chain it to the global market's processes of production and consumption. And the Latin American liberationists' vision of a Church of the poor, a Church that opts for the languishing masses of marginalized and excluded, is unable to fund resistance. It is in crisis because it misconstrues both the nature of the struggle and the resources that Christianity may provide in waging that struggle. Its vision is simply not radical enough to meet the challenge of a savage capitalism that wages war against humanity on all fronts – at the level of ontology, desire – and not just at the level of political economy.

We need not concede Fukuyama's point, however, and join the ranks of capitalism's suitors. At least not yet, for even as the liberationists falter, rays of hope emanate from the excluded spaces of Latin America. As the last chapter suggested, around the liberationists Christian communities that appear to be throwing off the shackles of politics as statecraft are emerging from the dark violence of the last several decades. Instead they are embodying forms of resistance and struggle that refuse to submit to the control of the state and its civil society. This chapter and the one that follows develop an account of Christian resistance to the capitalist order analogous to the witness of these communities.[1] Christianity is displayed as something other than the apolitical custodian of disembodied moral values like "love" or the religious repository of a grammar, even one as compelling as the "preferential option for the poor," that is supposed to inspire Christians to leave the stain-glassed realm of the sacred and enter the material world of social and political struggle. Instead, Christianity is reclaimed as a fully material or embodied reality ("The Word became flesh"), whose practices – such as baptism, catechesis,

Eucharist, discipline, prayer, and discipleship – do not merely mediate "ideas" and "values" but rather transform the material circumstances of Christian (and, more generally, human) existence. In opposition to savage capitalism and the governmental logic of its subservient state-form, Christianity is cast as the exemplary form of human community, the true politics.[2] This is to say, Christianity is reclaimed as an ensemble of technologies that reforms or shapes desire in ways that counter the capitalist discipline of desire. The first chapter asserted that contemporary capitalism is not merely an economic system but rather constitutes a discipline of desire. The second chapter displayed the futility of Christian resistance to contemporary capitalism when that resistance fails to recognize the nature of capitalism as a discipline of desire. Now I argue that Christian resistance to capitalism is contingent upon Christianity's enactment as a counter ensemble of technologies of desire. Christianity may fund resistance to capitalism only if it is reclaimed as a fully material (social, political, economic) formation that constitutes nothing less than a therapy of desire.

This argument proceeds in several steps, beginning with the retrieval of Christianity as an ensemble of technologies of desire. At the conclusion of the previous chapter I argued that some of the Latin American base communities appear to be living Christianity as a social, political, economic formation. Now I argue that as such a material formation, Christianity is rightly understood as a therapy of desire. While my argument ultimately rests on the claim that the Church of the poor in Latin America may be embodying just such a therapy, for the sake of simplicity and clarity I begin with an historical example of Christianity as an ensemble of technologies of desire. Christian history is replete with examples. I draw upon the practice of Bernard of Clairvaux and the Cistercian order he led. The example of Bernard and the Cistercians, although not without its difficulties, is particularly illuminating not only because the account of human desire for God found in Bernard's sermons on the Song of Songs remains a classic portrayal of Christianity as fundamentally a matter of desire, but also because the Cistercian practice of Christianity, in particular, is amenable to conceptualization as an ensemble of technologies that does not repress but heals and renews the desire of God.

Having retrieved Christianity as a technology of desire, the next step, to which the bulk of the final two chapters is devoted, involves an inquiry into the character of the therapy of desire that constitutes Christianity. With specific regard to its ability to resist capitalism, what kind of therapy does Christianity proffer? The banner behind which much of capitalism's opposition rallies today is "justice." Is the therapy of desire that Christianity offers called justice? Is justice the name of that ensemble of technologies that holds the most promise for resisting capitalism? Does Christianity's witness against savage capitalism revolve around the formation of just persons? This chapter focuses on the desire for justice in Latin America as that desire has been articulated by the liberationists. Justice is perhaps second only to liberation as the concept most readily associated with the Latin American liberationists and it is they who are largely responsible for the increased emphasis on justice in contemporary Christianity. After presenting the liberationists' conception of justice, the chapter closes with an analysis of that account, an analysis that reveals several weaknesses, which in turn suggests that justice so conceived does not accurately describe the therapy that Christianity offers in the hopes of liberating desire from capitalist discipline.

Christianity and desire

Christianity is not an apolitical custodian of moral values that need to be translated into social and political practices. Rather, it is a fully social, political, economic reality. It is not a spiritual reality properly juxtaposed to capitalism as a material reality. On the contrary, it is, no less than capitalism, an ensemble of technologies of desire. Given the dismal history of the Church's direct political engagement in Latin America, it is understandable that the liberationists would continue to heed the barriers modernity erects between politics and religion. Nevertheless, given the nature of contemporary capitalism, such a means of protecting the people from the Church comes at too high a price. As the previous chapters displayed, such a model of the Church and politics cripples Christianity's ability to resist capitalism. As Deleuze and Foucault show, capitalism is an ensemble of technologies that disciplines desire and if it is to be resisted then such resistance must take the form of nothing less than a counter-ensemble of technologies. Values and preferential options are insufficient. The "end of history" has brought this weakness into sharp relief and, if the accounts of liberationists and others are accurate, many poor Christian communities in Latin American appear to have learned the lesson. They have begun to reassert themselves as immediately political formations. Specifically, they have begun to reclaim Christianity as an ensemble of technologies of desire that stands against capitalist discipline.

Such a claim is, of course, not one that those communities would necessarily advance themselves. Indeed, the claim that Christianity is an ensemble of technologies of desire is not likely to strike a chord among many Christians today. It is a distinctly alien note, clearly the product of juxtaposing the work of Deleuze and Foucault to Christianity. The claim, therefore, demands justification; the legitimacy of construing Christianity as an ensemble of technologies of desire is not self-evident. Indeed, the impersonal, even mechanical connotations of the concept "technology" strike one as antithetical to the more interpersonal tone appropriate to Christianity. Foucault's understanding of technologies as heterogeneous assemblages of discourses, institutions, architectural forms, regulatory decisions, laws, administrative measures, scientific statements, philosophical, moral and philanthropic propositions, and so forth certainly seems worlds apart from a first-century Jew who gathered followers by uttering the simple words, "Follow me." Perhaps Alasdair MacIntyre's notion of a "practice" would be more amenable to the human tenor of Christianity?[3] The notion of practice has proven helpful in some construals of Christianity; nevertheless, in this case "technology" is preferred precisely because of its impersonal, or one might say "extrapersonal," connotations.

Foucault's concept of technology is helpful in casting Christianity as an alternative or antigen to capitalist modes of disciplining desire insofar as it is a reminder that resistance is more than a matter of individual practices. The display of Christianity as a therapy of desire is not just another retrieval of personalist politics.[4] Just as capitalism captures desire and rules by means of a whole host of technologies, by means of a vast array of assemblages of knowledges, instruments, persons, systems of judgment, buildings and spaces, so too Christianity must be conceived as a multitude of inter-, intra-, and extra-personal technologies if it is to fund resistance and liberate desire.

Likewise it is not readily apparent that Christianity ought to be construed in terms of desire. Modern Western Christianity has imbibed deeply from the well of the Enlightenment, and as a result reason and rationality have taken pride of place in Christian moral psychology.[5] This is not to say that modern Christianity has vanquished desire. On the contrary, modern Christianity could be characterized as obsessed with desire. Modern Christianity is obsessed with subduing desire, with controlling desire, understood as the natural passions and reactions of the body to external stimuli. Far from leaving desire behind, modern Christianity seeks to subdue desire and bring it before the bar of reason. According to this view, desire, understood as a largely negative phenomenon, is something to be restrained and suppressed.

Such a singularly negative view of desire, however, is a relatively recent development. Prior to the advent of modernity, Christianity took a decidedly more nuanced approach to desire. Indeed, it is not too much to say that for much of its history the end of Christianity was conceived in terms of the cultivation of a desire or passion for God. Recall the statement of Augustine, who is often invoked by moderns as a paradigmatic example of early Christian contempt for desire, that humanity was created with a natural desire for God and that it remains anxious and restless until that desire finds its home in God. Likewise, the great theological treatise of the Middle Ages, Thomas Aquinas' *Summa*, is best read as the systematic working out of the dual claim that humanity naturally desires God and that its supreme good or happiness resides in the mutual pleasure of shared desire with God.[6]

Bernard of Clairvaux and the Cistercians

One of the great exemplifications of pre-modern Christianity's positive concern for desire is Bernard of Clairvaux and the Cistercians.[7] Born in 1090 into a family of noble knights in the duchy of Burgundy and educated by the canons of St Vorles, Bernard entered the insignificant "New Monastery" at Cîteaux in his early twenties (around 1113). A few years later he was nominated as abbot of Cîteaux's third foundation, named Clairvaux. The next ten years of his life were spent establishing this community. His literary career began around 1125 as he wrote treatises addressing the controversies between the established monastic orders and the Cistercians, produced devotional literature for the Knights Templar (a knighthood of soldier monks Bernard was instrumental in forming), and penned theological works on such topics as humility, the necessity of loving God, and grace. In the 1130s he became widely known as an advocate for reform – the laxity of ecclesiastical and monastic life during that period is well known – and was a supporter of Innocent II against the anti-Pope Anacletus. During this time he also began his greatest work, a series of sermons *On the Song of Songs*, a project that would remain unfinished at his death eighteen years later in 1153. In the 1140s, at the height of his influence, when he could as easily have interposed himself into the affairs of heads of state as defy heads of state,[8] Bernard threw himself into the effort to defeat both the innovative theology of Peter Abelard and the infidels in the Holy Land: he was a prominent proponent of the Second Crusade. In this regard, it is not insignificant that one of the distinctive emphases of Bernard's efforts was his conviction that the Church, as an eschatological witness to the true polity – the Kingdom of God – was properly a political presence, conceding nothing to the secular lords.[9] With the failure of the crusade, he withdrew from public life to concentrate on writing for his order, which had flourished in large part through his efforts, and died several years later.

In considering Bernard's writing on desire, perhaps the first thing to be said is that it was of a piece with his leadership of the monastic community at Clairvaux and throughout Europe; that is, it was part of a single all-consuming effort to build up and strengthen the lives of the faithful, "to teach thirsting souls how to seek the one by whom they are themselves sought."[10] Bernard was not primarily an exegete or theologian. His task in writing was not simply to illumine the great mysteries of the faith. He was first and foremost a pastor of souls, interested in communicating to those under his care something that might help them in their journey to God.[11] Consequently his writings, especially his sermons on the Song of Songs, provide a particularly clear display of Christianity as an ensemble of technologies of desire, particularly when those writings are positioned within twelfth-century monastic life as displayed among the Cistercians.

The passage just cited provides a fitting entrance into Bernard's and the twelfth-century Cistercians' practice of Christianity. He is concerned with Christian lives insofar as they thirst for God. Clearly this is a reference to the psalmist who wrote, "O God, you are my God, I seek you, my soul thirsts for you; my flesh faints for you, as in a dry and weary land where there is no water" (Psalm 63:1). Standing in the rich tradition that runs from the biblical writers through Augustine to Aquinas after him, Bernard envisions the human being as constituted by the desire of God. What is desire? First, it should not be confused with a feeling or an instinctual reaction to an external stimulus, the sort of reaction that Descartes and later rationalists were to attempt to subordinate to the rational mind. Desire is a basic movement of the human being. According to medievals like Bernard, humanity was created in motion. Desire is movement. Second, this movement that is desire should not be construed in primarily negative terms. It is not uncommon for desire to be portrayed in an essentially negative hue, in connection with a sense of privation. Desire is often accorded the status of a lack, a yearning for something that is absent, a void or vacuum that is pulled forward in search of the only thing that can fill that space, namely God. Whereas Bernard does use the language of "lack" and "absence" in connection with desire, and commentators frequently describe Bernard's account of desire in those terms,[12] such descriptions are, at best, misleading and, at worst, ontologically superficial. As we shall see, those who persist in describing desire fundamentally in negative terms, such as lack and privation, conflate Creation and Fall and fail to heed the medieval distinction between the image and likeness of God in humanity.

According to Bernard, the human being is not constituted by a lack, an absence, a privation but by a fullness, a presence, an excess. This fullness is God. Human desire is a gift of God. Indeed, says Bernard, it is God's desire that creates human desire.[13] Human desire is nothing less than a mirror of the positive, creative desire of God. Hence this desire is more accurately described as a presence, not a void or absence. In *De diligendo Deo*, Bernard describes the human condition thus: "No one has the strength to seek you unless he has first already found you. For it is a fact that you will to be found in order that you may be sought and you will to be sought in order that you may be found. It is possible, therefore, to seek you and to find you, but it is not possible to anticipate you."[14] Human desire is the positive effect of God's creative desire. Human desire is a consequence of God's presence. Thus, Bernard speaks of human desire continuing in heaven, where "we find a desire to penetrate deeper which is never quenched, yet which has no sense of unrest about it. Here we experience that eternal and incomprehensible desire which knows no lack."[15] Human desire is not the product of a deficiency or privation, but an excess in the sense that, among Bernard and the Cistercians, desire was synonymous with love, understood as a positive, productive, self-giving force. As an expression of charity, desire is not so much an acquisitive drive, characteristic of a lack, but a generosity and donation expressed in the many forms of charity.

The human being is constituted by a positive movement of desire. Such was humanity and its desire in the pristine condition of Creation. However, Bernard acknowledges, in accord with the Christian tradition's teaching, since the Fall desire has been corrupted. Human nature has been distorted by sin. In his sermons on the Song of Songs, Bernard argues that humanity's desire of God is a correlate of the Divine Image that has been imparted to humanity through the Holy Spirit.[16] Humanity desires God because it has been graciously created in the image of God.[17] However, with the advent of sin, the likeness of God with which humanity was created was lost. As a consequence of the Fall, humanity is in a condition of dissimilarity.[18] Humanity is dwelling in the region of "unlikeness."[19] Here the medieval distinction between the image and likeness of God is pertinent. For centuries theologians had pondered the significance of the phrase "image and likeness" in Genesis 1:26 and by the Middle Ages a consensus emerged that this phrase indicated two distinct features of humanity. The "image" was deemed a reference to a fundamental ontological reality, in Bernard's case, desire. The "likeness," in turn, was equated with an ethical orientation, with the direction of this desire in harmony with God. Hence when Bernard asserts that humanity lost its likeness, he is saying that human desire is no longer in harmony with the desire from whence it came. Desire no longer conforms to God but rather conforms to the world.[20] Bernard invokes the psalmist's contrast between uprightness and being bent to describe this deformation or corruption of desire. Humanity, he says, insofar as it was created in the image and likeness of God was "upright," that is, without iniquity.[21] Desire moved or flowed freely as it was created to do. With the advent of sin, however, humanity was deformed, bent from its true path. Desire was captured and subjected or enslaved to alien powers. Desire now finds pleasure in what debases it; it is attracted to that which defaces the Image. This is to say that with the occurrence of sin, desire's direction is distorted; it now moves in a different direction. Its original likeness or direction was exchanged for an alien one.[22]

At this point, and only at this point, is characterizing desire as privation appropriate. The equation of desire with an absence or privation does not hold for desire in its free, created state, but only for desire in its captive, corrupt state.[23] Furthermore, this privation or absence, Bernard makes clear, is a matter of direction. Desire – the positive, creative movement with which God has endowed humanity – lacks direction. In other words, this lack is an ethical, not an ontological, matter; it concerns the likeness and not the Image of God in humanity. Desire remains positive, productive. Only now it finds joy in the wrong productions; it takes pleasure in the wrong goods. As will become evident shortly, grasping the positive sense of desire is crucial to appreciating the way in which monastic Christianity functioned as an ensemble of technologies of desire for Bernard and the Cistercians.

Desire has been captured, corrupted, misdirected. Of course, Christianity asserts that humanity has not been left to languish in this condition. God in God's grace has sought to redeem desire. Indeed, says Bernard, the Word has come to heal desire.[24] Jesus is our light, food, and medicine.[25] Jesus restores our desire, leading it on the path of virtue, of wisdom, justice, and holiness, of life and fruitfulness.[26] Of course, for Bernard and the monks under his guidance, this healing of desire was not something God accomplished in any immediate and straightforward manner. Reflecting on his own experience as well as that of his monks, Bernard stressed repeatedly that the renewal of desire was marked by periods of advance and retreat, strength and weakness.[27] Spiritual growth is a dialectic in which desire moves between the poles of the destructive, distorting power of sin on one hand and the gracious, restorative power of God on the other. In other words, the healing of desire, no less for the monastic than for the secular, occurs in the midst of the drama of life, which means it is subject to the vicissitudes of sin and temptation.

More specifically, Bernard asserts that this dialectical process of growth in grace whereby God renews and restores desire is characterized by the triad *disciplina : natura : gratia*.[28] The dialectical rehabilitation of desire by the grace of God is marked by a certain pattern. First, once the corruption of desire is recognized, it is subject to *disciplina*. In the first stage, human beings respond to God's grace by forcing themselves to do what is right. Through self-constraint and willpower human beings counter the contrary movements of the soul that, under the power of a distorted desire, does not move in harmony with God. The bonds that hold desire captive are being broken. Second, after some time, over the course of which repeated practice has led to the formation of certain habits, humans find that acting virtuously is less dependent upon external constraints. One could say that desire is beginning to flow freely again. Finally, in a third stage, which Bernard notes is perfected only in the next life, humans find that they are able to act virtuously without much of a struggle. Virtuous behavior is both easier and gives rise to delight while the contrary movements of desire are increasingly unattractive.

At this point we can begin to appreciate the way in which Cistercian Christianity functioned, in Foucault's terms, as an ensemble of technologies of desire. The monastery was not an enclave in which the pure withdrew, safe and secure from the vicissitudes of sin and temptation that batter life in the secular world. Nor was it a means by which those who sought holiness could master or squelch desire. Rather, the monastery was a *schola caritatis*, a school of charity, where desire was redeemed, where the dialectical experience of spiritual growth was fostered with the purpose of redirecting love. The monastery was the site of a divine pedagogy whereby desire underwent not annihilation but rehabilitation. The goal of the rigorous life of the monastery was not the loss of one's desire; it was not about evacuating a space or creating a void into which God would step. On the contrary, monastic Christianity as practiced by Bernard and the Cistercians was about the formation and shaping of virtuous desire. Cistercian life was not about the suppression of desire but the healing or transforming of desire that had been bent, distorted, deformed. "Far from being a constraint upon nature or a restraint in due freedom," writes Michael Casey, "[Cistercian life] works for the liberation of nature from the alien bondage of sin."[29] In other words, as it functioned for Bernard and the Cistercians under his care, Christianity amounted to a vast array of assemblages of knowledges, instruments, persons, systems of judgment, buildings and spaces all focused on giving a certain direction to desire. Monastic Christianity was an ensemble of technologies that functioned to redirect desire, that sought to release desire from its bondage so that it might freely flow as it was created to do, in harmony with the desire of God. Far from being a place where desire was eliminated, monastic Christianity was a veritable economy of desire.

A window into this economy of desire and its character as an ensemble of technologies of desire is opened when its distinctive pattern of recruitment is considered. The two distinct social settings of twelfth-century monasticism have already been mentioned. One of the major differences between the traditional orders and the newer orders, of which the Cistercians were a part, lay in their manner of recruitment. The traditional monastic orders usually acquired novices from among the oblates, children who had been offered to the monastery by their parents. In contrast, the newer orders deliberately put an end to this type of recruitment; they recruited among adults. The principal reason for this was that they sought a greater observance of asceticism, poverty, and disciplined living, and they hoped to avoid the burden of educating young novices.[30] The Cistercians, in particular, drew heavily from the aristocracy, the knights and nobles. Indeed, it is likely that most of the twelfth-century Cistercians whom Bernard supervised had previously been formed in the life of knighthood and nobility. The significance of this shift lay in the fact that unlike the recruits of the traditional orders, who had been raised almost from birth in the cloister, the recruits of the new orders had participated fully in a secular order that bent desire in ways that celebrated violence, pride, vanity, and sensuality.[31]

What is remarkable about Cistercian spirituality is that it is precisely this distorted desire that is the material for exercising virtue.[32] The monastic program at Clairvaux was not aimed at obliterating or replacing this desire; rather, the task was to reorder it. Jean Leclercq describes the sublimation of distorted desire among Bernard and the Cistercians in this way:

> Thus, anger, when controlled, becomes the vehicle of good zeal; pride brought low can be pressed into service in defence of justice . . . If a strong sexuality is brought under control and disciplined by the practice of works of mercy, the very quarter whence people are exposed to the darts of wickedness becomes itself an incitement to solicitude for others.[33]

The disordered impulses that monks had acquired in their previous lives as knights and nobles were sublimated, redirected or rechanneled into a spiritual engagement: doing battle and winning glory for the sake of divine love and the Divine Lover.[34] Hence, Bernard's works are replete with martial imagery: his treatment of the Song of Songs begins by comparing the monastic life to military service and the monastic community to a militia doing battle for the king.[35] In the Cistercian communities, desire that had strayed from its true course and subsequently been bound by violence and pride and sensuality was given a new direction and enlisted in the service of Christ.

A vast matrix of technologies, including both those of the self and of others,[36] were involved in bringing about this transformation of desire. According to the *Rule* of St Benedict, which was the cornerstone of Cistercian life in general and of Bernard's in particular, chief among the various rites and tasks that shaped monastic life was the liturgy. The liturgy, however, was not merely the principal end of monastic activity; it was also one of the instruments of the monk's spiritual craft and thus integral to the rehabilitation of desire.[37] Talal Asad describes the liturgy's functioning as a technology of desire in terms of the construction of memory. Through the rich language and imagery of the liturgy, and in particular through the sermons that gave authoritative exegesis of biblical texts, Asad argues, the monks were given a new vocabulary that enabled them to "redescribe, and therefore in effect reconstruct, their memories in relation to the demands of a new way of life."[38] In other words, the liturgy functioned as a technology of desire through the assembly of memory.[39] This is perhaps nowhere more evident than in the frequent references Bernard's sermons make to the "memory of heaven."[40] By invoking the memory of heaven, a memory that his proclamation explicitly creates – describing in some detail the nature and features of eternal life[41] – Bernard was freeing desire from its captivity to vice by inciting a new movement of desire in the direction of its true end.

Care must be taken, however, not to reduce the liturgy's assembly of memory to a matter of linguistic inscription. The liturgical reformation of desire is not simply a matter of symbolic overcoding or linguistic renarrating. The claims advanced here for Cistercian worship are not reducible to the notion that humans are "constituted by language" and that the liturgy is fundamentally a linguistic performance. The divine office is not first and foremost a linguistic convention. As Asad points out, "Although the formation of moral sentiments is dependent on a signifying medium, we cannot read off the formation from the system of significations that may be authoritatively identified and isolated as a distinctive semiotic phenomenon."[42] The production, reading, and proclamation of sacred texts as well as the singing of sacred song and reciting of prayer are more than linguistic phenomena. Such intellectual technologies are situated within a matrix of technologies of the body, and so forth, to which they relate in manifold ways, sometimes as the product, sometimes as the condition of possibility. This is to say that the reading and proclamation of sacred text and song in the divine office are embedded in an ensemble of technologies that act on and shape material bodies in particular ways, forming such things as Bibles, altars, psalters, Churches, abbots and monks. Indeed, the concept "assembly of memory" is meant to ward off any linguistic reduction of the liturgical construction of memory to matters primarily of language, discourse, or symbol. It is meant to suggest that the construction of memory includes more than linguistic representation, involving as it does – in the case of twelfth-century monastics – the construction of worship space, the production of books, stained glass, and artwork, the placement and use of various apparatuses such as altar, Host, Scripture, abbot's chair, relics, and baptismal font, and the various techniques of the body involved in reading, preaching, prayer, song, and silence.[43] In other words, only by means of a combination of a series of intellectual technologies and technologies of the body did the twelfth-century Cistercian liturgy function as a central mechanism through which desire was renewed in the likeness of God.[44]

The divine office did not stand alone, however, as the sole instrument of the restoration of desire. On the contrary, the liturgy was only one strand of the fabric of monastic life out of which the divine pedagogy was woven. The liturgy was embedded within the wider network of relationships, daily rituals, and institutional configurations that constituted Cistercian Christianity. Indeed, as Asad points out, the liturgy could not perform its task of assembling memory apart from a whole host of relations and technologies:

This redescription of memories depends on a long and complex process. In it (1) the authoritative preacher and the monk addressed, (2) the monk interacting with fellow monks, (3) the confessor and the monk in confession, and (4) the remembering religious self and the secular self remembered, all contribute in the production of a moral description by which the monk's desires and feelings are reconstructed.[45]

The entire spectrum of monastic rituals and rites, from meditation and obedience to manual labor, functioned as technologies of desire. Chief among these other rituals and rites was the sacrament of penance, which, as we have already seen, Foucault singled out for particular scrutiny as a technique of the self. Recall that Foucault described the monastic practice of confession as a technology geared toward the renunciation and sacrifice of the self. Yet the account of Cistercian monasticism presented here suggests that Foucault's usually perspicacious analysis has faltered on this point. The monastic practice of confession, no less than monastic ritual as a whole, was not geared towards the rejection of any presocialized (real) self.[46] Confession is clearly part of a process whereby sinful desire is renounced, but the renunciation of sinful desire should not necessarily be equated with the denial or repression of desire, as a closer look at the Cistercian practice of confession reveals.

Foucault's analysis is correct insofar as he places the sacrament of penance at the heart of the monastic program of the rehabilitation of desire. And Foucault is correct in his assertion that the verbalization of self-knowledge is crucial to this technology. However, this verbalization is not the exposure of an authentic desire that is sacrificed under the imposition of another, artificial desire. Confession is not concerned with the social control and repression of a primordial desire. On the contrary, it is part of a process of recognizing that desire has already been captured and controlled, that desire's present orientation or direction in the world is not an ontological given. According to Bernard, the recognition that desire has been captured is crucial to its renewal. Reflecting on the Vulgate rendition of Song of Songs 1:7, where the bride is told that if she does not know herself she must be exiled to a life dominated by gratifying the needs of the senses, Bernard writes:

> There must be no dissimulation, no attempt at self-deception, but a facing up to one's real self without flinching and turning aside. When a man thus takes stock of himself in the clear light of truth, he will discover that he lives in a region where likeness to God has been forfeited, and groaning from the depths of a misery to which he can no longer remain blind, will he not cry out to the Lord as the Prophet did: "In your truth you have humbled me"?[47]

Once persons see that they are oppressed, they will cry out to God; once persons begin to walk on this way of self-knowledge, then the divine likeness begins to be renewed and restored.[48] Recognition of the bondage of desire is a prerequisite of "sowing righteousness," of repentance, prayer, and works of mercy, all of which are part of the triadic process, *disciplina : natura : gratia*, whereby desire is redeemed:

> You therefore have sown righteousness for yourself if by means of true self-knowledge you have learned to fear God, to humble yourself, to shed

tears, to distribute alms and participate in other works of charity; if you have disciplined your body with fastings and prayers, if you have wearied your heart with acts of penance and heaven with your petitions. This is what it means to sow righteousness.[49]

In summary, the Cistercian practice of confession functioned in the Middle Ages in a manner not unlike Foucault's genealogical project functions for Western liberal society; that is, it uncovered those technologies of knowledge, power, and the self that had assembled desire in a particular way. More specifically, it revealed the contingent, precarious nature of the medieval technologies that assembled desire in terms of violence, pride, and sensuality. In so doing, it also contributed to the construction of a moral space where righteousness was sown, where the divine likeness could flourish, where once again desire could flow charitably.

Objections

Insofar as the twelfth-century Cistercians succeeded in providing the moral space for the release of desire from the bonds of violence, pride, and sensuality, they stand as an exemplification of Christianity as an ensemble of technologies, the end of which is the healing or liberation of desire. At this point, if I were suggesting that Cistercian Christianity was the form that contemporary Christian resistance to capitalism ought to take, then a series of objections would need to be addressed, objections concerning, among other things, the extent to which Cistercian Christianity really accomplished the redirection of desire, the Cistercians' relation to patriarchy, or Bernard's role in various and sundry political intrigues (not the least of which was his outspoken support of the Crusades). The purpose of this section, however, is much more modest. Far from being an argument for the restoration of Cistercian monasticism, or, for that matter, the Christendom mentality that sanctioned the Crusades,[50] the example of Bernard and the Cistercians stands only as a concrete display of Christianity as an ensemble of technologies of desire. In other words, the Cistercian example is meant only to aid in unthinking the modern prejudices against desire, thereby carving out a space for the possibility that contemporary Christian communities may function as ensembles of technologies of desire.

Yet even such a modest goal cannot evade one objection; namely, that whatever the cogency of the example, it ultimately falters on the distance between the "privileged" position of monks who lived in a social order that provided the possibility of inhabiting the rather rarefied moral spaces of the cloister and the situation of contemporary Christians. Put bluntly, there may well be many Christians who would enter such "prisons without doors," but the geopolitical landscape of the early twenty-first century hardly favors such enclaves. Unquestionably there are poor Christians who currently suffer in capitalism's clutch, who would gladly enter such moral spaces – even if only in hopes of finding sanctuary from the weapons of capitalism's security forces – but where are they? A reply to this question constitutes the task of this entire project and hence must await its completion; even so, a response that nudges us in the direction of that conclusion is possible.

Such a response begins with an assessment of the nature of the distance that separates medieval monastics and contemporary Christianity. Perhaps the significant distance is not the distance separating medieval feudal and modern liberal polities. Perhaps the difference that matters is not that which is created by the absence of monastic institutions but that which is rooted in the limitation of Christians' willingness to have their everyday lives shaped by the grace of God.[51] In other words, the real obstacle to living Christianity as an ensemble of technologies of desire is not the dearth of monastic orders but the lack of persons who are willing to place themselves in the types of relations with others and with God that characterized Cistercian life. Behind this suggestion is the recognition that what was perhaps the most significant monastic technology – penance – neither began in the monastery nor stayed there. As Foucault has shown, that technology of the self spilled over into society as a whole when the medieval era gave way to the modern and subsequently helped give birth to modern disciplinary societies.[52] Although it is an admittedly negative example, it does suggest that there is nothing intrinsic to conceiving of Christianity as an ensemble of technologies of desire that requires the presence of cloistered communities.[53]

Hence it is possible that Christian communities that shape desire in ways analogous to the twelfth-century Cistercians exist even in the absence of monastic institutions. The remainder of this chapter and the next explore one such possibility, namely that some Christian communities in Latin America may be creating moral spaces where desire is being freed from its bondage to the capitalist discipline in a manner that is analogous to the way in which Cistercian monasteries functioned as a therapy for desire captured by the feudal violence of the Middle Ages. Before turning to such spaces, however, there remains one specter to dispel, that of the therapist.

At first glance the argument that Christianity is rightly conceived as a therapy of desire might appear profoundly *passé*. After all, Western culture has been acutely attuned to the value of therapy in addressing the ills of modernity for years. Three decades have passed since Philip Rieff announced the triumph of the therapeutic mindset.[54] Almost two decades have passed since MacIntyre observed that the therapist functioned in our culture as a sort of moral exemplar that underwrote a mode of social existence.[55] In those decades the therapeutic mode of existence has only deepened its penetration into our culture, including Christianity. As Rieff predicted, clergy have become predominantly therapists and the Gospel has been adapted to the therapeutic mentality.[56] The current pervasiveness of this mode of existence is perhaps nowhere more evident than in the recent explosion of interest in spirituality, a phenomenon that Rieff foresaw with uncanny accuracy when he wrote thirty years ago that as a consequence of the triumph of the therapeutic:

> In the emergent culture, a wider range of people will have "spiritual" con-
> cerns and engage in "spiritual" pursuits. There will be more singing and
> more listening. People will continue to genuflect and read the Bible, which

has long achieved the status of great literature; but no prophet will denounce the rich attire or stop the dancing. There will be more theater, not less, and no Puritan will denounce the stage and draw its curtains. On the contrary, I expect that modern society will mount psychodrama far more frequently than its ancestors mounted miracle plays, with patient-analysts acting out their inner lives, after which they could extemporize the final act as interpretation.[57]

Given the prominence of the therapeutic today, my argument would appear to be terribly outdated if not entirely misplaced.

More troubling, however, than the charge of being dated is the unsettling observation that therapy seems to be flourishing at precisely the moment when capitalism has taken its "savage" turn. Just as capitalism was shedding its human face – its developmentalist facade – therapy was coming into its own. As Nikolas Rose has cogently argued, following Foucault, this is no mere coincidence.[58] On the contrary, the therapeutic gaze is an integral component of current capitalist modes of governmentality and its triumph was made possible by the problematics that underpin that governmentality, namely, the need for an indirect form of authority that operates on individuals in, with, and through their freedom, autonomy, and choice. Therapy embodies that form of authority (called "expertise") that is particularly well suited to the logic of savage capitalism; that is, it is that form of authority necessary to govern persons in a society that abhors all authority. By means of an elaborate complex of managers, social workers, nurses, teachers, and counselors, as well as a host of emotional, interpersonal, and organizational techniques, therapy organizes the practices of everyday life according to the logic of the market: freedom, autonomy, and choice. Therapy is government through freedom; its end is the formation of the entrepreneur of oneself. In other words, far from being an antidote to capitalist distortions of desire, therapy is an essential component in the promotion and maintenance of the capitalist order.

Obviously, if Christianity is to bring about the liberation of desire from the capitalist order, it must distance itself from those forms of therapy that amount to little more than a sedative for persons hooked on (or bound to) the capitalist order. Its efforts must not be directed toward helping persons become better "entrepreneurs of themselves," with the direction of one's desire being arbitrarily and subjectively chosen (within the spectrum of permissible market choices). Rather, in accord with the best of the Christian tradition, Christianity as a therapy of desire operates under the "burden" (which is a light one) of a direction that is given desire by virtue of its being the gift that is the desire of God. "Our hearts are restless until they rest in Thee."

But such giftedness and such direction should not be equated with a direction that is uncovered or recovered through an act of self-knowledge. Such a gift – knowledge of the genuine "core" reality of the self – would not yet distinguish Christianity as a therapy of desire from capitalist modes of therapy; indeed, contemporary capitalist therapeutics frequently operate on the assumption that there exists some given, true identity located deep in the heart of the "self."[59] The direction that is given desire by virtue of its being the desire of God is not a direction that is discovered or uncovered at the heart of a true "self." Desire's true direction is not a matter of puncturing a calloused exterior layer of the "self" and getting in touch with a pre-given, originary desire lurking at the heart of some uncompromised interiority. A certain knowledge does attend Christian technologies of the self, as the Cistercian practice of confession showed and Foucault analyzed, but this knowledge is not the knowledge of a true self or uncorrupted desire. On the contrary, as suggested earlier, such knowledge does not arrive at a hidden, authentic direction that should replace the current misdirection of desire, but at a sense of one's irreversible immersion in a flow – a sense of one's being always already in movement – with no fixed points. Such knowledge teaches us not what we must do to be true to our nature but simply to be endlessly iconoclastic about the ends of desire. While such knowledge is an important component in the healing and reorientation of desire, such healing and reorientation ultimately do not come about through an act of self-knowledge. Rather, such redirection occurs as desire is shaped by means of a host of technologies that constitute ensembles such as capitalism or Christianity.

Of course, this does not answer the question of whether or not Christianity as a therapy of desire is a genuine source of resistance to capitalist discipline. For that answer we must return to the liberationists and the poor Christian communities in their midst.

The desire for justice

Capitalism is an ensemble of technologies that disciplines desire according to the logic of production for the market. As the example of Bernard of Clairvaux and the Cistercians suggests, Christianity is also amenable to construal as an ensemble of technologies of desire. No less than capitalism, Christianity is a material formation that by means of a host of knowledges, instruments, persons, systems of judgment and spaces assembles desire. The task that now confronts us is that of naming the technologies that Christianity offers desire in the hopes of liberating it from the cancerous logic of savage capitalism. What therapy of desire does Christianity embody that stands a chance of resisting the deformations of capitalist discipline? How does Christianity form persons to defy the capitalist order? Today by far the most common cry raised against capitalism is that of justice. A widespread sense exists that injustice is the central issue of our day. Although other eras and epochs have been stained with the brush of cruelty, the age of savage capitalism is unique in the extent to which it has been so thoroughly painted by the cruelty of injustice. The reversal of the principle of justice has become the order of the day and the system of the state; injustice has been set up as the quintessential standard of the new world order.[60] Reacting against this situation, in recent decades some Christians have asserted that Christianity is fundamentally about justice. Indeed, in certain sectors of Christianity the cry for justice has become the defining mark of discipleship. The synod of bishops of the Catholic Church, for example, declared in 1971: "Action on behalf of justice and participation in the transformation of the world fully appear to us as a constitutive dimension of the preaching of the gospel, or, in other words, of the Church's mission for the redemption of the human race and its liberation from every oppressive situation."[61]

In what follows I take up the contemporary cry for justice and ask if it is an adequate characterization of the therapy that Christianity enacts to resist capitalism. Taking my cue from the liberationists, who scrutinize theological reflection in terms both of its fidelity to revelation and its historical effect, I approach the issue of adequacy from two angles. On one hand, the contemporary cry for justice is evaluated theologically. Does it accurately portray the heart of Christian resistance to capitalism? Does it accurately name those technologies that Christianity brings to bear against capitalist discipline? Is this vision of justice faithful to Christianity's vision of who God is and how God acts (and has acted through the Incarnation) in the world? The second angle involves questions of efficacy and practical effect. Is this justice capable of generating and sustaining resistance to capitalism? Is resistance to capitalism nourished insofar as Christianity forms persons and communities who seek this justice? Is this justice the Christian antidote to capitalism, the counter-logic that stands against the madness of the capitalist axiomatic of production for the market?

The point of departure for this inquiry is the work of the Latin American liberationists. Such a choice is justified because the impetus for the heightened significance of justice within the Christian tradition in recent decades comes in large part from the Third World, where "a deafening cry pours forth from the throats of millions asking . . . for a liberation that reaches them from nowhere else."[62] As the previous chapter displayed, the Latin American liberationists have been particularly attuned to this cry. Hence it comes as no surprise that their work has been at the forefront of the recent reappraisal of the place of justice in the Christian life. "There is a terrible injustice in today's world, one which, slowly or quickly, brings the great majority of humanity closer to death," writes Jon Sobrino. "Justice and truth, therefore, are fundamental and urgent demands."[63] Indeed, according to the liberationists, justice is the key concept for the Christian conscience of our day; the promotion of justice is the essential requirement of the Gospel message today.[64] In the current situation of injustice, the struggle for justice is elevated to the crucial proof of the validity and authenticity of Christianity.[65] "The God of Biblical revelation is known through interhuman justice," Gustavo Gutiérrez writes. "When justice does not exist, God is not known; God is absent."[66] The importance bestowed upon justice in liberationist accounts of contemporary Christianity is such that justice becomes synonymous with salvation.[67] Thus Gutiérrez can write, adding a new twist to an old adage, "Without justice there is no salvation."[68]

What justice?

During Advent on the island of Hispaniola in the year 1511, the Dominican friar Antonio de Montesinos mounted the steps to the pulpit and, looking out over rows of *encomenderos* and soldiers, issued the challenge, "Tell me, by what right or justice do you hold these Indians in such a cruel and horrible servitude?"[69] The liberationists place justice at the forefront of the Christian witness against capitalism, but what do they mean by justice? To what justice are they referring? In the West, justice has been broadly conceived in terms of the ancient phrase *suum cuique*: to each what is due. Yet how this has been understood is far from monolithic. Implicit in Montesinos' challenge and made explicit more recently by Alasdair MacIntyre, is the recognition that justice is pluriform. What is due can be calculated according to a host of discordant logics; "what is due" can be determined by some measure of merit, need, rank, works, legal entitlement, and so forth.[70] Moreover, not every conception of justice, notes Ignacio Ellacuría, is commensurable with Christianity.[71] On the contrary, some accounts of justice may underwrite social orders that create and perpetuate the very poverty and misery that liberationists seek to combat. As Leonardo Boff notes:

> Justice, in the classical definition, consists in giving to each his own. Evidently, this "his own" presupposes a given social system. In slave society, giving to each his own consists in giving to the slaves what is theirs and to the masters what is theirs; in bourgeois society it means giving to the owners what is theirs and to the workers what is theirs; in neocapitalist systems it means giving to the magnates what is theirs and to the proletarians what is theirs.[72]

As a consequence, the first question that confronts the liberationists as they highlight the place of justice in Christian resistance to the capitalist order is, "What justice?"

The answer to this question is not as simple as the prominence of the concept in the liberationists' work would lead one to expect. As Ismael García has noted, although issues of justice are central to the pastoral and theological work of Latin American liberationists, they provide neither a clear statement nor an explicit definition of what they mean by the term.[73] One might attempt to circumvent this silence by making the claim that when liberationists speak of justice, the reference is predominately social justice. As was the case with integral liberation, they recognize that justice relates to all dimensions of life: the social/political, the personal, and the theological. Nevertheless, they focus most of their attention on issues of social, economic, political justice. While certainly accurate, such an observation does not provide much traction. We are still left without a clear statement of what constitutes social justice. One looks in vain for a full-fledged "theory of justice" comparable to that of Rawls or Nozick. While this noticeable lacuna has fed the fires of critics who dismiss the liberationists as "lyrical leftists" who toss around hollow slogans, the absence is not the product of some supposed theoretical deficiency in their work. In fact, the absence is not an absence at all. As Clodovis Boff suggests, the social teaching of the Church is the theological field in which the theology of liberation is properly situated.[74] When the liberationists refer to justice they are taking for granted the long tradition of shared meanings that constitutes modern Catholic social teaching on justice. Hence, in order to properly understand what liberationists say about justice, it is necessary to begin with an overview of that tradition.

Catholic social teaching on justice

The temptation is to begin that overview in the year 1891, when the era of modern Catholicism began in earnest with the promulgation of Leo XIII's encyclical *Rerum novarum*. Leo XIII inaugurated a new era in the social and political self-understanding of the Roman Catholic Church that was marked by the Church's deliberate effort constructively to engage with the problems associated with the modern world's economic development. Leo XIII's stated goal in issuing *Rerum novarum* was to identify the "principles which truth and justice dictate" for dealing with the "misery and wretchedness" caused by the new industrial growth. Such principles would be followed by the elaboration of "the relative rights and mutual duties of the rich and the poor, of capital and labor."[75] Yet to begin with Leo XIII and the enunciation of "rights" is to have eclipsed much of the story of the emergence of "social justice" as a central tenet of Catholic social thought. A full appreciation of all that the term justice entails requires retreating several steps, to the medieval vision out of which the modern teaching on justice emerged.

The medieval Christian understanding of justice finds its most definitive articulation in the work of St. Thomas Aquinas. In accord with the tradition of the Church, which had appropriated the classic notion of justice as *suum cuique*, Aquinas defines justice as "the perpetual and constant will to render to each one his right."[76] As he elaborates on this, it quickly becomes clear that "justice" is actually an umbrella term encompassing both a general and a particular virtue. As a general virtue, justice is that virtue which coordinates the proper good or end of individual persons with the common good or end of the human community. Human beings are endowed by God with a certain destiny or end. This destiny or end, however, is not the destiny or end of the person as an isolated individual. Rather, human beings are created as social beings. They are endowed with a certain dynamism that compels them to enter into society, not only for the sake of meeting material needs but also to satisfy a God-given longing for completeness or wholeness that can only be found in communion with other persons. Society, in turn, is understood as a grouping of persons joined together in an orderly way for the pursuit of certain ends (including material goods, the temporal ends of the political community, and the final end of all humanity, namely the beatific vision) that can be collectively labeled the "common good." Justice as a general virtue arises in the midst of the effort to articulate the relation between the common good of society and the particular good of the individual. According to Aquinas, the common good is not an "alien good" juxtaposed with the particular good of the individual person, in the sense that the person is set over against society. Rather, society's common good, rightly understood, is at the same time the proper good of its particular members. The relation between the common good and the particular person's good is so intimate that "whoever promotes the common good of the community, by that very fact promotes his own good as well . . ., for the proper good simply cannot exist outside of the family, or of the city or Kingdom."[77] The name of the general virtue charged with the task of coordinating these goods is general justice. More specifically, justice as a general virtue operates by commanding and directing the actions of particular virtues toward the common good: "the good of any virtue whether such virtue directs man in relation to himself, or in relation to certain other individual persons, is referable to the common good, to which justice directs, in so far as it directs man to the common good."[78]

In addition to this general virtue of justice, Aquinas recognizes justice as a particular virtue as well. As a particular virtue, justice is further divided into the commutative and distributive species, with which we are more familiar.[79] The two types of justice – general and particular – are related insofar as particular justice – commutative and distributive activity – is always subordinated to the operation of general justice. The general virtue oversees the activity of the particular virtue, commanding and orienting its activity to the preservation of the common good. In other words, justice, for Aquinas, functions as more than a calculus of what is due; it is a matter of righteousness, of conformity with the common good. As such it is a principle of unity that arises out of the source of all unity, the shared love called the common good.

Every theology presupposes a sociology and the vision of justice that Aquinas articulated was most clearly displayed in medieval monastic communities, like the Cistercians. Insofar as those communities were about persons joining together in the common pursuit of perfection, insofar as they were ordered toward nurturing a shared love or solidarity in the common good, they were paradigmatic embodiments of the medieval vision of a just community. Yet as the Middle Ages gave way to modernity and Christendom retreated before Leviathan, these communities declined and the Thomistic vision underwent dramatic change. The story of the emergence of justice in the modern social teaching of the Catholic Church is the story of the adaptation of the Thomistic conception of justice to a different way of life, namely life in modern liberal societies. It is the story of the gradual and subtle move away from justice as the principle of a community's solidarity, in a robust sense of the common good, to justice as a fundamentally distributive force that secures rights in societies distinguished by the absence of anything but the thinnest of conceptions of the common good. As we shall see, this adaptation was not simply the product of the Church's open-armed embrace of modernity and advancing liberalism. On the contrary, it occurred even as elements of the Church sought to retrieve the Thomistic sense of justice in order to resist the advance of liberalism. Indeed, the adaptation occurred precisely through those elements that sought to retrieve the Thomistic vision of justice for the sake of combating what they perceived to be the grievous wrongs perpetrated by the liberal economy.

By the nineteenth century, liberalism had effectively reduced the rich medieval vision of the common good as a shared love embracing material, social, and spiritual goods, to the temporal good of the secular state. Justice likewise suffered at the hands of the modern state as it became only a particular virtue that governed the relationship between citizens and the state, and dictated that citizens obey the laws of that state.[80] Justice, in other words, had become a matter of the positive laws of the modern state.

In an effort to counter the spread of this reductionistic conception of justice, in 1840 an Italian Jesuit by the name of Luigi Taparelli d'Azeglio published an essay in which he coined the term "social justice." With this term he sought to recover the Thomistic conception of justice as a general virtue that coordinated all activity with the common good. Social justice, as d'Azeglio described it, embraced not only the positive laws of state but the entire social order: the totality of relations that touched upon the intellectual, moral and material development of persons. Yet even as he sought to reclaim Aquinas, d'Azeglio was not immune to the influence of modernity. As d'Azeglio attempted to reassert the link between justice and a common good that was much broader than the ends of the secular state, his vision of the common good reflected the subtle influence of modern contract theories of the state and justice. When d'Azeglio referred to the common good he tended to cast it as a good alien or external to the members of society that must be distributed to them. In other words, the common good was no longer, as in the case of Aquinas, a good that was commensurate with the proper good of the individual. Rather, it was the sum total of individual goods, and as such constituted an abstract good that was other than the proper good of the individual. In this situation justice was transmuted into the arbiter of claims of the individuals against society for their share of the common good. In other words, social justice was acquiring the distinctly distributive hue of one of Aquinas' species of particular justice and losing its character as a general unitive principle that presupposed a community founded on a strong sense of the common good as a shared love.

The term "social justice" was soon picked up and developed further by many who were influential in the emergence of "social Catholicism" in the late nineteenth century. The social Catholics continued to press the notion of "social justice" as a means of expanding the scope of then current conceptions of justice. Indeed, there were many – including a growing number in the Church – who, caught in the rising tide of *laissez-faire* economics, argued that the strictures of commutative justice exhausted the obligations of justice. For example, liberal Catholics of the time argued that commutative justice ought to be the primary form of justice that governed human relations. Thus, with regard to a just wage, justice demanded only that owners pay workers the agreed upon wage. Of course, liberals recognized that by itself commutative justice was not capable of addressing adequately all the social ills of the day. This shortcoming, however, was not properly a matter of justice. Rather, it was a matter of charity and, as such, best addressed by acts of liberality, benevolence, and almsgiving. Against the liberals, social Catholics raised the banner of social justice, asserting that almsgiving and benevolence were not always a matter of charity, but sometimes fell under the purview of justice.

In the course of making the case for social justice, social Catholics eventually adopted the modern discourse of rights. They essentially embraced the conclusions of modern social contract theorists, namely that society was rightly understood as constituted by a conglomeration of rights and duties adhering to individuals over against the whole. The medieval vision that Aquinas articulated and the Cistercians embodied had construed rights in terms of the divine ordering of the human community as that order was spelled out in a series of divine, natural, and human laws. As such, right was fundamentally a matter of consent to or participation in the divine order and the individual was understood as possessed by Christ and a recipient of all the good that one is, has, and does.[81] In the newer tradition, God's right established discrete rights possessed originally by individuals – by virtue of their creation in the image of God and endowment with a certain dignity – and then derivatively by communities. According to this conception, the individual occupies the central position as right is associated with a human power to control and dispose of temporal things.[82] Individuals, in other words, became essentially proprietors.

As a consequence of these changes in the understanding of both rights and persons, the social Catholics increasingly conceived of social justice as the virtue that maintained societal equilibrium by insuring that those rights and duties were honored. Justice was cast as the external force deemed necessary to hold individuals together in a society where human social relations were increasingly acquisitive, atomistic, and competitive – a far cry from the medieval vision of Aquinas and the Cistercians of a society united by the shared love that is the common good. This is not to say that social Catholics abandoned the notion of the common good or that their notion of justice was nothing more than a contractarian notion of procedural justice in holy drag. The point is that social Catholics had clearly slipped away from an account of justice anchored in a thick account of community united by a robust conception of the common good – justice understood in the Thomistic sense of solidarity in a shared love. Their account of society as an amalgamation of proprietary individuals endowed with rights and of justice as the guarantor of those rights, clearly reflects a much thinner conception of the common good, one better suited to the realities of advancing modernity where there was increasingly little hope of securing agreement on more than a minimal standard of basic "rights" and certainly no hope of society coming together around a shared love. In other words, for all of their effort to reclaim and renew the Thomistic vision, the social Catholics' conception of justice did not succeed in escaping the advancing liberalism's discipline. Such an observation, however, does not diminish the social and moral force generated by the concept of social justice. In the late nineteenth century it was a powerful concept, fueling a movement that sought to alleviate the plight of the working masses in an age when even a thin conception of the common good as a cache of rights could appear prophetic. Moreover, its appearance was to mark indelibly the life and teaching of the Catholic Church in the coming years.

The next milestone in the Catholic Church's reflection on justice was the development of the "social teaching" or "social doctrine" of the Church. This teaching took shape in a series of papal encyclicals, dating back to Leo XIII's *Rerum novarum* (1891), that attempted to fortify the Church's increasingly tenuous ties to the masses by bringing the weight of the magisterium to bear on the social problems afflicting those masses. The idea of justice plays a prominent role in that effort. Much of what the popes have to say about the social problems of the day is expressed in the language of justice. For example, it is to the "principles which truth and justice dictate" that Leo XIII appeals when denouncing the wretched condition of the working class. Likewise, in the course of addressing the social order in the wake of the great depression of 1929, Pius XI invokes "social justice" numerous times in the second great social encyclical, *Quadragesimo anno* (1931), and in the midst of the cold war, John XXIII lays out a vision of true peace built on justice in another great social encyclical, *Pacem in terris* (1963).[83]

The conceptual framework that underwrites what the popes say about justice in the social encyclicals was essentially adopted from the tradition of reflection on social justice initiated by the social Catholics of the late nineteenth century.[84] That is, the modern social teaching of the Catholic Church puts forward an understanding of justice that is broader than mere commutative justice, that is oriented toward the common good, and that is spelled out primarily in terms of rights.

The commitment to a conception of justice that extends beyond the narrow path of commutative justice is particularly evident in the prominent social encyclicals of three pontiffs. Although in *Rerum novarum* Leo XIII was concerned with only a narrow aspect of the social problem of the day, namely the "condition of the working classes," nevertheless a broad conception of justice, akin to the social Catholic's notion of "social justice," is apparent in the attention he devotes to a whole host of issues related to the working class's condition, from poor working conditions, to long hours, to the abuse of child and female labor, to the disregard of workers' spiritual needs and their right to organize. In leveling his criticism of these practices and pointing out an obligation of employers to respect the good of laborers' souls, to use their surplus for the relief of the poor, to respect the peculiar capacities of women and children, clearly Leo XIII is operating on the basis of an understanding of justice that exceeds the commutative justice of the unrestricted market. Indeed, in a statement that has become symbolic of the Church's resistance to any notion of justice reduced to the commutative dimension, Leo XIII writes that "there underlies a requirement of natural justice higher and older than any bargain voluntarily struck: the wage ought not to be in any way insufficient for the bodily needs of a temperate and well-behaved worker."[85] In all of this Leo XIII is recalling the distributive dimension of justice, a dimension that condemns the concentration of property in the hands of "a tiny group of extravagantly rich men [who] have been able to lay upon the great multitude of unpropertied workers a yoke little better than slavery itself."[86] Justice demands that all persons share in the benefits and goods that accrue to a prosperous society.[87]

Unsurprisingly, perhaps, because it was a deliberate reflection on and extension of the principles of *Rerum novarum*, Pius XI's *Quadragesimo anno* advances a similar, broad notion of justice. The first use of the term "social justice" is in the midst of a discussion of just distribution. The increase in riches that attend to socio-economic development, Pius XI says, ought to be so distributed among persons and classes that the common advantage of all is served. "By this law of social justice, one class is forbidden to exclude the other from sharing in the benefits."[88] Social justice is also invoked in support of Leo XIII's argument for a living wage and denunciation of the abuse of women and child laborers.[89] Finally, in a passage that echoes Leo XIII's blunt denunciation of justice limited to its commutative species, Pius XI states:

> Just as the unity of human society cannot be founded on an opposition of classes, so also the right ordering of economic life cannot be left to a free competition of forces . . . [F]ree competition, while justified and certainly useful provided it is kept within certain limits, clearly cannot direct economic life . . . Therefore, it is most necessary that economic life be again subjected to and governed by a true and directing principle.[90]

That principle, Pius XI asserts, is the lofty and noble principle of social justice.

If Leo XIII is noteworthy for initiating papal reflection on social justice and Pius XI for legitimating the use of the term and reinforcing that commitment, John XXIII is remarkable for two significant changes in the Church's vision of social justice. Like his predecessors, John XXIII advocated a conception of justice in *Mater et magistra* (1961) that encompassed a distributive as well as commutative dimension. Following in their footsteps, he insisted that laborers not be treated as commodities, that they be allowed to organize, and that they be paid a living wage. He also denounced unrestricted competition as the principal law of the economy.[91] However, John XXIII also introduced two innovations in the tradition's understanding of social justice. First, he expanded the vision of social justice beyond national boundaries and shook off the traditional preoccupation with property and socialism. He was the first pope to take up in any depth the issue of international relations in a world that was growing more interdependent. In particular he took up the issue of the disparity of wealth between nations, arguing that justice demands that countries that produce an excess of goods distribute that surplus to less developed countries, and that they do so without thought to furthering their own interests and control, which is denounced as a new form of colonialism.[92] Likewise, he redirected the Church's focus to the concerns of the poor. Second, he severed the tie between papal teaching on justice and a semi-feudal, corporatist model of society. Both Leo XIII and Pius XI were convinced that a just social order was a hierarchical one that distributed resources unequally. As Leo XIII wrote in *Rerum novarum*, "men must put up with the human predicament: in civil society it is not possible for those at the bottom to be equal to those at the top . . . [and] this is clearly of advantage both to individuals and to society."[93] John XXIII abandoned this commitment to a paternalistic framework for the realization of justice and distanced the social teaching of the Church from a commitment to any particular social model, a move that was followed by the Second Vatican Council when it declared, "in virtue of her mission and nature, [the Church] is bound to no particular form of human culture, nor to any political, economic or social system."[94] Instead, the Church subjects all models to scrutiny in light of the demands of social justice.

In addition to adopting a broad notion of justice, the social teaching of the Church also appropriates the link between justice and the common good that is prominent in both Aquinas and the social Catholics. The popes are emphatic that the administration of justice is not to be carried out in accord with the precepts of personal interest or national gain. Rather, justice is intimately bound up with the common good. Indeed, at times social justice is so intimately related to the common good that the two concepts appear to be almost interchangeable. For example, Pius XI writes in *Quadragesimo anno*, "To each, therefore, must be given his own share of goods, and the distribution of created goods . . . must be effectively called back to and brought in conformity with the norms of the common good, that is, social justice."[95]

In asserting the connection between justice and the common good, however, the social teaching more closely resembles the social Catholics than Aquinas. That is, the idea of the common good that most frequently appears in the social encyclicals is not that of a shared love, particularly not a shared love that finds its object in the beatific adoration of the Trinity, and justice is not a matter of unity in that shared love. Rather, the common good is most often cast as the condition of possibility from which a shared love may subsequently arise, and justice is presented as the guarantor of that condition of possibility. Put more concretely, the common good is a matter of access to a minimal amount of social and material goods, and social justice is the principle that secures that access.[96] This comes out in the social encyclicals in various ways. Sometimes social justice and the common good are described in terms of securing "public and private prosperity," or in terms of guaranteeing the personal development of the members of society, or the achievement of social, cultural, economic advancement.[97] Other times the common good and justice are presented as a matter of insuring that all persons share in the benefits that come with a society's socio-economic advancement, or as a matter of securing the tranquility, stability, and security of human life.[98]

By far, however, the most prominent image of the relation between the common good and justice is that of the securing of certain fundamental rights of persons.[99] The common good is conceived of as a body of rights that justice secures and protects. "Justice," wrote Pius XII, "demands that all recognize and respect the sacred rights of liberty and of human dignity."[100] "Rights must be held sacred wherever they exist," declares Leo XIII.[101] And John XXIII asserts that society is a moral order founded on the recognition of the inalienable rights of persons, and that this order is "brought into effect by justice."[102]

The adoption of rights language is a striking development in the social teaching of the Church since traditionally the Church had been suspicious of the various democratic and socialist movements that first struggled on behalf of certain "rights."[103] Nevertheless, in the social encyclicals the language of rights abounds. Leo XIII identified several in *Rerum novarum*, including the right to possess private property; the right of citizenship; the right to care and protection by the state; the right "to obtain those things which are needed to sustain life;"[104] and the right of association. As the social teaching of the Church develops in the decades after Leo XIII, these rights are reinforced and others added, until the enumeration of rights reaches its pinnacle in John XXIII's encyclical *Pacem in terris* and the Second Vatican Council that he called.

In the midst of Vatican II, John XXIII issued *Pacem in terris*, which begins with a strong statement recognizing humanity as fundamentally rights-bearing creatures:

> Any well-regulated and productive association of men in society demands the acceptance of one fundamental principle: that each individual man is truly a person. His is a nature, that is, endowed with intelligence and free will. As such he has rights and duties, which together flow as a direct consequence from his nature. These rights and duties are universal and inviolable, and therefore altogether inalienable.[105]

This statement is immediately followed by a list of some of these rights. Among the rights that John XXIII puts the Church on record as recognizing are a right to life; a right to bodily integrity and to the means necessary for the proper development of life, particularly food, clothing, shelter, medical care, and rest; a right to education; freedom of conscience; a right to a just wage; the right to private property; the right to self-determination. Following John XXIII's lead, Vatican II affirmed the existence and the Church's support of human rights stating in *Dignitatis humanae*: "this sacred Synod intends to develop the doctrine of recent Popes on the inviolable rights of the human person and on the constitutional order of society."[106] The Council went on to affirm the full array of human rights articulated in the social encyclicals as the norm to which all societies should be held accountable.

Even as it increasingly presented social justice in terms of rights, the Church was careful to distance itself from the liberal tradition of rights, which it still suspected of granting a freedom from religion. Such distance was sought through the careful articulation of both the source of these rights and the responsibilities or duties that were their correlate. The social teaching is careful to identify the source of these rights as God. These rights are not intrinsic to humanity in itself; rather, they accrue to persons on account of their God-given dignity. Hence the recognition of the rights of others is not simply something one does out of respect for the intrinsic humanity of others. Such respect is rooted in a recognition of a divine mark or claim upon the person, as Leo XIII notes: "The rights which are at stake are not at a man's own disposition. They are duties owed to God and must be scrupulously observed."[107] Rights may also be understood as duties. The flip side of the recognition of rights is the recognition of duties. The social teaching of the Church carefully couples rights with duties. One cannot simply assert one's rights and then ignore the rights of others. "[I]n human society," writes John XXIII, "one man's natural right gives rise to a corresponding duty in other men; the duty, that is, of recognizing and respecting that right. Every basic human right draws its authoritative force from natural law, which confers it and attaches to it its respective duty."[108] What distinguishes this reciprocal recognition of rights from the liberal theory of rights that the Church abhorred was that this recognition was not satisfied with mere non-interference. According to the Church, it is not enough that one acknowledge that others have certain rights; one has a duty to offer positive aid. "For example, it is useless to admit that a man has a right to the necessities of life, unless we also do all in our power to supply him with means sufficient for his livelihood."[109] Justice, in other words, demands that both the rights and the duties that are correlative to the God-given dignity of humanity be respected.

Such was the understanding of justice prevalent in the Church when Latin American liberationists were first awakened to the plight of the poor in their midst. Justice was a matter of securing human beings' fundamental rights, generally understood as the civil and political rights associated with Western democracies coupled with the socio-economic rights stressed in socialist societies. Although justice was still linked to the common good, as it had been in the medieval vision, it is clear that the nature of that relation had been significantly reconfigured to correspond better with the realities of life (and the Church's new position) in modern liberal societies. As an amalgamation of rights, the common good was much thinner than the "shared love" that animated the Cistercians and found expression in Aquinas.[110] Consequently, justice was no longer envisioned primarily as an instrument of unity that nourished human solidarity in that shared love. Instead it functioned more as a civil peace keeper, as Pius XI makes clear in *Quadragesimo anno*: "For justice alone can, if faithfully observed, remove the causes of social conflict but can never bring about union of hearts and minds."[111] In other words, justice is at best the condition of possibility for unity, which is a product of charity, in contrast with Aquinas for whom the shared love was justice's condition of possibility. Without the shared love, the general virtue of justice has no end and hence is defunct; one is left with only the particular virtue of justice in its distributive and commutative dimensions. This explains why the social teaching's effort to foster a commitment to "social justice" so often looks like the addition of a distributive dimension (distributing goods commensurate with rights) to a prior narrow conception of justice as strictly commutative.

Justice in Latin American liberation theology

It is against the backdrop of the modern Catholic social teaching on justice that the lack of a full-fledged, systematic treatment of justice among the Latin American liberationists must be understood. The impact of this teaching on the Church in Latin

America was belated and largely indirect. Initially the social teaching was suppressed. Even the modest steps taken by Leo XIII in *Rerum novarum* were viewed with alarm by those who had a vested interest in the status quo. The later social encyclicals, however, fared much better and the teaching of Pius XI and John XXIII, in particular, influenced the progressive members of Catholic Action groups and the Christian Democrats. However, the most important vehicle for papal teaching on social justice in Latin America was the work of Jacques Maritain. The liberationists were thoroughly steeped in Maritain's New Christendom and through that theology they absorbed the conception of justice promulgated in the Church's social teaching. In particular, Maritain's 1943 book, *The Rights of Man and Natural Law*, which was widely read in Latin America, articulated the vision of social justice that was then emerging in the social encyclicals. Like the papal encyclicals just considered, Maritain's vision of a just society was one that recognized the God-given rights of persons and that was organized in a way that encouraged the ever wider participation of all in the full enjoyment of those rights.

When viewed in light of the tradition of social teaching on justice, it is possible to discern a coherent conception of justice in the liberationists' work. Specifically, it is now possible to see in the narrative of liberation that underwrites the liberationists' account of the "irruption of the poor" a theory of justice, even though justice is rarely mentioned.[112] Recall that that narrative begins with the premise that a "broad and deep aspiration for liberation inflames the history of humankind in our day, liberation from all that limits or keeps human beings from self-fulfillment, liberation from all impediments to the exercise of freedom."[113] As this tale is told by Gutiérrez, the flame of freedom was ignited with the early Christians' struggle with the Roman government for religious freedom. They struggled for religious autonomy, for the freedom to practice the religion of their choice without state interference. This struggle emerged from a keen sense that religious freedom was an inalienable right and that political powers were incompetent in religious matters. Even though these principles would be discarded when Christianity attained power and itself defined the status quo, Gutiérrez nevertheless acknowledges the signal contribution of early Christianity to the recognition of human rights. The narrative of freedom then moves forward to the birth of modernity in the eighteenth century. At that time several forces for freedom came together under the banner of the Enlightenment. The scientific and industrial revolutions marked the birth of a new era of freedom from the forces of nature. The development of psychology opened up new horizons of personal freedom. Finally, the French Revolution heralded the emergence of various social freedoms or rights. After first resisting it, the Church gradually came to terms with and, during the pontificate of John XXIII and the Second Vatican Council, eventually embraced this drive for freedom and recognized the various rights of humanity.

At this point the liberationists' narrative can be interrupted in order to draw at least a tentative conclusion about their conception of justice. When it is positioned within the larger context of the modern social teaching of the Church, that narrative suggests that the liberationists have adopted the model of justice that is present

111

in the social teaching. The story of the gradual spread of the flame of liberation is the story of the gradual recognition of the basic rights of humankind. By implication, the struggle for justice is, following the social teaching, the struggle for a society where the basic rights of humankind are respected. Such a conclusion is reinforced by the references to rights found dispersed throughout liberationists' writings. "To be righteous or just," writes Gutiérrez, "means to acknowledge the rights of others,"[114] and Sobrino, reflecting on Amos 5:23–24 (". . . let justice surge like water . . ."), asserts, "The conclusion would be obvious. For anyone who believes in God, the struggle for human rights is an inescapable imperative."[115]

The liberationists' embrace of the understanding of justice found in the social teaching of the Church, however, is not uncritical. Even as they take up the basic notion of justice as the recognition of rights, they push it in new directions. Such development is necessary, according to the liberationists, on the grounds that the social teaching suffers from several crucial flaws. While the social teaching is in many ways an important advance beyond previous ecclesiastical positions that dismissed rights out of hand, it suffers from being too abstract, too disconnected from the realities of a world in the clutches of savage capitalism. In a particularly sharp indictment of this abstraction, Clodovis Boff remarks, "This is in fact what happens when one approaches the [social teaching of the Church]: one finds that it agrees with practically everything. But once the texts are studied, practically nothing stays in mind."[116] In a bit more charitable and nuanced description of the weakness of the social teaching, particularly as it was manifested in the documents of the Second Vatican Council, Gutiérrez writes:

> With moderation and reserve, the great demands of modernity are accepted: the rights of the human person, subjective values, freedoms, social equality, the value of human progress. Social conflicts, on the other hand, are touched upon only in general terms of the presence of misery and injustice in the world. Although a certain distance is taken from some aspects of the individualistic roots of bourgeois society, there is no serious criticism of the implications of the monopolistic domination of the popular classes, especially the poor, by capitalism. . . . The fact that . . . society, far from being a harmonious whole, is shot through with confrontations between social classes, is not a circumstance falling in the council's direct line of sight.[117]

The temptation is to reduce the charge of "abstraction" to a complaint that the social teaching is limited by being rooted predominantly in the ethos of the developed world. While it is certainly true that some of the social teaching reflects a reality far removed from that of the vast majority of the Third World and that the liberationists do raise this point,[118] this is not the real substance of their difficulty with the social teaching on justice. Getting to the heart of the charge of "abstraction" requires picking up once again the liberationists' narrative of liberation.

According to the liberationists, the march of freedom did not end with the modern era. On the contrary, the 1960s marked the beginning of a new era, one in which the flame of liberation attained a new intensity. "We are," the Latin American bishops observed at Medellín, "on the threshold of a new epoch in the history of [Latin America]. It appears to be a time of zeal for full emancipation, of liberation from every form of servitude, of personal maturity and of collective integration."[119] This new zeal is found specifically among the dispossessed and marginalized, among the "absent of history" who at that time were beginning to make their voices heard. It is this "irruption of the poor" that the liberationists herald as the next milestone in the history of freedom.

The irruption of the poor stands as a milestone in the sense that it marks the emergence of a demand for socio-economic rights, for the right to life that has been trampled upon as savage capitalism has advanced across the globe, hand in hand with modernity. As the poor rise up and cry out in anguish, they are demanding that social and economic rights be accorded the same recognition in practice as has been granted to civil and political rights in the modern world. Reflecting from amidst the absent of history on modernity and the rights it championed, Gutiérrez notes:

> Today we see clearly that what was a movement for liberty in some parts of the world, when seen from the other side of the world, from beneath, from the popular classes, only meant new and more refined forms of exploitation of the very poorest – of the wretched of the earth. For them, the attainment of freedom can only be the result of a process of liberation from the spoliation and oppression being carried on in the name of "modern liberties and democracy."[120]

From the underside of history a significant gap between the professions and practices of modernity is visible. Rights are vociferously proclaimed by various governments and enshrined in venerated documents, yet modernity has not brought freedom to much of the world. Specifically there remains a qualitative difference in the respect accorded political and socio-economic rights.

The source of this discrepancy, the origin of the gap between the rhetoric and practice of modernity, is the "unsatisfied Enlightenment."[121] From the discussion of the previous chapter, recall that according to the liberationists, the advance of liberation that the birth of modernity signaled was side-tracked by a radical individualism that came on the scene with the rise of the capitalist class – the bourgeoisie with their belief in the right of private ownership. The French Revolution was a prime example. On the one hand, the French Revolution proclaimed the right of every human being to participate in the society to which they belonged. Thus it embodied the human desire for a truly democratic society, which is rightly celebrated as an achievement of modernity. On the other hand, such proclamations remained largely ambiguous and declarative, given that they were not necessarily tied to just economic conditions.[122] According to Gutiérrez, it was

113

the emergence of a radical individualism that blocked the full working out of the logic of the Enlightenment, a logic that would have made the connections between the modern freedoms and the economic conditions of their possibility. In a similar manner, Sobrino argues that the Enlightenment consisted of two distinct phases. One, represented by Kant, was concerned with freedom from authority – essentially political freedoms and rights. The second phase, represented by Marx, was concerned primarily with liberation from the wretched conditions of the real world – social and economic rights. As modernity has played itself out, the first phase has been granted pride of place both by the secular and theological powers of this world.[123]

It is fashionable in some circles to accuse liberation theology of being unconcerned with human rights in general and political rights in particular.[124] On the one hand, this claim rings hollow in light of the narrative of liberation that undergirds liberationist thought, especially when that narrative is accompanied by such statements as "the struggle for human rights is not only a categorical ethical demand incumbent on each and every individual, or merely a crucial part of the mission of the Church and the praxis of Christians, but a demand and a mission with a divine dimension. . . ."[125] On the other hand, there is a grain of truth in the charge. But that grain of truth stands not as an indictment of liberationists so much as it turns against those who level it by bringing to the fore the breach between the rhetoric and practice of human rights in modernity. Take, for example, Juan Luis Segundo's argument that human rights language is little more than a weapon used by the West to legitimate the perpetuation of unjust economic practices on a global level. Speaking of what he considers "perhaps the most inhumane and anti-evangelical element in the defense of human rights," namely the West's invocation of human rights language to bludgeon Latin American governments, he writes:

> What those wealthy countries are not willing to see is that we are the ones who have to pay the cost of their respect for these rights, with the economic and political crises provoked by the plunder of the planet, which oblige our governments to maintain a minimum of order by means of more and more barbarous and inhumane methods. We are accused of not being democratic, when we are prevented from being so. If my country could apply to the rich nations the economic and political measures that are applied to us today, it would be *we* who would go and investigate, today – hypocritically, of course – the violations of human rights in *those* countries. The tragic thing about the situation is that those who shape and control the defense of human rights – despite undeniable good will – are the same persons who make that defense impossible on three-quarters of the planet.[126]

Human rights are profoundly inhumane and anti-evangelical when they are brought to bear, for example, on the issue of political prisoners in Latin America while the gross violation of more basic human rights, which affects two-thirds of humanity, is ignored, or worse, minimized as if the socio-economic conditions that produce throughout an entire population the deprivation not only of expression but of instruction and consequently of thought itself, were attributable to "natural causes."[127]

The question arises at this point concerning the link between the criticism of modernity present in the narrative of liberation and the liberationists' charge that the Church's social teaching is deficient. If we grant that modernity has indeed failed to embody the rights its lofty rhetoric exalts, what has this to do with the Church's teaching? Where is the error in the Church's teaching in this regard? Indeed, as David Hollenbach suggests and the brief survey earlier supports, the social teaching of the Church, particularly as it developed during the papacies of John XXIII and Paul VI, could be characterized as an "integral theory of rights," embracing both political and socio-economic rights.[128]

The problem with the Church's teaching on human rights, according to the liberationists, is quite simply that its defense of human rights is not sufficient to bring about the concrete realization of those rights. Its abstract, universal doctrine of human rights at best has little effect and in the worst case only props up the current order. Indeed, Segundo asserts, "to the extent that, by its words and actions, the Church intimates that the gospel today is identified with human rights, it conveys the sorrowful news of its attachment to international capitalism."[129] The social teaching's conception of justice as respect for human rights is of a piece with its generally developmentalist, reformist approach to social change; that is, it is a conception of justice that is fundamentally at home in a capitalist world. The social teaching never condemns the capitalist system in principle, only what are deemed its excesses or aberrations. For this reason, Clodovis Boff argues that "in theory [the social teaching of the Church] is anti-capitalist, but in practice it collaborates with this system."[130]

How can the social teaching demand justice and simultaneously embrace a developmentalist agenda that advocates the reform of capitalism? This is only possible, according to the liberationists, if the social teaching does not actually start from the reality of global capitalism, from the reality, in Gutiérrez's words, of "the monopolistic domination of the popular class, especially the poor, by capitalism."[131] Instead the social teaching reflects the lingering influence of the neo-scholastic methodology that begins with metaphysical reflection on natural law and seeks to apply the conclusions deduced from such reflection to reality.[132] Speaking in abstract, atemporal principles that seem to hover over concrete history like some sort of spiritual luminary, the social teaching, in the words of one commentator, "lectured the world from outside it."[133] The magisterium was the repository of truth; what could be learned from the profane world? This tendency was only reinforced by the strong ultramontanist current in the early twentieth-century Church, with the result that little attention was given to the diversity of situations in which Christians lived and struggled around the world.

This stringent neo-scholastic method underwent revision beginning with John

XXIII.[134] His encyclical *Mater et magistra* introduced into the social teaching the see-judge-act method of Catholic Action and he began to speak of discerning the "signs of the times," which both Vatican II and the liberationists adopted. Henceforth the social teaching of the Church would refrain from endorsing a single model of society and would broaden its vision with regard to the diversity of the situations to which it spoke; for example, both John XXIII and Paul VI brought an international horizon to the tradition. Yet, as the comment from Gutiérrez reminds us, too much should not be made of this change. In spite of the language, the social teaching still tends to read more as a call for simple obedience than as an initiator of historical analysis and careful judgment at the local level. Any doubt in this regard fades in the light of the 1966 papal address, *Libentissimo sane animo*, where Paul VI reaffirms the traditional position of the Church that both theology and the magisterium have as their fundamental purpose the preservation of the sacred deposit of revelation and its explanation in accord with the dictates of reason and the Spirit's enlightenment.[135] Thus, even when the social teaching does offer analysis of concrete historical reality, the portrait it paints is surreal. It bears little resemblance to the harsh reality of life under capitalist discipline as it is endured by the masses of poor Latin Americans.

The residual neo-scholasticism that taints the social teaching's methodology, however, does not in itself account for the surreal portrait of a humane capitalist order that genuinely serves the common good, that is dedicated to fostering the development and welfare of all peoples. At best this method, by attending to eternal verities accessible through metaphysics, enables the Church to overlook the normative (as opposed to aberrant) destructiveness of capitalism. What seals the Church's partnership with the capitalist order, according to the liberationists, is the particular social theory that underwrites the social teaching. Although the social teaching may have developed to the point that it prescinds from explicitly endorsing any particular model of society, it nevertheless remains committed at a more general level to a particular social theory. Specifically, the social teaching remains committed to an organic social theory that traces its roots to the medieval vision of society as a hierarchically organized, harmoniously functioning body.[136] If the neo-scholastic method is the magisterium's technique, organic social theory is what the magisterium applies to the canvas of the Church's social teaching. This continued commitment to organic social theory is the soft underbelly of the Church's social teaching that makes it vulnerable to incorporation into the capitalist order in at least two ways.[137] First, organic social theory's affinity for hierarchical order is replicated by capitalism insofar as capitalism tends to generate socio-economic hierarchies in both the family and economy.[138] Hence it is not surprising that, as the liberationists suggest, in practice if not in theory the Church has come down on the side of so-called free markets in the great ideological struggle of modernity between capitalism and socialism's more egalitarian notions of economics. Second, its emphasis on social harmony and cooperation is by nature conservative, tending to favor the status quo and slow reform over the open conflict and confrontation associated with more radical patterns of social change.

Organic social theory operates on the assumption that social conflict is to be overcome by integrating the different factions into a hierarchically structured social order held together by the coordinating authority of the state. According to this model, conflict tends to be sublimated or denied rather than resolved.[139] As Gutiérrez said, the recognition of social conflict was simply beyond the horizon of the social teaching's vision.

Taken together, then, the method and the social theory of the social teaching hinder that teaching from developing what the liberationists see as an adequate account of justice, one that is actually capable of funding resistance to capitalism and securing the basic rights of all persons. Instead, that method and theory lead the social teaching, perhaps in spite of the best intentions of its authors, into the jaws of capitalism.[140] At best the social teaching's vision of justice amounts to a call for the reform of capitalism and the curbing of its worst excesses and abuses. At worst, the social teaching is wielded like a club to beat down those who seek the rights espoused by the social teaching but who no longer believe that capitalism can be reformed in any significant way and that the social conflict it generates cannot be resolved through denial and sublimation. In either case, the social teaching's theory of justice reflects the same deficiency as the rights rhetoric of the modern West: as that rhetoric unfolds, socio-economic rights are eclipsed in practice.

As a result of the irruption of the poor, liberationists were awakened to the shortcomings of the social teaching's reformist and developmentalist conception of justice and in turn began to articulate an alternative vision of justice, one that built upon the social teaching while simultaneously seeking to be faithful to the irruption of the poor. Appealing to the social teaching's effort to discern the "signs of the times," the liberationists shaped a conception of justice that took as its starting point, not philosophical deductions from natural law informed by organic social theory, but the experience of the long-suffering peoples of Latin America. As the liberationists put it, in attempting to discern the signs of the times, they were attending to the movement of the Holy Spirit not in new cogitations of the mind, but in the struggle of women and men for life.[141] Thus, Gutiérrez begins his famous work, *A Theology of Liberation*:

> This book is an attempt at reflection, based on the gospel and the expe-
> riences of men and women committed to the process of liberation in the
> oppressed and exploited land of Latin America. It is a theological reflec-
> tion born of the experience of shared efforts to abolish the current unjust
> situation and to build a different society, freer and more human . . . My
> purpose is not to elaborate an ideology to justify positions already
> taken . . . It is to reconsider the great themes of the Christian life within
> this radically changed perspective and with regard to the new questions
> posed by this commitment.[142]

In other words, in marked contrast with the social teaching, the liberationists' reconceptualization of justice is rooted in a concrete experience. Their theory of justice is a second step, a response to a particular situation that arises out of a prior commitment and activity.

More specifically, the liberationists' revision of the social teaching's theory of justice begins from the experience of injustice. It is rooted in reflection on the dismal poverty that submerges the majority of Latin Americans in conditions of inhuman wretchedness. In place of abstract ideals and deductions from natural law, liberationists' reflection on justice begins with the world as it is now. "Justice," says Sobrino, "takes seriously the primordial fact of the *created world* in its given form; that is to say, it takes seriously the existence of the oppressed majorities. The existence of these majorities is not a fact that can be lightly passed over in speaking of the essence of the Christian message."[143] For this reason the Medellín document on Justice, drafted by several liberationists, begins with an assessment of the "pertinent facts," among which is included the recognition of the "misery that besets large masses of human beings in all our countries" and that is identified as "injustice which cries to the heavens."[144] Likewise, Segundo Galilea asserts that the starting point of liberation theology's reflection is the present situation, in which "the vast majority of Latin Americans live in a state of underdevelopment and unjust dependence," and Leonardo Boff identifies the basic question of liberation theology as the question presented to Christianity by poverty that exists on a continental scale, that is not an innocent or neutral phenomenon, and that amounts to a moral injustice demanding heavenly vengeance.[145] In a passage that echoes their understanding of justice as the recognition of rights rooted in human dignity, Gutiérrez describes the situation from which theological reflection must begin:

> The true face of Latin America is emerging in all its naked ugliness. It is not simply or primarily a question of low educational standards, a limited economy, an unsatisfactory legal system, or inadequate legal institutions. What we are faced with is a situation which takes no account of the dignity of human beings, or their most elemental needs, that does not provide for their biological survival, or their basic rights to be free and autonomous.[146]

Careful attention to the signs of the times, particularly the dominant sign constituted by the misery of the masses and their cry for justice, is the first distinctive of the liberationists' account of justice.

This distinctive starting point, in turn, gives rise to several other novel features of the liberationists' account of justice, features that distance that account from the social teaching in important ways. Among these is the liberationists' recognition of social sin, or, more specifically, structural injustice. Immersion in the struggle of the poor for their rights has awakened liberationists to the full reality of sin. They have come to see that the power and profundity of sin are not adequately grasped if it remains confined to the language of individuals. On the contrary, sin has a structural dimension that exceeds the activities of isolated persons.[147] Injustice is manifest in social structures, as the Medellín documents acknowledge:

... in many instances Latin America finds itself faced with a situation of injustice that can be called institutionalized violence, when, because of a structural deficiency of industry and agriculture, of national and international economy, of cultural and political life, "whole towns lack necessities, live in such dependence as hinders all initiative and responsibility as well as every possibility for cultural promotion and participation in social and political life," thus violating fundamental rights.[148]

Injustice is not confined to individuals; it can be "institutionalized." As such, injustice becomes a matter of structures and institutions – such as governments, businesses, and markets – that oppress human beings by violating their God-given dignity and trampling on their basic rights. Structural injustice encompasses the internal colonialism of one class within a nation dominating another and the external neocolonialism of developed countries dominating underdeveloped countries. Also included under the rubric of structural injustice are the situations and structures that promote and facilitate both individual acts of injustice and the passive complicity of persons with injustice.[149]

According to the liberationists, structural injustice is the most prominent form of sin in Latin America. It is the most pervasive form of violence and the most important cause of all other forms of violence on that continent.[150] Therefore, an adequate theory of justice must denounce not only individual acts of injustice, individual violations of human rights, but also the structures and institutionalized patterns of behavior that systematically violate human rights. If a theory of justice does not take seriously "social sin" and structural forms of injustice, then it comes as little surprise that that theory should endorse reformist and developmentalist palliatives as the means to the full recognition of fundamental human rights.

Because the liberationists do attend to the social or structural dimension of injustice, their account of justice cannot be reconciled with a system that perpetrates and perpetuates the poverty and suffering of the poor. Consequently, unlike the social teaching, it is open and explicit in its denunciation of and resistance to capitalism. Although the liberationists acknowledge that not all poverty and suffering are caused and/or perpetuated by capitalism,[151] having watched capitalism spread and several "decades of development" pass while the condition of the poor continues to deteriorate, they are convinced that the global capitalist order is at the heart of the vast majority of the suffering. Under the impact of their encounter with the world of the poor, and with the aid of dependency theory, they have concluded that capitalism does not alleviate but rather exacerbates the plight of the poor masses. Indeed, according to the liberationists, capitalism is intrinsically unjust. Its fundamental logic of production for the market is neither interested in nor capable of meeting the fundamental requirements of justice – respect for human rights.

Given this rejection of both capitalism and conceptions of justice that effectively amount to little more than efforts to dull its teeth, it is unsurprising that conflict is, in the words of Hugo Assmann, "a constant rather than occasional theme" in the alternative vision of justice that liberationists propose.[152] Social conflict is accorded a much more prominent place in liberationists' account of justice than is found in the social teaching. Whereas the social teaching seeks justice through the sublimation of conflict in a hierarchical social order, the liberationists insist that true peace and genuine justice are incompatible with such means and such an order. A realistic view of the world leaves no room for the social teaching's optimism and facile forms of conciliation.[153] Indeed, from the vantage point of Latin America, particularly in the late 1960s and early 1970s, when national security apparatuses were spreading like a malignant tumor and harshly crushing the forces of progressive social change, the liberationists could dismiss the gradual and reformist vision of change propagated by the social teaching as rather ingenuous and naive. Justice, the liberationists insisted, demands that conflict be brought into the open and faced, not subsumed or denied.

This means that the Christian who is concerned with justice cannot shy away from conflict. Christians who would pursue justice can neither ignore conflict nor attempt to remain above conflict in a stance of pseudo-neutrality. "It is not possible to remain neutral in the face of poverty and the resulting claims of the poor; a posture of neutrality would, moreover, mean siding with injustice and oppression in our midst."[154] Justice demands that one enter the fray, that one enter into conflict and choose sides for some and against others. As Gutiérrez observes, those who seek justice cannot avoid conflict because in a society scarred by injustice and the exploitation of one social class by another, the proclamation of justice will transform history into something challenging and conflictual.[155]

The close association of the struggle for justice with social conflict has drawn the ire of the magisterium and others who accuse liberationists of a range of offenses from making class struggle the engine of history to being apologists for terrorism. Such charges, however, are misplaced. Far from being a call to arms, the liberationists understand the recognition of social conflict to be nothing more than simply the acknowledgment of a painful historical fact:

> No one agrees with a situation in which human beings come into conflict. And in fact the situation is not "acceptable," either humanly or in a Christian perspective. Conflict is undoubtedly one of the most painful phenomena in human life. We should like things to be different, and we ought to look for ways of getting rid of these oppositions, but on the other hand – and this is the point I want to make – we cannot avoid facing up to the situation as it actually is, nor can we disregard the causes that produce it.[156]

Social conflict is a reality that the liberationists, as long as they do not avert their eyes from the misery and squalor that surrounds them, cannot escape.

Thus when the liberationists highlight the connection between the struggle for

justice and social conflict, they are neither asserting the ontological necessity of violence nor establishing conflict as a law of history.[157] Far from blessing conflict, they
are critical of any theology that would baptize revolution or promote conflict.[158]
They do not believe that the juxtaposition of oppressors and oppressed is inevitable
and that justice can come only at the point of a sword or through the barrel of a
gun. On the contrary, social conflict is ultimately the product of sin; it is the historical consequence of collective sin.[159] As such, liberationists understand it to be
a historically contingent reality. Humanity need not live in conflict; persons do not
need to oppress their sisters and brothers. Conflict need not be sublimated or
denied; it can be resolved. The resolution of social conflict, in fact, is precisely why
the liberationists give conflict such a prominent position in their work. They seek
to resolve it by uncovering and then eliminating the cause of the conflict, namely
injustice.

Closely associated with the recognition that justice demands acknowledging
and entering into social conflict is the liberationists' assertion that justice is partisan. If justice demands that one enter into conflict, choosing sides and opposing
some, then clearly it cannot feign neutrality or objectivity. "Genuine justice," says
Sobrino, "is partisan justice."[160] Although it is concerned with the recognition
and securing of the fundamental rights all persons, justice is particularly concerned with the rights of the poor. In a world plagued by the injustice of oppression
and exploitation, justice as the defense of human rights becomes the imperative to
struggle first of all for the trampled rights of the poor. "Human rights must be primarily the rights of the oppressed," declares Ellacuría. "It is only by doing justice
to the oppressed peoples and classes that an authentic common good and truly universal human rights will be fostered."[161] Not the disinterested activity of a neutral
arbitrator, true justice is the offspring of solidarity with the suffering poor, as the following passage from Sobrino makes clear:

> Justice, operating within history, urges the adoption of a *partisan and sub-*
> *jective perspective* in the practice of love and in the development of Christian
> existence. This perspective is from below, from the standpoint of
> wretchedness and oppression, from the underside of history. By taking
> this approach, one effectively adopts the evangelical perspective, which
> avoids succumbing to an idealist and alienating universalist attitude by
> taking as its point of reference the weak, the poor, and the oppressed.[162]

In this sense justice is a correlative of the well-known preferential option for the
poor. Justice is preferential; it privileges the rights of the poor. Specifically, it privileges the right to life, which is the first and fundamental human right and which
is supremely the right of the impoverished majority of this world.[163] "We must
insist," says Sobrino, "that the most basic human right of all remains the right of
whole peoples, peoples forming the major portion of humanity, to their endan-
gered lives."[164] Hence, when liberationists speak of justice as the defense of rights,
they always do so in the context of the right of the poor to life.

At first glance this may appear to compromise the universality of justice insofar as such an emphasis on the rights of the poor implies less importance being given to the human rights of the wealthy. Does the partisan nature of the liberationists' account of justice entail a retraction of the rights of the comfortable minority? Many (wealthy) critics have voiced this concern, fearing that the characterization of God as partisan somehow jeopardizes God's love and concern for all of humanity. The partisan nature of justice, liberationists concede, does admit a certain prioritization of rights:

> . . . the promotion of the common good cannot progress by denying the individual rights of the human person, precisely because the promotion of those rights is an integrating part of the common good. But it can happen in a specific historical situation that it is necessary to establish priorities in the enjoyment of individual human rights. For example, the refined cultural activities of the few cannot have primacy over the fundamental education of the majority of the people, and even less can the enjoyment of some convenience have primacy over the right to have what is necessary for survival. Since almost everything in human life is superfluous in the countries which suffer from extreme poverty, anyone who wishes to enjoy superfluities should join a society where this massive poverty is absent and where the voice crying to heaven of those in need cannot be heard. But although human rights should be regulated by the common good, it is impossible to conceive of a common good which would require the permanent and grave violation of human rights in order to maintain itself.[165]

Nevertheless, as this passage shows, the critics' fears are unfounded. The partisan nature of justice and the prioritization of rights that it entails do not lead to the dismissal of the rights of the wealthy. They do not legitimate a crusade against the oppressor or the use of terror in the struggle for the rights of the poor.[166] What the partisan nature of justice does accomplish is the anchoring of human rights in concrete reality, thereby increasing the chance that the rights of all will actually be respected in practice and not merely declared in theory:

> A declaration of the rights of the poor does not overlook the universality of human rights, as some seem to fear. On the contrary, a proclamation of the rights of the poor bestows on human rights in general an authentic universality – through enhanced historical concretion and evangelical realism, which are the foundation of all authentic prophecy.[167]

The rights of the poor provide a palpable, measurable standard that protects the struggle for human rights from the danger of becoming mere abstract declarations and formulations. Their rights, especially their right to life, function as a societal barometer of sorts. A society's respect for human rights in general can be gauged by the treatment accorded to the least of its members. Moreover, the emphasis on the rights of the poor also insures a more universal scope to the quest for human rights insofar as that emphasis places the focus of that quest on the rights of the majority of humanity.[168]

Not only is the partisan nature of justice a more effective means of securing the rights of all, according to the liberationists, but it is also more faithful to the biblical witness than dispassionate and abstract conceptions of justice. The biblical witness as read by the liberationists presents a God who does justice. Indeed, justice is at the center of the biblical witness of who God is. The justice that God does, however, is not neutral. As José Miranda has shown in a study used extensively by liberationists, in the Bible to do justice and to judge are directly linked to the protection of the rights of the poor.[169] When the Bible portrays God acting in the name of justice, it presents God acting to redeem the poor and the downtrodden. God's justice is not a matter of dispassionate adjudication; God is not enthroned in the heavens, wearing a blindfold. Rather, God is partisan; the Incarnation was a partisan act – God took on poor flesh. Divine intervention and judgment are a matter of protecting the weak, the poor, the widow, the orphan. Thus, when God instructs the faithful to do justice, the expectation is that they too will defend the rights of the poor. In this way, the biblical conception of justice parts company with the classic Western image of justice as the disinterested rendering to each what is due. Instead, biblical justice is a matter of rendering to the poor the rights that are due them, and it is to this witness that the liberationists appeal in defense of their conception of justice as partisan.

Such is the basic shape of the liberationists' account of justice. Like the social teaching out of which it emerges, it is a theory of rights. Justice is fundamentally a matter of rendering to each what they are due in accord with their rights. Moving beyond the social teaching, however, the liberationists insist that the full import of justice as the securing of rights can only be grasped if one is immersed in the harsh reality of the world of the poor. Such immersion reveals dimensions of justice that are invisible from the lofty heights of neo-scholastic theology. Specifically, the true nature of justice as partisan engagement in conflictual situations is revealed. Justice compels Christians to enter into conflict against capitalism and its unjust structures for the sake of the rights of the poor majorities.

The terror of justice

Is this account of justice adequate, theologically and practically, as a description of Christian resistance to capitalism? Does justice as the guardian of rights accurately name the technologies that Christianity brings to bear against capitalist discipline? Is this account of justice capable of funding Christian resistance to capitalism? Let us begin with the practical question.

Practical efficacy?

The liberationists accuse the social teaching of an abstraction that renders its effectiveness against the capitalist order doubtful. Does the liberationists' account of justice fare any better? Little would be accomplished by denying that the liberationist vision of Christian involvement in the struggle for justice has inspired many to join that struggle. That vision prompted the social teaching to move, at least for a while, in the direction of a new openness to the movement of the Spirit at the base of the Church and it has contributed to the magisterium's taking up concepts like liberation and the preferential option for the poor. The impact of the liberationists' passion for justice on the Church as a whole is such that justice has become a pervasive theme. While the liberationists deserve praise for their ability – often in the face of brutal repression – to bring justice to the forefront of the Church's deliberations on its mission in the contemporary world, nevertheless there are grounds for questioning whether their conception of justice is ultimately up to the task of sustaining resistance to the capitalist order.

First, there is the difficulty created by the liberationists' conception of the Church of the poor as an apolitical custodian of values. In terms of justice, the construal of the principal task of the Church as instilling values or principles, such as the respect for basic human rights, is insufficient for the formation of just persons. Long ago Aristotle noted that actions are called just when they are the kind of actions that a just person would perform. However, he noted, the just person is not one who simply performs just actions; the just person also performs those actions in the way that just persons do.[170] Justice requires a capacity to judge and to do the right thing in the right place at the right time in the right way. The exercise of justice, in other words, is much more complex than the routinizable application of a value or rule like "respect human rights."[171] The formation of just persons involves a great deal more than consciousness raising on the issue of human rights. It involves the very reformation of desire, which, as we have seen, entails the assembly of a whole host of technologies that act upon and through not only minds, but hearts and bodies and languages and institutions and architectural forms, and so forth. The formation of just persons is not primarily a matter of getting their values right; it is a matter of redirecting desire, with all that involves, so that it flows the way just persons' desire flows. The liberationists' theory of justice, in other words, is inadequate insofar as it lacks sustained attention to the host of technologies of desire necessary for the formation of just persons. In this way it suffers from the same deficiency as the social teaching – it is too abstract. This should come as no surprise, however, given that in its essentials liberationist ecclesiology resembles the social teaching's ecclesiology. Both intentionally distance themselves from the substantive accounts of Christianity articulated by the likes of Aquinas and embodied in communities like the Cistercians. In neither case is Christianity recognized as a fully material reality – that is, a social-economic-political formation – in its own right. As a consequence, Christianity can amount to little more than a cluster of values that awaits material incarnation in secular ensembles of technologies like capitalism or socialism.

This weakness, however, is not something that liberationists could mend by simply turning more attention to specific technologies of desire, for the weakness in their account of justice runs deeper than the absence of such attention. Even if they did attend to those technologies that were aimed at forming persons who respected and struggled for the rights of others, and especially the rights of the poor, their conception of justice would still be inadequate for the reason that it is not good enough. Their conception of justice is not just enough. Forming persons to respect rights is not enough to repel capitalism. In other words, their conception of justice is undermined by its being guided by too thin an account of the common good.

The earlier sketch of the evolution of the common good showed a gradual movement away from Aquinas' thick conception of the common good as a shared love of God towards a thinner notion of the common good, to the point that the common good amounted to little more than the sum total of rights to which individuals were entitled by virtue of their God-given dignity. With the thinning of the common good, justice likewise underwent transformation. If the medieval conception of justice can be characterized as the co-ordination of all activity in the public pursuit of perfection, as modernity unfolded and the pursuit of perfection was privatized, and as the Church reluctantly adapted itself to this new situation, justice was reduced to a matter of the adjudication of claims to society's resources expressed in the language of rights. Justice and the common good no longer had much to say, beyond the injunction to respect the rights of others, about how persons use those resources and exercise those rights.[172] No longer the principle of unity in a common good, justice was merely the facilitator and enabler of the pursuit of private goods. This retreat cannot accurately be described as the repudiation of the good in favor of the right, the simple capitulation of the Church to the forces of liberalism. Nevertheless, it was clearly a diluting of the good that precedes the right, insofar as it was, as Hollenbach indicates, an acknowledgment of the plurality of goods that persons may pursue.

As we have seen, the liberationists' conception of justice is underwritten by this thin conception of the common good as a cache of rights. For the many significant changes they make to the social teaching's conception of justice and their reservations about pluralism, they have not reclaimed justice in the more substantial, Thomistic sense as the principle of unity in the public pursuit of perfection. And this abiding commitment to the modern notion of justice as the guardian of rights suffers from at least two fatal flaws that rob it of the ability to stand against capitalism and liberate desire.

First, the discourse of rights that underwrites that conception of justice cannot provide a strong enough foundation on which to build a community that could assemble the technologies needed to reclaim desire from capitalist discipline. As Ronald Beiner and Alasdair MacIntyre have cogently argued, the modern discourse of rights is not capable of supporting the character-building formations required to resist capitalism.[173] Even when it is remade in theological form, such discourse can neither create the bonds of friendship necessary to inspire and maintain such resistance nor resolve the conflicts of claims on resources that often reside at the heart of situations of poverty. In other words, it cannot generate and sustain the solidarity that the liberationists recognize is essential to withstanding capitalism; such solidarity issues only from a more substantial account of the common good.[174] At best, the liberationists' account of justice as respect for rights may result in societies that look a great deal like modern liberal societies which, incidentally, is precisely what the architect of the liberationists' basic vision of rights, Jacques Maritain, thought.[175]

Second, justice as the guardian of rights is problematic because capitalism is quite compatible with such justice, even when it focuses on the rights of the poor. In other words, justice as a matter of rights is not radical enough. Modern rights discourse is vulnerable to capitalist cooptation and incorporation, as the liberationists themselves acknowledge when they critique the social teaching. Actually, given the historical trajectory of modern rights discourse, the more appropriate question is not that of its possible incorporation into the dominant formation but whether or not it can be anything but part of the dominant formation. In this regard it is not coincidental that rights discourse took hold precisely as the capitalist order was establishing itself. Liberationists tell the story of the emergence of rights as part of the great march of freedom through history. Yet, when set against the backdrop of Foucault's account of liberal governmentality, the emergence of modern rights appears much more complex. Indeed, far from marking a milestone in the struggle to overcome "all that limits or keeps human beings from self-fulfillment"[176] as the liberationists assert, rights are more plausibly understood as but one component of the host of technologies that developed for the sake of governing persons "through freedom," in accord with the demands of emergent market forces. As such, rights discourse appears less as a milestone in freedom's progress than as the concomitant of a desire that has been shorn of its divine *telos* and distorted into the economic self-interest of *homo economicus*.[177] This less benign reading of rights discourse finds support in the work of scholars such as Anthony Arblaster and Ian Shapiro, who present accounts of the emergence of rights that suggest such rights were not first articulated with the radical meaning that liberationists attribute to them, and then "hijacked" as it were by the emergent bourgeois capitalist class.[178] On the contrary, the modern discourse of rights was *originally* articulated by the emergent bourgeois class. Moreover, it was articulated with the intent of securing new forms of wealth and property (commercial, financial, as well as landed) against the traditional, feudal forms of wealth embodied in the aristocracy. In other words, rights were first and foremost about removing obstacles not to human self-fulfillment but to trade and commerce. In this sense, Shapiro notes, the liberal conception of rights legitimates capitalist market practices.[179] In other words, the modern discourse of rights is an element of the capitalist discipline of desire; justice as the guarantor of rights is but one component in the capitalist deformation of desire. Thus, that discourse's adaptation by the liberationists serves as another example of how their revolutionary vision has been disciplined by the capitalist order.

Consequently, the burden of proof is on those who would argue that "human rights" is, in fact, an oppositional discourse. Indeed, although the liberationists critique the social teaching for implicitly embracing welfare state capitalism, it is more likely that the social teaching is only carrying the advocacy of modern rights to its logical conclusion and that the liberationists are wagering on a dead horse, namely, that the modern rights discourse can stand against capitalism. It may well be the case that the best that modern rights language can do is prop up a welfare state that reins in the worst excesses of capitalism. If so, then the clarion call for human rights is properly understood as an alternative – operating at the fringe of the dominant order – and not a truly oppositional discourse.

The practical difficulties that attend the notion of justice as the guarantor of rights unfortunately do not exhaust the problems that afflict the liberationists' account of justice. Several other weaknesses arise with regard to both its distributive emphasis and its upholding the traditional notion of justice as *suum cuique*.

Prominent among these is the fact that justice, as the liberationists have conceived it, does not break the cycle of violence that is endemic to the capitalist order. Earlier the historical overview of the development of the concept of social justice displayed a gradual shift in the nature of justice, from its functioning primarily as a unitive force that coordinated the activities of society in the common project of perfection to its operating predominately in a distributive mode whereby the resources of society were made available to all in accord with their due rights. This distributive conception of justice is particularly well suited to a society that is no longer united in the pursuit of a shared love but is hopelessly fragmented as a conglomeration of persons who are devoted to the pursuit of their own private goods and ends. In adapting itself to this situation, however, justice relinquishes its connection with a genuine peace that comes from the harmonious interaction of persons who share a common good. Justice that is primarily distributive rather than unitive essentially becomes simply the regulator of conflict; it becomes a matter of maintaining the peace between the multiple private goods that compete for society's resources. This peace, however, is a fragile peace that does not so much resemble genuine harmony as it does a temporary cessation of strife, a tenuous balance of power that could at any moment issue in renewed conflict and violence. Earlier it was suggested that justice as the guardian of rights is incapable of resolving conflicts that result from the inevitable clash of rights. Liberationists are aware of this problem and as a result they suggest that in certain circumstances a hierarchy of rights is (temporarily) permissible, with the right to life of the poor at the forefront of that hierarchy. Such a solution, however, is only of limited usefulness. After all, given that the majority of the world's population is impoverished, the range for possible conflicts of rights has not been diminished significantly. How does the assertion of the primacy of the right to life of the poor aid in adjudicating conflicts between the poor? Indeed, it is precisely this ambiguity that capitalism has long exploited, pitting workers against workers for low wages and terrible jobs, hiring the poor to kill the poor, and so forth.

The extent of justice's inability to resolve conflict goes even further, however, than the inevitable clash of rights. Justice in the distributive sense that liberationists invoke may actually exacerbate conflict and violence precisely in the name of restoring violated rights. The liberationists acknowledge the possibility of the legitimate use of violence, within very narrow boundaries, in the name of justice.[180] This possibility raises the specter of the pursuit of the rights of the poor culminating in the reversal of roles in which the oppressed and the oppressors merely switch places. How does justice keep from inflicting new injustice? Christian Duquoc, a theologian intimately acquainted with and sympathetic to the work of the Latin American liberationists,[181] argues that it cannot. The idea of justice linked with violence, he argues, ultimately precludes genuine peace and harmony among peoples. Indeed, he goes further and suggests that such justice issues in terror:

> Terror results from the combination of violence and the idea. Now, contrary to any spontaneous notion, the idea that is expressed in violence is not, in itself, necessarily perverse. . . . It is often moral, as in the case of the desire for flawless justice or for unblemished social transparency. A little earlier I recalled Robespierre's phrase: "Terror is the emanation of a virtue." The utopia of a world without corruption, and taking concrete shape in the exercise of power, becomes terror until justice is in principle realised and the pure find themselves back together. And since nobody is pure when measured against the utopia of justice, violence is unleashed limitlessly.[182]

Justice so conceived only perpetuates the violence and prolongs the conflict that afflicts people. This holds true even when it is successful in reasserting violated rights and re-establishing the volatile equilibrium between competing claims on the fruits of society. Even when successful it does not pave the way for new relations among peoples, relations that might transcend the truce of mutual advantage. Instead it keeps humanity trapped in an agonistic logic, where the mutual recognition of rights is constantly threatened by the pull of competing visions of the good.

Not only does this essentially distributive conception of justice suffer from its failure to break the spiral of violence, it also falters inasmuch as it replicates the very capitalist discipline that it is put forward to combat. Previously it was noted that the capitalist discipline is best characterized as an axiomatic that distorts desire in accord with the dictates of production for the market and that it is a mistake to identify this axiomatic with any single capitalist subject, such as an acquisitive and consuming subject. Nevertheless, it can hardly be disputed that a dominant characteristic of capitalism is its penchant for distorting desire into a proprietary power that is acquisitive and consumptive. The liberationists' conception of justice as primarily a principle of distribution mimics in important ways this acquisitive discipline and hence hardly portends the liberation of desire from capitalism. Specifically, justice as a matter of rendering to everyone that portion of societies' prosperity that is due them by virtue of their rights reinforces capitalist discipline insofar as it both construes desire as essentially proprietary and encourages desire to claim its rights, to acquire what is due it. Justice so understood forms desire to be acquisitive, just as capitalism does. The liberationists face capitalism and demand that it render what is due; capitalism responds that that is exactly what it does. Liberationists face the poor and encourage them to become acquisitive; so, too, does capitalism.[183] Of course, the fact that there is a parallel formation of desire does not mean that little separates the liberationists and the capitalists. The constraints that liberationists place on acquisitive desire in the form of the duty to respect the rights of others, particularly the right to life of the poor, does distinguish the acquisitive desire generated by the liberationists' conception of justice from that generated by savage capitalism.[184] Nevertheless, a troubling family resemblance remains.

A contrasting example is helpful in illuminating the way the liberationists' conception of justice mirrors capitalist discipline with regard to the formation of acquisitive desire. Consider justice in the unitive sense that Aquinas used it. Far from simply directing desire to acquire what is due, the general virtue of justice might well intervene to prevent, for the sake of the common good, the particular virtue of distributive justice from rendering what is due. In this way, justice in the unitive sense wards off the proprietary individual[185] and forms desire in such a way that it may well forego the acquisition of what is due in the name of the common good. Lacking as they do a strong conception of the common good that might trump rights claims, there is nothing comparable in the liberationists' account of justice. Consequently, their justice leaves desire as an essentially acquisitive force, again, hardly something that bodes well for the liberation of desire from capitalism.

In addition to the practical deficiencies that stem from justice being principally a distributive force, the liberationists' embrace of justice in the traditional sense of *suum cuique* is also problematic. The problem with granting justice so conceived pride of place in the struggle against capitalism is that it must always fail. Justice so conceived is impossible.[186] As Duquoc suggested, it is a utopian ideal that cannot be realized. Hence, to pin one's hopes for liberation on the advent of this justice is to set off on the path to failure from the outset. This is the case, not simply because humanity cannot be that good but because injustice is irreversible. Once injustice has been committed, no future can ever make good the suffering of the past. Granted that in some cases, when the violation of rights is not particularly grave, justice can re-establish the precarious balance of rights. But even then the offense is not offset. This problem comes into high relief when the injustice is a matter of the masses of tortured and murdered. Nothing can be set on the scales of justice opposite an infant victim of the Contras that will somehow balance it out, that will render that death amenable to a calculus of "what is due" for the simple fact that precisely as an act of injustice it is irretrievably "that which is *not* due." There is nothing (not even a final judgment[187]) that can transmute that situation, that death, into "what is due"; hence justice as a calculus of what is due is defeated. Justice as "rendering what is due" eternally impales itself on Ayacucho.[188]

In defense of justice, some liberationists invoke the resurrection. Does not the resurrection of Jesus amount to the victory of justice over injustice? "[T]he resurrection of Jesus," asserts Sobrino, "shows *in directo* the triumph of justice over injustice. It is the triumph not only of God's omnipotence, but also of God's justice. . . . Jesus' resurrection is thus transformed into good news, whose central content is that once and for all justice has triumphed over injustice, the victim over the executioner."[189] This, however, is incorrect. The resurrection, no less than the crucifixion, is a profoundly ambiguous event. For example, just as the cross need not be interpreted as an act of injustice – on the contrary, some popular accounts of the atonement make it an act of justice – so, too, the resurrection is not self-evidently a sign of justice. Indeed, given the presence of so much injustice and the striking absence of justice in today's world, what is to keep us from seeing the resurrection as nothing more than an indication of the victim's stamina and endurance? "Look," the executioner (capitalist) exclaims, "the victim has returned. More suffering (labor, debt) can be extracted!"

Whatever the resurrection signifies, it does not annul the cross. The one who is raised remains the crucified one and injustice is as irreversible as the cross on which the crucified hung. Whatever the future brings, whatever restoration God may effect, the cross is not undone. The healing of the nail's mark is not its undoing. Therefore, if the resurrection is to be understood, in line with Sobrino and the liberationists, as the overcoming of the wound of injustice, then it must be understood as an overcoming that is something other than justice conceived as *suum cuique*. If desire is to be liberated from capitalist discipline and the wound of injustice healed, it must be through the operation of a strange therapy, one that resists capitalist incorporation, breaks the cycle of violence, and wards off the temptation to acquire.

Theological adequacy?

The question of the proper interpretation of the resurrection introduces the issue of the theological adequacy of the liberationists' conception of justice. If there are grounds to suspect that the resurrection is not about justice in the classic sense of "rendering what is due," is it possible that the whole effort to place such a conception of justice at the center of the Christian witness against capitalism is misguided? Is the primacy liberationists accord such justice a faithful reflection of the Christian vision of God?

Liberationists defend the primacy of justice by appealing to the Bible. As we have seen, they emphasize that the God of the Bible is fundamentally a God who establishes justice. Nothing is gained by disputing this claim. Justice is certainly a prominent theme in the Bible and God is clearly portrayed as working to establish justice. What is arguable, however, is the meaning and significance that libera-tionists bestow upon this particular divine attribute in the struggle against injustice generally and capitalism in particular. When God acts to counter injustice, God does not simply enact justice in the sense of settling accounts with a strict render-ing to each what is due. The paradigmatic example of this is the atonement. The traditional claim is that God's act of atonement in Christ is foremost an act of grace. The offer of redemption that comes to humanity in Christ is an offer that is unmerited, undeserved. Humanity has no claim upon such redemption; there is no right to which it corresponds. When it arrives it cannot be synchronized with any calculus that attempts to "render what is due." In this sense, when viewed through the lens of a strict calculus of what is due, redemption is an act of injustice. God is patently unjust, refusing to deal with humanity in the manner it deserves. What is due fallen humanity is death, yet God in God's grace gives life. Pressing the point, in the context of the liberationists' account of justice as a rendering what is due in accord with rights, one could argue that God redeems humanity *from* justice.[190] The atonement amounts to the displacement of justice in the classic sense of "ren-dering what is due" by grace. Consequently, whatever is said about God and God's justice must be said against the backdrop of the amnesty of grace, an amnesty that extinguishes the terror of justice as it puts in place a new economy to deal with injustice. To this economy of grace we now turn.

Notes

1 I couch my objective this way because I do not presume to theorize for these com-munities, although they are the foil for much of my argument.

2 This claim need not preclude the rightful recognition of Israel that Christianity too often occludes. For more on this, see Scott Bader-Saye, *The Church and Israel After Christendom* (Boulder, CO: Westview Press, 1999), and Bruce Marshall, "Christ and the cultures: the Jewish people and Christian theology," in *The Cambridge Companion to Christian Doctrine*, ed. Colin Gunton (Cambridge: Cambridge University Press, 1997), 81–100.

3 MacIntyre defines a practice as follows: "By a 'practice' I am going to mean any coherent and complex form of socially established cooperative human activity through which goods internal to that form of activity are realized in the course of trying to achieve those standards of excellence which are appropriate to, and partially definitive of, that form of activity, with the result that human powers to achieve excel-lence, and human conceptions of the ends and goods involved, are systematically extended." *After Virtue*, 2nd edn (Notre Dame: University of Notre Dame Press, 1984), 187.

4 This is not to suggest that MacIntyre is necessarily guilty of a personalist reduction of the notion of practices. My point is only that the term "technologies" brings institu-tional and other elements to the foreground and thus wards off personalist misreadings to which "practices" may be more susceptible. As Latin American liber-ationists might say, the concept of technology more obviously incorporates the "structural" dimension of human activity.

5 For accounts of this see MacIntyre *After Virtue*; Charles Taylor, *Sources of the Self* (Cambridge: Harvard University Press, 1989); G. Simon Harak, *Virtuous Passions* (New York: Paulist Press, 1993).

6 Harak, *Virtuous Passions*, 82. Aquinas is often read as the progenitor of the modern dualism of reason/passion. For a corrective, see 67, 77, 90–92, 96.

7 The biographical summary that follows draws primarily on Michael Casey, *A Thirst for God: Spiritual Desire in Bernard of Clairvaux's Sermons on the Song of Songs* (Kalamazoo, MI: Cistercian Publications, 1987), 3–17.

8 Casey calls him the most famous and influential person of his age. See Casey, *A Thirst for God*, 1, 16.

9 Rowan Williams, "Three Styles of Monastic Reform," in *The Influence of Saint Bernard*, ed. Benedicta Ward (Oxford: SLG Press, 1976), 34, 36.

10 Bernard of Clairvaux, *On the Song of Songs*, sermon 84.7, quoted in Casey, *A Thirst for God*, 53.

11 Casey, *A Thirst for God*, 244.

12 Casey provides a good example, when he describes desire as "a deep inner void which can only be filled through an intimate interpersonal relationship with God . . ." or when he writes, "only God himself is large enough to be able to satisfy the immense craving for love which the human heart experiences." See *A Thirst for God*, 61, 140.

13 Bernard of Clairvaux, *On the Song of Songs*, 4 vols., trans. Kilian Walsh (Kalamazoo, MI: Cistercian Publications, 1971–1980), sermon 57.6.

14 Quoted in Casey, *A Thirst for God*, 85.

15 Quoted in Casey, *A Thirst for God*, 228.

16 Bernard of Clairvaux, *On the Song of Songs*, sermons 8, 14.

17 Ibid., sermon 11.

18 Ibid., sermons 11.5, 82.5.

19 Ibid., sermon 36.5.

20 Ibid., sermon 21.6.

21 Ibid., sermon 24.5.

22 Ibid., sermon 82.

23 The notion of desire as a "lack" can only be used of unfallen desire in a benign, analogous sense, for it is not about an absence or void but an inexhaustible divine plenitude or surplus that always gives more, in the sense of the Psalmist who writes "my cup runneth over" (Ps. 23:5). Such a "lack" has to do with the lure of God to participate ever more deeply in the triune love of God.

24 Ibid., sermon 83.

25 Ibid., sermon 15.

26 Ibid., sermons 13, 22, 48.

27 Ibid., sermons 17, 21, 32, 51, 74.

28 What follows is drawn from Casey, *A Thirst for God*, 250–251. See Bernard of Clairvaux, *On the Song of Songs*, sermon 23.6. See also Bernard's *On Grace and Free Choice*.

29 Ibid., 143.

30 Jean Leclercq, *Monks and Love in Twelfth Century France* (Oxford: Clarendon Press, 1979), 10. What follows draws heavily on Leclercq.

31 Ibid., 21, 88–89.

32 Talal Asad, *Genealogies of Religion: Discipline and Reasons of Power in Christianity and Islam* (Baltimore, MD: Johns Hopkins University Press, 1993), 142.

33 Leclercq, *Monks and Love in Twelfth Century France*, 16–17. He is quoting P. A. Cusack's description of Benedict's spirituality. See P. A. Cusack, "The Temptation of St Benedict: An Essay at Interpretation through Literary Sources," *American Benedictine Review* 27 (1976): 162. The conflation is apt, as Benedict definitively influenced Bernard. See Casey, *A Thirst for God*, 28.

34 Ibid., 92–93. For a fascinating reading of the great medieval literary work, *Quest of the Holy Grail*, as an exemplification of Cistercian formation in this regard, see Isabel

Mary, "The Knights of God: Citeaux and the Quest of the Holy Grail," in *The Influence of Saint Bernard*, ed. Benedicta Ward (Oxford: SLG Press, 1976), 53–88.

35 Ibid., 91. See 86–98 for a study of the martial imagery in Bernard.

36 This point bears emphasizing. To a modern reader the ways in which monastic rituals involved what Foucault called technologies of power or domination are readily apparent. An abbot lecturing his captive audience, the vow of obedience, confession to another, such practices clearly embody "acting upon the actions of another." What might not be as obvious is the ways in which the monastic space was also occupied by technologies of the self – actions whereby one acted upon oneself. Bernard once referred to the monastery as a "prison with open doors": no one held the monks there, the doors were open, they could (and some did) leave. In this sense the monastery could be understood as one great instrument whereby monks remade themselves. However, the monastery functioned as a technology of the self in a more immediate sense as well insofar as monastic ritual was not about filling passive subjects with new content. The monks were actively involved in this remaking and, moreover, this remaking entailed not the suppression of the self or will, but their transformation. In other words, what occurred in the monastery was not merely the imposition of a new self, but self-transformation. Even the vow of obedience, rightly understood, was not about the loss or constriction of one's will so much as it was about redirecting the will in a common project. For this reason the monastery should be distinguished from disciplinary institutions to which it sometimes has been compared, like prisons and hospitals (Asad, *Genealogies of Religion*, 126).

37 Asad, *Genealogies of Religion*, 136–137.

38 Ibid., 144. Benedict Anderson notes that artwork and stained glass accomplished the same purpose. See his *Imagined Communities* (New York: Verso, 1991), 22–24.

39 On the assembly of memory, see Nikolas Rose, *Inventing Our Selves* (Cambridge: Cambridge University Press, 1996), 179–181; Rowan Williams, "'Know Thyself': What Kind of an Injunction?," in *Philosophy, Religion, and the Spiritual Life*, ed. Michael McGhee (New York: Cambridge University Press, 1992), 221.

40 For several references, see Casey, *A Thirst for God*, 229.

41 Ibid., 208–231.

42 Asad, *Genealogies of Religion*, 131.

43 Rose, *Inventing Our Selves*, 181. In more contemporary terms, says Nikolas Rose, "one's memory of oneself as a being with a psychological biography, a line of development of emotion, intellect, will, desire is produced through family photograph albums, the ritual repetition of stories, the actual or 'virtual' dossier of school reports, and the like, the accumulation of artifacts, and the attachment of image, sense, and value to them, and so forth" (180). See also Marcel Mauss, "Techniques of the Body," *Economy and Society* 2 (1973): 70–88.

44 In this regard, see Catherine Pickstock's comments on the Eucharistic liturgy as a means of forming desire in her essay, "Thomas Aquinas and the Quest for the Eucharist," *Modern Theology* 15 (1999): 159–180.

45 Asad, *Genealogies of Religion*, 144.

46 Ibid., 140. John Milbank makes a similar observation, arguing that the equation of discipline with Christian confession reflects not the success of Christianity, but, contra Foucault, its distortion and failure on the eve of modernity. See John Milbank, *Theology and Social Theory* (Cambridge: Basil Blackwell, 1990), 290–294.

47 The rendition of Song of Songs 1:7 comes from Williams, "Know Thyself," 218. Sermons 35–37 deal with this passage. The passage quoted is from Bernard of Clairvaux, *On the Song of Songs*, sermon 36.5.

48 See Bernard of Clairvaux, *On the Song of Songs*, sermon 36.6; Casey, *A Thirst for God*, 157–158.

49 Bernard of Clairvaux, *On the Song of Songs*, sermon 37.2.

50 In the final chapter the difference between my proposal for a politically active Christianity and Bernard's vision of Christendom, as well as how the Cistercian technologies' failure with regard to facilitating the Crusades might be accounted for, will become clear.

51 L. Gregory Jones, "A Thirst for God or Consumer Spirituality? Cultivating Disciplined Practices or Being Engaged by God," *Modern Theology* 13 (1997): 23.

52 This shift is undoubtedly related to the ways in which in the Middle Ages the practice of penance was privatized. For more on this as well as the ways in which developments in Christianity opened the door to a disciplinary society, see Catherine Pickstock, *After Writing: On the Liturgical Consummation of Philosophy* (Malden, MA: Blackwell Publishers, 1998).

53 More positive examples of Christianity as an ensemble of technologies of desire that is not dependent on feudal monastic orders might be provided by some strands of the radical Reformation, or early British Methodism, or twentieth-century Catholic Worker houses.

54 Philip Rieff, *The Triumph of the Therapeutic* (New York: Harper & Row, 1966).

55 MacIntyre, *After Virtue*, 27–35.

56 Rieff, *The Triumph of the Therapeutic*, 251–252.

57 Ibid., 26. See also Jones, "A Thirst for God or Consumer Spirituality?," 3–28.

58 See Nikolas Rose, "Engineering the Human Soul: Analyzing Psychological Expertise," *Science in Context* 5 (1992): 351-369; Nikolas Rose, "Expertise and the Government of Conduct," *Studies in Law, Politics, and Society*, 14 (1994): 359–397; Peter Miller and Nikolas Rose, "On Therapeutic Authority: Psychoanalytical Expertise under Advanced Liberalism," *History of the Human Sciences* 7 (1994): 29–64. Rose is critical of Rieff in this regard, suggesting that Rieff tends to cast therapy as a sign or effect of other more fundamental changes, instead of understanding how therapy functions as a mode of government.

59 What follows relies heavily on Williams, "'Know Thyself'": What Kind of an Injunction?," 211–227.

60 Emil Brunner, *Justice and the Social Order*, trans. Mary Hottinger (New York: Harper and Brothers, 1945), 4.

61 Synod of Bishops, "Justice in the World," in *Liberation Theology: A Documentary History*, ed. Alfred T. Hennelly (Maryknoll, NY: Orbis Books, 1990), 138.

62 Second General Conference of Latin American Bishops, *The Church in the Present-Day Transformation of Latin America in the Light of the Council*, "Document on the Poverty of the Church," §2. Text found in *Liberation Theology: A Documentary History*, ed. Alfred T. Hennelly (Maryknoll, NY: Orbis Books, 1992), 114–119.

63 Jon Sobrino, *Compassion: The Shaping Principle of the Human and of the Christian* (Regina: University of Regina Press, 1992), 1. See also Ignacio Ellacuría, *Freedom Made Flesh*, trans. John Drury (Maryknoll, NY: Orbis Books, 1976), 110.

64 Jon Sobrino, *The True Church and the Poor*, trans. Matthew J. O'Connell (Maryknoll, NY: Orbis Books, 1984), 78–79. Note that the liberationists conceive of justice as the historical form of love. See Sobrino, *The True Church and the Poor*, 47–48.

65 José Ignacio González Faus, "Justicia," in *Conceptos Fundamentales de Pastoral*, eds. Casiano Floristan and Juan-José Tamayo (Madrid: Ediciones Cristiandad, 1983), 514.

66 Gustavo Gutiérrez, *A Theology of Liberation*, rev. ed., trans. Sister Caridad Inda and John Eagleson (Maryknoll, NY: Orbis Books, 1988), 111; see also Sobrino, *The True Church and the Poor*, 53, 55.

67 Gustavo Gutiérrez, *The God of Life*, trans. Matthew J. O'Connell (Maryknoll, NY: Orbis Books, 1991), 28, 94. See also Ignacio Ellacuría, "Fe y Justicia," in *Fe, Justicia y Opción por Los Oprimidos*, eds. Ignacio Ellacuría, Arnaldo Zenteno, and Alberto Arroyo (Bilboa: Desclée de Brouwer, 1980), 21.

68 Gustavo Gutiérrez, *Las Casas*, trans. Robert R. Barr (Maryknoll, NY: Orbis Books, 1993), 235.

69 Quoted in Bartolomé de Las Casas, *Witness: Writings of Bartolomé de Las Casas*, ed. George Sanderlin (Maryknoll, NY: Orbis Books, 1992), 67.

70 See Alasdair MacIntyre, *Whose Justice? Which Rationality?* (Notre Dame: University of Notre Dame Press, 1988); Chaim Perelman, *The Idea of Justice and the Problem of Argument* (London: Routledge, 1963).

71 Ignacio Ellacuría, "The Church of the Poor, Historical Sacrament of Liberation," in *Mysterium Liberationis: Fundamental Concepts of Liberation Theology*, eds. Ignacio Ellacuría and Jon Sobrino (Maryknoll, NY: Orbis Books, 1993), 556.

72 Leonardo Boff, *Jesus Christ Liberator*, trans. Patrick Hughes (Maryknoll, NY: Orbis Books, 1978), 71.

73 Ismael García, *Justice in Latin American Theology of Liberation* (Atlanta: John Knox Press, 1987), 1, 11.

74 Clodovis Boff, "The Social Teaching of the Church and the Theology of Liberation: Opposing Social Practices?" *Concilium* 150 (1981): 20.

75 Cited in David Hollenbach, *Justice, Peace, and Human Rights* (New York: Crossroad Publishing Co., 1990), 18.

76 St Thomas Aquinas, *Summa Theologica*, trans. Fathers of the English Dominican Province (Westminster, MD: Christian Classics, 1981), II–II.58.1. Note that in asserting that the Christian tradition appropriated the classic notion of justice as *suum cuique*, I am not suggesting that the Christian tradition simply adopted the classic notion without significant change. On the contrary, in at least some strands of the tradition, *suum cuique* was altered beyond recognition, such that "rendering what is due" was no longer an operation of desert in the classic sense but rather essentially transmuted into its opposite, namely, an operation that presupposed God's unmerited grace. Aquinas is a case in point. By positioning justice, as he does, firmly within the economy of divine grace (see I–II.109), the classic notion of rendering what is due is subverted into something that the classic authors such as Aristotle and Cicero would not recognize. As MacIntyre says, it is no accident that the account of the cardinal virtues, of which justice is one, in the *Secunda Secundae* had to have as its prologue an inquiry into the supernatural virtues, for "just as and because justice is continually the victim of the vice and sin of pride, so justice cannot flourish, cannot indeed, so it turns out, even exist as a natural virtue, unless and insofar as it is informed by the supernatural virtue of *caritas*. Charity is the form of all virtue; without charity the virtues would lack the specific kind of directedness which they require. And charity is not to be acquired by moral education; it is a gift of grace, flowing from the work of Christ through the office of the Holy Spirit (*S.T.* IIa–IIae, 23 to 44)." (*Whose Justice? Which Rationality?*, 205)

77 Ibid., II–II.47.10.ad 2. Quoted in Normand J. Paulhus, "Uses and Misuses of the Term 'Social Justice' in the Roman Catholic Tradition," *The Journal of Religious Ethics* 15 (1987): 265.

78 Ibid., II–II.58.5.

79 Ibid., II–II.61.1.

80 Paulhus, "Uses and Misuses of the Term 'Social Justice' in the Roman Catholic Tradition," 268. A more complete history of the term "social justice" can be found in Jean-Yves Calvez and Jacques Perrin, *The Church and Social Justice* (Chicago: Henry Regnery Company, 1961), and Leo W. Shields, *The History and Meaning of the Term Social Justice* (Notre Dame: University of Notre Dame Press, 1941). See also John Finnis, *Natural Law and Natural Rights* (Oxford: Clarendon Press, 1988); Ernest Fortin, "The New Rights Theory and the Natural Law," *Review of Politics* 44 (1982): 590–612; Bernard Brady, "An Analysis of the Use of Rights Language in Pre-Modern Catholic Social Thought," *The Thomist* 57 (1993): 97–121.

81 Joan Lockwood O'Donovan, "Natural Law and Perfect Community: Contributions of Christian Platonism to Political Theory," *Modern Theology* 14 (1998): 36.

82 Joan Lockwood O'Donovan, "Historical Prolegomena to a Theological Review of 'Human Rights'," *Studies in Christian Ethics* 9 (1996): 54, 56; O'Donovan, "Natural Law and Perfect Community: Contributions of Christian Platonism to Political Theory," 19–23. See also C. B. Macpherson, *The Political Theory of Possessive Individualism* (Oxford: Oxford University Press, 1962); Ian Shapiro, *The Evolution of Rights in Liberal Theory* (Cambridge: Cambridge University Press, 1986).

83 See Pius XI, *Quadragesimo anno*, §57–58, 71, 74, 88, 101, 110, 126. Note that Pius X did invoke the term without elaboration or development in *Iucunda sane*, §3; see John XXIII, *Pacem in terris*, §167.

84 This was no sheer coincidence. In the years immediately preceding the release of *Rerum novarum*, which set the terms for the developments of the next century, Leo XIII had established close ties with the various leaders of social Catholicism. See Calvez and Perrin, *The Church and Social Justice*, 79–80.

85 Leo XIII, *Rerum novarum*, §45. All references are to the encyclical as it is found in Michael Walsh and Brian Davis, eds., *Proclaiming Justice and Peace*, rev. and enl. edn (Mystic, CT: Twenty-Third Publications, 1991), 15–41.

86 Ibid., §2.

87 Ibid., §34. Note that although Leo XIII asserted that justice was distributive and that all persons ought to share in the prosperity of society, he was not an egalitarian. His vision of justice was semi-feudal. A rightly ordered society was a hierarchical one in which the common good was distributed in proportion to one's rank or position in that society (see §49). Hence the subtle qualifier with regard to the obligation to distribute one's surplus, "when necessity and *seemliness* have been satisfied, there is the duty of using what is over to relieve the poor" (§21; italics added).

88 Pius XI, *Quadragesimo anno*, §57. All references are to the encyclical as it is found in Michael Walsh and Brian Davis, eds., *Proclaiming Justice and Peace*, rev. and enl. edn (Mystic, CT: Twenty-Third Publications, 1991), 41–80.

89 Ibid., §71, 74.

90 Ibid., §88. Pius XI's vision merits the same caveat as Leo XIII with regard to the non-egalitarian nature of his notion of distributive justice. His corporatist vision of a hierarchically ordered society entailed the unequal distribution of authority, status, and wealth.

91 "We are filled with an overwhelming sadness when we contemplate the sorry spectacle of millions of workers in many lands and entire continents condemned through the inadequacy of their wages to live with their families in utterly subhuman conditions . . . [I]n some of these lands the enormous wealth, the unbridled luxury, of the privileged few stands in violent, offensive contrast to the utter poverty of the vast majority . . . We therefore consider it our duty to reaffirm that the remuneration of work is not something that can be left to the laws of the marketplace; nor should it be a decision left to the will of the more powerful. It must be determined in accordance with justice and equity." John XXIII, *Mater et magistra*, §68, 69, 71; see also 18. All references are to the encyclical as it is found in Michael Walsh and Brian Davis, eds., *Proclaiming Justice and Peace*, rev. and enl. edn (Mystic, CT: Twenty-Third Publications, 1991), 81–124.

92 John XXIII, *Mater et magistra*, §161, 170, 171, 172.

93 Leo XIII, *Rerum novarum*, §15.

94 The Second Vatican Council, *Gaudium et spes*, §42.3. All references are to the encyclical as it is found in Michael Walsh and Brian Davis, eds., *Proclaiming Justice and Peace*, rev. and enl. edn (Mystic, CT: Twenty-Third Publications, 1991), 157–220. David Hollenbach notes that this move by John XXIII had been gradually developing since Pius XII. See his *Justice, Peace, and Human Rights*, 29. Note that John Coleman suggests

that this development was in fact not novel, but rather a return to the Leonine tradition. See John Coleman, "Development of Church Social Teaching," in *Readings in Moral Theology No. 5*, eds. Charles E. Curran and Richard A. McCormick (New York: Paulist Press, 1986), 173.

95 Pius XI, *Quadragesimo anno*, §58, see also 110.

96 The Second Vatican Council's declaration *Gaudium et spes* captures this sense well when it describes the common good as "the sum of those conditions of social life which allow social groups and their individual members relatively thorough and ready access to their own fulfillment" (§26). See also David Hollenbach, *Claims in Conflict: Retrieving and Renewing the Catholic Human Rights Tradition* (New York: Paulist Press, 1979), 152.

97 Leo XIII, *Rerum novarum*, §33. See 47 and 49 where the same function of the state is described as the pursuit of the common good. See also John XXIII, *Mater et magistra*, §74, 151. In all of these ways, justice and the common good come to resemble the promotion of (Western) civilization. Several of the popes acknowledge this link and celebrate the Church's accomplishments in this regard. Leo XIII, for example, wrote: "It is not the Rome of Scipio or of Caesar but the Rome of Christ which has spread the light of true civilization throughout the globe, which has reformed laws and customs, brought peoples and classes to live together as brothers, made men better both in their private and social lives. . . . Christian Rome, the indefectible teacher of sound faith and good works, shines and will continue to shine like a heavenly lighthouse until the end of time, guiding men along the road to eternal life. As for goods of the temporal order, you all know well that were it not for the work and merits of papal Rome, Italy and all Europe would have been irremediably lost in the darkness and misery of barbarism." (Letter to delegates of the Catholic societies of Rome, December 17, 1893. Quoted in Calvez and Perrin, *The Church and Social Justice*, 28.)

98 Pius XI, *Quadragesimo anno*, §57; Pius XII, "Speech to the Tribunal of Rota", October 3, 1941. Cited in Calvez and Perrin, *The Church and Social Justice*, 114.

99 It should be noted that the modern social teaching includes as a vital component of rights language, correlative duties. These duties, however, are inevitably overshadowed by the rights. Joan Lockwood O'Donovan suggests why when she writes: "A common thread throughout rights theories from their inception is the idea of the bearer of rights as a self-transcending will who *uses* the world around and his own body and capacities to achieve certain self-referential ends. Even if these ends and the means of realising them are given in divine and natural law, the rights-bearer is still regarded as the primary source of political meaning, social worth, and positive law. . . . It is precisely on account of the supposed sovereignty of the rights-bearing subject, relative or absolute, that the concept of rights is not simply coordinate with that of obligations, as some more conservative apologists for rights wish to argue." ("Historical Prolegomena to a Theological Review of 'Human Rights,'" 63–64).

100 Pius XII, *Quoniam paschalia*, quoted in Calvez and Perrin, *The Church and Social Justice*, 157.

101 Leo XIII, *Rerum novarum*, §38.

102 John XXIII, *Pacem in terris*, §9, 37. All references are to the encyclical as it is found in Michael Walsh and Brian Davis, eds., *Proclaiming Justice and Peace*, rev. and enl. edn (Mystic, CT: Twenty-Third Publications, 1991), 125–156.

103 Gustavo Gutiérrez notes that this change was initiated by Leo XIII when he reluctantly acknowledged the liberal Catholic argument that the modern liberties were a "lesser evil." See his "Freedom and Salvation: A Political Problem," in *Liberation and Change*, ed. Ronald H. Stone (Atlanta: John Knox Press, 1977), 47–49.

104 Leo XIII, *Rerum novarum*, §45. The specific reference is to a just wage.

105 John XXIII, *Pacem in terris*, §9.

106 The Second Vatican Council, *Dignitatis humanae*, §1. Text found in Joseph Gremillion, ed., *The Gospel of Peace and Justice* (Maryknoll, NY: Orbis Books, 1976), 337–350.

107 Leo XIII, *Rerum novarum*, §41.

108 John XXIII, *Pacem in terris*, §30.

109 Ibid., §32.

110 In acknowledging this change, David Hollenbach, a major proponent and inter-preter of modern Catholic teaching, insists that this not be understood as a "retreat" so much as a theologically informed response to "social and ideological pluralism." He does, however, admit that this change resulted in the Church's being able to advance only "modest" claims about what constitutes a just social order. Hollenbach can maintain this claim – that rendering the Church capable only of making "modest" claims about what constitutes a just social order is not a retreat – because he sees in the more modest standards a move that severed the Church's *explicit* ties to a semi-feudal corporatist order. What Hollenbach fails to realize is that such a move only severed the Church's explicit ties to that order. Nothing in the more "modest" human rights standard rules out Church support for semi-feudal political orders; it only insists that such orders defend themselves in the language of rights (and several pontiffs, as the tradition of social encyclicals shows, had no trouble articulating such a defense). Indeed, the more modest standards only level the playing field, in the sense that with this shift any political order is potentially legitimate so long as it can defend itself in terms of respect for human rights. To be fair to Hollenbach, he does seem to be aware of this ambiguity in the new standard when he writes, "The strengths of such a universal and integrative approach . . . may also be a weakness. . . . It can be asked whether some of the more recent statements from the Holy See do not show unmistakable signs of using abstract comprehensiveness as a substitute for concrete choice and action in the midst of conflict." For examples of this he points to statements by Paul VI as well as the Third General Conference of Latin American Bishops. See Hollenbach, *Justice, Peace, and Human Rights*, 90–91, 94. Jon Sobrino offers a Latin American appraisal of the embrace of pluralism, saying: "Pluralism was originally a way of regaining freedom in the face of an imposed uniformity; in present-day Latin America, however, it often becomes an alibi for not moving effectively along the lines set down by Medellín. To put it another way, the appeal to pluralism . . . often becomes a weapon of ecclesial politics in defense of clearly conservative attitudes and interests." Sobrino, *The True Church and the Poor*, 198.

111 Pius XI, *Quadragesimo anno*, §137.

112 The most complete account of this history is provided in Gutiérrez's "Freedom and Salvation: A Political Problem." A much abbreviated account appears in Gustavo Gutiérrez, *The Power of the Poor in History*, trans. Robert R. Barr (Maryknoll, NY: Orbis Books, 1983), 169–214 and Gutiérrez, *A Theology of Liberation*, 17–22. See also Sobrino, *The True Church and the Poor*, 10–18.

113 Gutiérrez, *A Theology of Liberation*, 17–18.

114 Gustavo Gutiérrez, "Option for the Poor," in *Mysterium Liberationis: Fundamental Concepts of Liberation Theology*, eds. Ignacio Ellacuría and Jon Sobrino (Maryknoll, NY: Orbis Books, 1993), 245; see also Gustavo Gutiérrez, *The God of Life*, trans. Matthew J. O'Connell (Maryknoll, NY: Orbis Books, 1991), 120.

115 Jon Sobrino, *Spirituality of Liberation*, trans. Robert R. Barr (Maryknoll, NY: Orbis Books, 1988), 104.

116 Clodovis Boff, "The Social Teaching of the Church," 19. He goes on to say that as a result, the social teaching resembles not so much a coherent system as a "box of spare parts" from which "inspirational nuclei" are selected and developed. Such is the origin, according to Boff, of the base communities and the "option for the poor."

117 Gutiérrez, *The Power of the Poor in History*, 182.

118 See Ricardo Antoncich, *Christians in the Face of Injustice: A Latin American Reading of Catholic Social Teaching* (Maryknoll, NY: Orbis Books, 1987); Ricardo Antoncich,

"Liberation Theology and the Social Teaching of the Church," in *Mysterium Liberationis: Fundamental Concepts of Liberation Theology*, eds. Ignacio Ellacuría and Jon Sobrino (Maryknoll, NY: Orbis Books, 1993), 103–122.

119 Second General Conference of Latin American Bishops, *The Church in the Present-Day Transformation of Latin America in the Light of the Council*, "Introduction to the Final Documents," §4. Text is found in *Liberation Theology: A Documentary History*, ed. Alfred T. Hennelly (Maryknoll, NY: Orbis Books, 1992), 94–96.

120 Gutiérrez, *The Power of the Poor in History*, 186.

121 Gutiérrez, "Freedom and Salvation: A political problem," 30.

122 Gutiérrez, *The Power of the Poor in History*, 49.

123 Sobrino, *The True Church and the Poor*, 10–15.

124 See, for example, Paul Sigmund, *Liberation Theology at the Crossroads: Democracy or Revolution* (New York: Oxford University Press, 1990), 189–195.

125 Sobrino, *Spirituality of Liberation*, 103; Alfred Hennelly suggests that while the issue of human rights does not constitute a "central *explicit* theme" in liberationists' work, "the *reality* of human rights (including socioeconomic rights as well as individual political rights) does have central importance." See Alfred T. Hennelly, "Human Rights and Latin American Theology," in *Human Rights in the Americas: The Struggle for Consensus*, eds. Alfred T. Hennelly and John Langan (Washington DC: Georgetown University Press, 1982), 25–26 (italics in original).

126 Juan Luis Segundo, *Signs of the Times*, ed. Alfred T. Hennelly (Maryknoll, NY: Orbis Books, 1993), 62 (italics in original). See also Franz Hinkelammert's essay, "La inversión de los derechos humanos: el caso de John Locke," *Pasos* 85 (1999): 20–35.

127 Ibid., 61.

128 See Hollenbach, *Justice, Peace, and Human Rights*, 93–98.

129 Segundo, *Signs of the Times*, 64. Obviously, Segundo does not give much credence to the claim that the social teaching of the Church has successfully articulated an alternative social and economic order that is a "third way" beyond capitalism and socialism. For more on the effort to articulate a "third way" and its failure, see Denis Goulet, "Economic Systems, Middle Way Theories, and Third World Realities," in *Readings in Moral Theology No. 5*, eds. Charles E. Curran and Richard A. McCormick (New York: Paulist Press, 1986), 340–365.

130 Clodovis Boff, "The Social Teaching of the Church," 21. Mary Hobgood suggests that the reason for this is that "Catholic social teaching has consistently ignored its own historical analysis of the effects of capitalist dynamics when it formulates strategies to respond to the consequences described." See her *Catholic Social Teaching and Economic Theory* (Philadelphia: Temple University Press, 1991), 236. It is worth noting that Hobgood argues that the social teaching did not reject capitalism (see pages 105, 113, 115, 121, 122, 132).

131 Gutiérrez, *The Power of the Poor in History*, 182.

132 Samuel Silva Gotay, *La Teología de la Liberación* (Santo Domingo: CEPAE, 1985), 74. See also Aloysius Pieris, "Human Rights Language and Liberation Theology," in *The Future of Liberation Theology*, eds. Marc H. Ellis and Otto Maduro (Maryknoll, NY: Orbis Books, 1989), 306–309; Calvez and Perrin, *The Church and Social Justice*, 36–53; Hollenbach, *Claims in Conflict*, 113–118.

133 Peter Hebblethwaite, "The Popes and Politics: Shifting Patterns in Catholic Social Doctrine," in *Readings in Moral Theology No. 5*, eds. Charles E. Curran and Richard A. McCormick (New York: Paulist Press, 1986), 264.

134 For a fuller, although not unproblematic treatment, see Hollenbach, *Claims in Conflict*, 118–133.

135 Paul VI cited in Christine Gudorf, "Major Differences: Liberation Theology and Current Church Teaching," in *Readings in Moral Theology No. 5*, eds. Charles E. Curran and Richard A. McCormick (New York: Paulist Press, 1986), 447. Gudorf points out

that it was only with Paul VI's encyclical *Octogesima adveniens* (1971) that the social teaching really embraces careful attention to the Spirit's prompting through the hopes and aspirations and activity of Christians at the base (§§448–451). See, in particular, Paul VI, *Octogesima adveniens* §4, 42. Note that according to Peter Hebblethwaite this shift was short-lived, insofar as John Paul II, even as he seeks to revive the tradition of social teaching, is moving the social teaching back towards its neo-scholastic roots. See his "The Popes and Politics," 273–281.

136 This holds even for the social teaching of pontiffs like John XXIII and Paul VI, whose vision of rights was still largely paternalistic, directed as it was largely at the wealthy and presupposing that moral appeals alone would be sufficient to spark their cooperation in the development of the underdeveloped peoples. It is worth noting that Catholic social teaching is more accurately described as an amalgamation of several different types of social theory, of which the organic is the oldest and perhaps predominant type. See Hobgood, *Catholic Social Teaching and Economic Theory*.

137 I do not mean to suggest that organic social theory does not also provide grounds for resisting capitalism. On the contrary, its communitarian values are the basis for what distance the social teaching does achieve from an uncritical endorsement of capitalism.

138 Hobgood, *Catholic Social Teaching and Economic Theory*, 6, 98.

139 Hollenbach, *Claims in Conflict*, 162.

140 Michael Novak's appeal to the social teaching in his book, *The Catholic Ethic and the Spirit of Capitalism* (New York: Free Press, 1993), is a good example.

141 In this way they undoubtedly contributed to the future direction of the social teaching, insofar as Paul VI in *Octogesima adveniens* reinterprets the methodology of that teaching in a manner strikingly similar to the way liberationists describe their own work. See *Octogesima adveniens*, §4, 42. However, Christine Gudorf is correct when she suggests that the social teaching only adapts or co-opts liberationist methodology on the grounds that whereas the liberationists insist that active commitment to the cause of the poor is a prerequisite for properly reading the gospel, according to Paul VI, the Church possesses the truthful message regardless of its commitment. See Gudorf, "Major Differences: Liberation Theology and Current Church Teaching," 451.

142 Gutiérrez, *A Theology of Liberation*, xiii.

143 Sobrino, *The True Church and the Poor*, 50 (italics in original).

144 Second General Conference of Latin American Bishops, *The Church in the Present-Day Transformation of Latin America in the Light of the Council*, "Document on Justice," §1. Text in *Liberation Theology: A Documentary History*, ed. Alfred T. Hennelly (Maryknoll, NY: Orbis Books, 1992), 97–105.

145 Segundo Galilea, "Liberation Theology and the New Tasks Facing Christians," in *Frontiers of Theology in Latin America*, ed. Rosino Gibellini (Maryknoll, NY: Orbis Books, 1979), 167; Leonardo Boff, "Christ's Liberation via Oppression: An Attempt at Theological Construction from the Standpoint of Latin America," in *Frontiers of Theology in Latin America*, ed. Rosino Gibellini (Maryknoll, NY: Orbis Books, 1979), 126.

146 Gutiérrez, *The Power of the Poor in History*, 28.

147 Note that there exists in the work of John XXIII and Vatican II the beginnings of an account of social sin and structural injustice, but it remains underdeveloped. See John XXIII, *Mater et magistra*, §59–67 and The Second Vatican Council, *Gaudium et spes*, §25. For a fuller history of this concept, see Peter Henriot, "The Concept of Social Sin," *Catholic Mind* 71 (1973): 38–53.

148 Second General Conference of Latin American Bishops, *The Church in the Present-Day Transformation of Latin America in the Light of the Council*, "Document on Peace," §16. Text in *Liberation Theology: A Documentary History*, ed. Alfred T. Hennelly (Maryknoll, NY: Orbis Books, 1992), 106–113. Note that this document was drafted by Gustavo Gutiérrez and Pierre Bigo.

149 It is no surprise that this conception of structural sin drew objections on the grounds of the "problems of conscience" it would create for the "children of good families." See Gutiérrez, *The Power of the Poor in History*, 135.

150 Jon Sobrino, "Unjust and Violent Poverty in Latin America," *Concilium* 195 (1988): 56.

151 Ignacio Ellacuría, *Conversión de la Iglesia al reino de Dios* (San Salvador: UCA Editores, 1985), 140; Sobrino, *The Principle of Mercy*, 22, 19; Jon Sobrino, "De una teología solo de la liberación a una teología del martirio," in *Cambio Social y Pensamiento Cristiano en América Latina*, eds. José Comblin, José Ignacio González Faus, and Jon Sobrino (Madrid: Editorial Trotta, 1993), 112; Ignacio Ellacuría, "The Church of the Poor, Historical Sacrament of Liberation," 556; Javier Jiménez Limón, "Suffering, Death, Cross, and Martyrdom," in *Mysterium Liberationis: Fundamental Concepts of Liberation Theology*, eds. Ignacio Ellacuría and Jon Sobrino (Maryknoll, NY: Orbis Books, 1993), 710.

152 Hugo Assmann, *Theology for a Nomad Church*, trans. Paul Burns (Maryknoll, NY: Orbis Books, 1976), 65.

153 Ibid.

154 Gutiérrez, *A Theology of Liberation*, 159.

155 Gutiérrez, *The Power of the Poor in History*, 207.

156 Gustavo Gutiérrez, *The Truth Shall Make You Free*, trans. Matthew J. O'Connell (Maryknoll, NY: Orbis Books, 1990), 67. See also 72–75; Gutiérrez, *A Theology of Liberation*, 157–158; Antoncich, *Christians in the Face of Injustice*, 127–128.

157 See Gutiérrez, *The Truth Shall Make You Free*, 38, 131.

158 See Gustavo Gutiérrez, *A Theology of Liberation*, 1st ed., trans. Sister Caridad Inda and John Eagleson (Maryknoll, NY: Orbis Books, 1973), 274; Gutiérrez, *The Power of the Poor in History*, 43–44.

159 Jon Sobrino, *Christology at the Crossroads*, trans. John Drury (Maryknoll, NY: Orbis Books, 1978), 54.

160 Jon Sobrino, *Jesus in Latin America* (Maryknoll, NY: Orbis Books, 1987), 178.

161 Ignacio Ellacuría, "Human Rights in a Divided Society," in *Human Rights in the Americas: The Struggle for Consensus*, eds. Alfred T. Hennelly and John Langan (Washington DC: Georgetown University Press, 1982), 63.

162 Sobrino, *The True Church and the Poor*, 51; see also 167.

163 Sobrino, *Spirituality of Liberation*, 106.

164 Ibid., 108.

165 Ellacuría, "Human Rights in a Divided Society," 64–65.

166 This is the case, in part, because the liberationists recognize that there is no simple and clear-cut oppressor/oppressed dichotomy. See, for example, Ignacio Ellacuría, "The Crucified People," in *Mysterium Liberationis: Fundamental Concepts of Liberation Theology*, eds., Ignacio Ellacuría and Jon Sobrino (Maryknoll, NY: Orbis Books, 1993), 591–592.

167 Gutiérrez, *Las Casas*, 44.

168 García, *Justice in Latin American Theology of Liberation*, 28.

169 José Miranda, *Marx and the Bible*, trans. John Eagleson (Maryknoll, NY: Orbis Books, 1974), 35–199.

170 Aristotle, *Nicomachean Ethics*, trans. Martin Oswald (Indianapolis: Bobbs-Merrill Co., 1962), 1105b5.

171 MacIntyre makes this point about virtue in general. See his *After Virtue*, 150.

172 This, of course, is not to say that the Church did not have anything to say about such matters, only that what it had to say was not a matter of justice or the common good.

173 See Ronald Beiner, *What's the Matter With Liberalism?* (Berkeley: University of California Press, 1992); MacIntyre, *After Virtue*.

174 The fact that the liberationists and their rights discourse have generated some resistance to capitalism does not refute my argument. Such resistance must stand the test of time. Moreover, liberationist practice and the practice of the poor Christian communities in their midst may very well be much better than their theory. In other

words, the liberationists misdescribe what it going on. A more accurate description, I suspect, would entail an account of the common good much thicker than mere respect for rights suggests. It would undoubtedly involve a vision of human perfection found in worshipping God.

175 See Jacques Maritain, *Reflections on America* (New York: Charles Scribner's Sons, 1958); Jacques Maritain, *Christianity and Democracy*, trans. Doris C. Anson (New York: Charles Scribner's Sons, 1944).

176 Gutiérrez, *A Theology of Liberation*, 17–18.

177 Albert Hirschman and Milton Myers both show how the emergence of "reason of state" entailed a distortion of the understanding of "desire" into "interest" and, furthermore, how under subsequent regimes of governmentality this interest became individual economic interest. See Albert Hirschman, *The Passions and the Interests: Political Arguments for Capitalism Before Its Triumph* (Princeton: Princeton University Press, 1981); Milton L. Myers, *The Soul of Modern Economic Man* (Chicago: University of Chicago Press, 1983).

178 Anthony Arblaster, *The Rise and Decline of Western Liberalism* (New York: Basil Blackwell Publishers, 1984), and Shapiro, *The Evolution of Rights in Liberal Theory*.

179 Ibid., 302–303.

180 See Daniel M. Bell, Jr., "The Violence of Love: Latin American Liberationists in Defense of the Tradition of Revolutionary Violence," *Journal for Peace & Justice Studies* 8 (1997): 17–36.

181 He was the director of Gutiérrez's dissertation at the Catholic Institute of Lyons. See Gutiérrez, *The Truth Shall Make You Free*, 1–52. His theological sensibilities have been recognized by Latin American liberationists as those of a kindred spirit. See Segundo, *Signs of the Times*, 91.

182 Christian Duquoc, "The Forgiveness of God," *Concilium*, 184 (1986): 39.

183 The accuracy of this assertion explains in part why Novak and company can be read and embraced by many well intentioned Christians. It is another example of the capitalist powers of incorporation, of the way rights language is not intrinsically oppositional.

184 The distance between the liberationists and the proponents of, say, welfare state capitalism, is less clear, however. In this regard, Gutiérrez's response to a question concerning the prospects for a capitalist liberation theology is interesting: "I don't believe the capitalist system as we know it today is good for the poor. But theoretically if it is a way out of poverty, I have no problem. My question is not about capitalism. My question is about poverty." (*The New York Times*, July 27, 1988; quoted in Sigmund, *Liberation Theology at the Crossroads*, 238.)

185 Note that Thomas was not entirely successful in this regard; the Franciscan vision may have been superior. See O'Donovan, "Natural Law and Perfect Community: Contributions of Christian Platonism to Political Theory," 38 and *passim*.

186 It is important to recall the parameters of my argument. I am challenging justice as the liberationists conceive of it. The impossibility of their justice does not preclude an alternative, truer form of justice from performing a vital role in the Christian life. I pursue this further in the next chapter under "The Redemption of Justice."

187 For more on the problems with justice conceived of in terms of "what is due" see Thomas Talbott, "Punishment, Forgiveness, and Divine Justice," *Religious Studies* 29 (1993):160–162; Miroslav Volf, "The Final Reconciliation: Reflections on a Social Dimension of the Eschatological Transition," *Modern Theology* 16 (2000): 98.

188 Ayacucho is a remote city in the mountains of Peru that is known for its extreme poverty and violence. The Quechua name means, "City of the Dead." Gutiérrez refers to it in the midst of a discussion of the fragility of theological language. He makes the point that it is not sufficient to ask how can God be discussed *after* Auschwitz. One must also ask how God can be discussed *during* Ayacucho. The same

question can be put to justice, which is precisely the point of my raising this series of practical questions. See Gutiérrez, "How Can God be Discussed from the Perspective of Ayacucho?," *Concilium* (1/1990): 108. See also Gustavo Gutiérrez, *On Job*, trans. Matthew J. O'Connell (Maryknoll, NY: Orbis Books, 1987), 102.

189 Sobrino, *Jesus in Latin America*, 149; Sobrino, *Compassion: The Shaping Principle of the Human and of the Christian*, 4.

190 There are prominent strands of the Christian tradition (Augustine, Anselm, Aquinas) that argue that the atonement is the completion of perfect justice. In the final chapter I consider in more detail both the atonement and this perfect justice.

4

THE REFUSAL TO CEASE SUFFERING

Forgiveness and the liberation of desire

In the effort to display the clash of capitalism and Christianity as one of discordant technologies of desire, thus far I have argued that contemporary capitalism is best understood as an ensemble of technologies of desire that exercises dominion over humanity and disciplines desire through the exercise of what Foucault called "governmentality," and that any effort to resist capitalism that fails to recognize capitalism as such a discipline of desire is futile. Hence, if it is to fund resistance to capitalism, Christianity must shed its (modern) identity as an apolitical custodian of abstract values and preferential options and assume its proper place in the temporal realm as the true politics, the exemplary form of human community. This is to say, the Christian community, in its sacraments and orders, its discipleship and prayer, must be retrieved as (no less than capitalism and its state-form) an ensemble of technologies of desire that can properly be characterized as a therapy of desire. Furthermore, the nature of the therapy enacted by Christianity to counter capitalist discipline is not adequately described as justice in the classic sense of *suum cuique* and its modern variant, "rights." For such justice is incapable of liberating desire from savage capitalism's discipline. At best, it may curb capitalism's most egregious abuses; at worst, it only intensifies the terror that plagues this world. Moreover, such justice does not faithfully reflect the way God acts in history to redeem humanity from sin. It was suggested that Christ's atonement for sin marks the ascendancy of grace over justice understood as *suum cuique*. Christ's work is the inauguration of a different economy for dealing with the sin of injustice, of a peculiar technology for healing desire of the wounds inflicted by capitalist discipline, namely, the refusal to cease suffering that is forgiveness.[1]

In this final chapter I defend the claim that forgiveness is the therapy of desire that Christianity enacts to counter capitalist discipline, that forgiveness is the name of the ensemble of technologies that God has graciously made available to humanity in Christian communities for the sake of healing desire of the madness that is capitalism.[2] Said a little differently, it is God's gift of forgiveness in Christ, and not the relentless pursuit of justice understood in the classic sense of rendering "what is due," that liberates desire and gives birth to communities capable of resisting capitalism. Through the reception and return of God's gift

144

of forgiveness – receiving and giving it – communities are formed where desire is liberated from capitalist discipline.

The Latin American liberationists and the communities of poor Christians in their midst remain central to my argument. The former do so because, in spite of their bold commitment to justice, several address the issue of forgiveness and what they have to say proves salutary to the effort to recover forgiveness as the font of Christian resistance to capitalism. Moreover, the liberationists are helpful insofar as they give a voice to the voiceless; which is to say, that in spite of the theoretical difficulties that mark their work, they have accomplished the extraordinary feat of creating an opening for the emergence of the witness of the Church of the poor. This witness suggests that many poor Christian communities in Latin America are living Christianity not as an apolitical repository of values but as a fully social and political presence that counters capitalist discipline. More specifically, some segments of the Church of the poor appear to be extending the divine gift of forgiveness as a therapy that liberates desire from savage capitalism.

I begin building the case for forgiveness by evaluating its theological adequacy and practical efficacy at precisely those points where the liberationists' justice was found lacking. Does forgiveness more adequately describe the way Christianity claims God acts in the world to overcome sin and does it avoid the pitfalls that undermine the ability of the liberationists' account of justice to resist capitalism? This contrast both reveals the promise of forgiveness as a mode of resistance to capitalism and raises several important issues that set the stage for what follows. Next, what the liberationists say about forgiveness is examined. Of particular interest is the way in which their relatively underdeveloped comments on forgiveness create a certain tension with their firm commitment to the primacy of justice understood as *suum cuique*. Recognition of this tension leads to consideration of the liberationists' reservations concerning forgiveness. The third section engages forgiveness as an ensemble of technologies that enable desire to resist capitalism. Consideration is given to the Church of the poor as a particular embodiment of this ensemble of technologies, to the "mechanics" of forgiveness, and to the place and function of justice within this economy of grace. Finally, I conclude with an assessment of the risks involved in this odd form of resistance to capitalism.

The gift of forgiveness

At the conclusion of the previous chapter I argued that justice as the guarantor of rights, in spite of its contemporary prominence, is not an adequate name for the ensemble of technologies that Christianity enacts to liberate desire from capitalist discipline. On theological and practical grounds, such justice fails to evoke and sustain resistance to the capitalist order. But does forgiveness fare any better? Specifically, does it break the cycle of violence and conflict? Does it form desire in a way that neither mirrors nor is easily incorporated by capitalist discipline? How does forgiveness deal with the irreversibility of injustice? Is it an appropriate characterization of both the way that God deals with sin and the way followers of God are expected to deal with sin? With regard to each of these issues, the answer is yes: forgiveness transcends justice conceived as *suum cuique*. Forgiveness avoids both the theological and practical problems that cripple such justice.

Theological adequacy

Theologically, the claim that God forgives is hardly a point of contention among Christians. "Every Christian," observes Christian Duquoc, "confesses that the God of Jesus is neither the guarantor of the moral law nor the guardian of civil order but that he is rather the one who, in his son, has intimated to men and women that he does not take strict account of their faults."[3] Asserting the primacy of forgiveness is decidedly not revolutionary. Indeed, it is God's forgiving character that is frequently invoked against those who take a strong stance against sin, and, as we shall see, it is precisely such invocations that prompt the liberationists to stress God's desire for justice instead of divine forgiveness. Does divine forgiveness really override the liberationists' vision of God as the just one who guarantees the rights of all, especially the poor?

As previously suggested, the claim that forgiveness more faithfully characterizes the way God overcomes sin than does the liberationists' account of justice rests upon an interpretation of the atonement. It rests upon a certain answer to the question addressed by Anselm in his classic, *Cur deus homo*. This is to say, the claim advanced for forgiveness here rests upon a certain reading of God's activity in Christ. What has God accomplished in Christ? God has given the gift of forgiveness. God has refused to render to humanity what is due sin, but instead graciously endures humanity's rejection and extends redemption and reconciliation in Christ. Justice in the classic sense of *suum cuique* would refuse to have suffered the injustice of sin and the cross; instead, God in Christ shouldered the cross and refused to cease suffering, defeating sin and injustice by forgiving it, by bearing it in order to bear it away. Accordingly, the atoning grace of God in Christ displaces such justice as the modality of God's overcoming of sin and sets in its place forgiveness. God confronts sin, injustice, capitalism, not with justice conceived in the liberationists' terms, but with the gift of forgiveness.

There is one glaring difficulty with this claim. I mentioned Anselm. Does not his classic work contradict the suggestion that the atonement operates according to a divine logic of forgiveness? Does not the prominent position granted justice in his work suggest that the liberationists are correct in asserting that God is primarily one who enforces justice understood as rendering what is due? In the face of human sin, the argument runs, God, as one who must uphold justice, cannot simply forgive sin but must enforce justice and a strict accounting of what is due. So, instead, the God-man, Christ, steps forward and fulfills justice, renders what is due, through his substitutionary death on the cross. Redemption is a result of the payment of a debt incurred through sin, the satisfaction of divine justice.

Although such a reading of Anselm and the atonement has become commonplace,[4] it is nevertheless a distortion of both. As David Hart has cogently argued,

Anselm does not set divine justice against mercy and forgiveness.[5] A careful read-ing of his account of Christ's atoning work reveals that he does not in fact assert that the atonement was a substitutionary sacrifice meant to pay a debt incurred or satisfy a justice that functions in accord with a strict logic of "what is due." Instead, Anselm's account of the atonement actually resonates with the vision of the early Church, whereby God in Christ is understood to be acting on humanity's behalf in order to redeem us from the powers to which we have delivered ourselves. It is a matter of God entering into a situation where sin has captured and distorted desire and liberating humanity from sin and death. As such, the atonement is not amenable to a strict calculus of what is due; rather it is a matter of donation and redonation, of God's giving and giving again. God has always given to humanity in the form of love, and when humanity rejected that gift, God gave again in the form of love incarnate, which is the Son. Christ's work is that of giving again, of communicating God's love and grace (which has never ceased to flow) to human-ity again (and again). The work of atonement is God in Christ bearing human rejection and extending the offer of grace again, thereby opening a path for humanity to return to the Father. In this sense, the atonement is identified not with a propitiatory sacrifice in the name of justice, but with the self-giving of the Son to the Father as an act of recapitulation that provides humanity with a positive means of return to its Creator, as Hart explains:

> Christ takes up the human story and tells it correctly, by giving the correct answer to God's summons; in his life and death he renarrates humanity according to its true pattern of loving obedience, humility, and charity, thus showing all human stories of righteousness, honor, and justice to be tales of violence, falsehood, and death; and in allowing all of humanity to be resituated through his death within the retelling of their story, Christ restores them to communion with the God of infinite love who created them for his pleasure.[6]

The atonement is not about meeting the demands of an implacable justice before which even God must bow, but the forgiveness that enables desire to return to its source. It is about humanity's being taken up into the divine life of the Trinity through participation in Christ, in Christ's body, the Church. There is a sacrifice involved in this atoning work and there is a substitution. But these are no longer positioned in an economy of *suum cuique*, of equity and retribution, but rather find their true meaning in the aneconomic order of divine forgiveness. Thus Christ's sacrifice becomes the donation of obedience and praise (the return of love) offered by the Son to the Father, and his role is substitutionary in that the Son offers the worship that we cannot. Again, Hart explains:

> [A]s Christ's sacrifice belongs not to an economy of credit and exchange, but to the trinitarian motion of love, it is given entirely as gift, and must be seen as such: a gift given when it should not have been needed to be

given again, by God, and at a price that *we*, in our sin, imposed upon *him*. As an entirely divine action, Christ's sacrifice merely draws creation back into the eternal motion of divine love for which it was fashioned. The violence that befalls Christ belongs to our order of justice, an order overcome by his sacrifice, which is one of peace.[7]

The aneconomic order of divine forgiveness overcomes – even as it refuses to cease suffering, suffering even to the point of death on the cross – the economy of human justice, with its strict calculus of what is due.

Insofar as the work of atonement is God in Christ opening (again) a path called forgiveness, by which desire returns to its true home, forgiveness not only names the way God in Christ defeats sin, it also characterizes the way Christians are called to meet sin. Desire is healed insofar as it receives the gift of forgiveness, which it does by participating in Christ, and being in Christ, desire participates in Christ's work, which is the gift of forgiveness. Hence, the gift of forgiveness is the gift of the capacity to forgive and the return of the gift is a sign of the gift's reception. Where it is not given, it has not been received ("Forgive us . . . as we forgive others"). Conversely, where it has been received, the gift of forgiveness that is love is returned. And love's return to its source is the end of forgiveness, reconciliation. Moreover, the gift of forgiveness is the *communally instantiated* capacity to forgive. Being in Christ is to participate in Christ's body, the Church. Hence, we learn to receive and return the gift in the Church, and the task of the Church is nothing other than the reception and transmission of this gift.

All of this is borne out by Scripture. To paraphrase the Gospel of Mark, because the reign of God has drawn near, forgiveness is possible (Mark 1:15). The advent of the Kingdom interrupts the progress of sin and creates spaces (called "Church") where desire can escape from its captivity to sin through the enactment of God's forgiveness. Moreover, as persons answer God's call and enter that space, not only are they forgiven, but they are empowered to forgive. Desire that has been healed of the wound of sin in turn seeks out the wounded and offers the healing balm of forgiveness. Thus, shortly before his death, Jesus promised to send the Holy Spirit to his disciples for the sake of empowering them to continue his work in the world (John 14:15–21, 26), and after the resurrection Jesus breathed on the disciples and said, "Receive the Holy Spirit. If you forgive the sins of any, they are forgiven them; if you retain the sins of any, they are retained" (John 20:21–23). As persons are gathered into communities by the Holy Spirit, they are forgiven and empowered to forgive. By receiving the gift of forgiveness and returning the gift of God's love by extending the gift of forgiveness to others, the Church carries out the ministry of reconciliation that has been given it by virtue of its participation in Christ (2 Corinthians 5:18–21).

Hence, forgiveness is a theologically more appropriate characterization of God's activity to overcome sin in the world than the liberationists' vision of justice. Whatever the nature and function of justice in Christ's atoning work and the

Christian life (matters to which we will return shortly), it operates within the horizon cast by the divine gift of forgiveness.

Of course, much more needs to be said about this forgiveness, lest it become an instance of "cheap grace" and God's amnesty is transformed into a license for impunity. Let us therefore turn to the question of practical efficacy.

Practical efficacy

Among the practical obstacles that the liberationists' account of justice was unable to surmount was the violence endemic to a world enthralled to capitalism. Their justice was unable to break the cycle of violence that torments humanity. Specifically, it was incapable of eliminating the conflict that arises from the inevitable clash of rights and it legitimated violence in the name of justice. Forgiveness, however, may gesture towards a genuinely novel future insofar as it interrupts the cycle of violence, which it does in two ways. First, forgiveness renounces the power of violence to bring it into being. Recall that justice is transformed into terror when it is linked to the violence to enforce it. "The first thing that forgiveness does," observes Duquoc, "is to break the link between violence and the idea."[8] Forgiveness refuses this connection because it perceives the futility of attempting to transform human relations by means of violence. The liberationists envision justice as the means of maintaining a balance of rights, such that when that balance is upset, justice exerts a force equal and opposite to the offense so that the equilibrium of rights might be restored. The problem is that equilibrium is not synonymous with transformation. Justice as an equivalent counter-force to injustice does not produce new relations; at best, it only restores old ones. The refusal of suffering by inflicting suffering on others – even suffering deemed just and deserved – does not constitute a mode of living that signals or anticipates the ultimate vanquishing of suffering and misery and transformation of human relations. Forgiveness, on the other hand, is precisely the refusal to cease suffering by shifting that suffering onto another by taking up the sword of justice. It refuses to respond to offense with an equivalent counter-force and by that refusal it creates the possibility for the emergence of something new. Commenting on Jesus' teaching to not resist evil, Duquoc notes:

> Jesus is not naive, he does not ask us to be passive, he does not require us to give up fighting against evil – but he shows us that equivalence in evil, even in the name of justice, does not transform human society. What is required is an attitude that is not determined by what has already been done, an innovative, a creative gesture. Otherwise enclosure within a repetitive logic is inevitable, and the term of this logic is the exclusion or the death of at least one of the parties. It is forgiveness that represents this innovative gesture: it creates a space in which the logic inherent in legal equivalences no longer runs.[9]

In so doing, forgiveness interrupts the cycle of violence and counter-violence that plagues justice and holds out the promise of a peace that is more than the uneasy truce of adversaries.

The renunciation of violence that forgiveness embodies bears emphasizing because it is at the heart of the difference between this effort to retrieve the Church as a material formation, as the true polity, and the bloody Christendom of a bygone era. To the extent that this vision is inextricably bound up with the enactment of forgiveness as the refusal to cease suffering by shifting that suffering onto another by taking up the sword of justice, a distance is created from the Christendom of Bernard of Clairvaux's era. The specter of the Crusades can only lurk in the shadows cast by a Christianity that has refused to suffer by embracing the sword. When Christianity forgets that being in Christ is synonymous with participating in Christ's affliction – refusing to cease suffering by taking up the cross – it declines the grace that liberates desire. When and where Christian technologies have as their end a holiness that is not cruciform, they no longer guide desire to its true end but instead perpetuate desire's captivity.

The refusal of an equivalent counter-violence is not the only way that forgiveness interrupts the cycle of violence. As Duquoc suggests, at the heart of forgiveness' disruption of the cycle of violence lies a rejection of the logic that fuels it. This second and more fundamental refusal has two dimensions. First, forgiveness amounts to a refusal of the logic insofar as it entails surrendering any claim to what is due. We have traced how justice became an agonistic struggle to secure rights and adjudicate between competing claims of rivalrous desires upon society's goods. Forgiveness overcomes the conflict by relinquishing any claim to such rights. The terror of justice is warded off by the refusal to assert one's rights to what is due against another. Recall the atonement, which initiates the flow of forgiveness. In place of the demand that humanity render what is due, in Christ God gives. God in Christ gives for us. Christ forgives by doing that which we could not: returning the gift of love as obedience and praise to the Father. This "giving-for" subsumes conflict generated by the effort to acquire what is due. Forgiven, desire gives; it does not acquire and possess.

This suggests the second dimension of the refusal of the logic that underwrites the cycle of violence. Forgiveness entails not just a renunciation; there is a substitution or replacement as well. Specifically, the agonistic logic of rights is replaced with the peaceable logic of reconciliation. The end of forgiveness is the return to God, reconciliation. God in Christ extends the gift of forgiveness to humanity for the sake of reconciling humanity to God, and Christians are empowered to receive and return the gift through its interhuman extension for the sake of reconciliation with God and one another. The goal of forgiveness, Jon Sobrino writes, is not merely the alleviation of guilt but is the goal of all love – positive reconciliation.[10]

In this way, the end of forgiveness is quite different from that of justice as the guarantor of rights. Unlike the liberationists' justice, forgiveness is not primarily a means of securing access to and the proper distribution of society's fruits in accordance with a logic of rights. Rather, forgiveness is about the overcoming of the sin

that lies at the heart of all oppression and injustice, a sin that is much more insidious than the language of rights conveys. As the liberationists themselves
acknowledge – which makes their account of justice all the more puzzling – what
divides oppressed from oppressor goes deeper than the violation of rights. The ultimate cause of poverty, injustice, and oppression, observes Gutiérrez, is the "breach
of friendship with God and others."[11] Injustice and oppression are principally
matters of a breach of communion, the severing of the filial bonds of friendship
that unite humanity as children of God. This is to say, injustice is not a sin because
it tramples on human rights. The sin of which capitalism is guilty, in the final analysis, is not that of the gross violation of basic rights, especially the right of the poor
to life. Rather capitalism is sin because it fractures the friendship of humanity in
God. It disrupts the original, peaceable flow of desire that is charity; it ruptures the
sociality of desire, which by nature seeks out new relations in the joyous conviviality that is love. Capitalism is sin because it harnesses the productive power of
desire in its original mode, which is donation or giving, to the market. In so doing
it corrupts it, rendering it proprietary, with the result that desire no longer flows in
the harmonic symphony of joy that is the fruit of the creation and extension of
non-proprietary (that is, participatory) relations of desire, but is submerged in the
agonistic struggle that is contemporary life under savage capitalism, where even the
excluded poor, who can hardly be characterized as driven by a passion to acquire
and consume, are nevertheless forced to compete with their brothers and sisters for
life.[12]

The gift of forgiveness leaves behind the agony of rights and opens a peaceful
path of reconciliation by restoring desire in its original mode of donation.[13] It
releases desire from the capitalist discipline that renders it proprietary, that bends
it into an agonistic force competing with others for insertion into the market,
instead renewing it as the flow of generosity that ceaselessly gives and receives.
Healing desire of the wounds inflicted by capitalist discipline, the gift of forgiveness
renews the possibility of a true mutuality and reciprocity of desire through non-
possessive participation in the other. In this way, the gift of forgiveness is the true
form of absolute deterritorialization, whereby desire is released from every captivity (including the bondage of anarchic self-assertion) in order to flow freely as it
was created to do, in the sociality of love that is the Trinity. Thus, by refusing the
logic and not only by refusing violence as a means of enactment, forgiveness interrupts the cycle of violence in which justice as the guarantor of rights remains
trapped.

With regard to its practical efficacy, that the gift of forgiveness renews desire in
its original mode of donation suggests that it also stands as an ensemble of technologies that may prove more resistant than the liberationists' construal of justice
to capitalist incorporation. Recall that justice as the guarantor of rights, to the
extent that it casts desire as proprietary and encourages persons to become acquisitive, mimics capitalist discipline and thus is particularly vulnerable to
incorporation. In contrast, forgiveness recovers desire as the excess that is God's gift
of charity. It recreates desire in Christ as the flow of conviviality that is a ceaseless

giving and receiving, never a taking or seizing. Precisely to the extent that forgiveness is successful in shaping desire in such a way that it does not mutate into a proprietary, acquisitive force, it represents an oppositional formation that may fund resistance to the capitalist order.

This is so because, as Franz Hinkelammert points out, capitalism does not know, short of repressing it, what to do with forgiveness; it simply cannot handle non-proprietary, participatory desire.[14] In defense of this assertion, he notes that at the end of the 1970s in Latin America, when the weight of the growing external debt was beginning to be felt, the liturgy of both Catholic and Protestant Churches across the continent underwent a subtle alteration. The language of the Our Father was altered from "Forgive us our debts" to "Forgive us our offenses." This change, he argues, was instigated by economic pressures. Capitalists feared that persons would begin to see that Christian forgiveness presented a direct challenge to the current economic order. They could not abide the Churches forming persons who, by receiving and extending the gift of forgiveness, would defy the justice of capitalism's markets and disrupt the flow of desire in accord with the capitalist axiomatic of production for the market. Leonardo Boff further reinforces this sense of the oppositional force of forgiveness when he argues that the Lord's Prayer, far from being merely a spiritual matter, is part of the divine effort to bring about the integral liberation of humanity in this world.[15] As such, forgiveness is intimately related to the triumph of the reign of God over the forces of evil, both personal and social, that currently dominate this world.

Before it can be asserted with too much confidence that forgiveness is indeed a fount of resistance to capitalist discipline, however, the issue of the irreversibility of injustice must be addressed. When confronted with the reality that nothing can "fix" injustice, nothing can transmute injustice into justice, the effort to counter injustice with justice grinds to a halt, mired in futility. How does forgiveness navigate this impasse? The promise of the gift of forgiveness lies in its being an expression of a divine logic of grace, of an aneconomic order of ceaseless plenitude that exceeds the human logic of reciprocity and desert. When discussing its rupturing the cycle of violence, forgiveness was characterized as an innovative gesture. Forgiveness overcomes the irreversibility of injustice precisely as an innovative movement, as the outflowing of the divine plenitude that ceaselessly gives more and gives again, graciously bearing the refusal that injustice embodies and the suffering it inflicts. When confronted with human sin, God in Christ bears the offense and gives again, not holding that sin against us, and in so doing opens the way for our return in Christ. In this way, forgiveness is innovative as it opens up the future, as it refuses to allow the injustice of the past to determine and therefore strangle the future. By abandoning calculi of reciprocity and desert, forgiveness sets both the victim and the victimizer free from the unbearable burden of injustice. The victim is freed from the enmity that is born of a violation that cannot be undone; the victimizer is freed from the guilt and loathing that comes from never being able to undo the violation. Forgiveness places them both in a position to risk a new relationship. Ultimately forgiveness is an act of hope that denies the destructiveness of injustice the final word, instead insisting that something else is always possible.

Such is the case for the theological and practical superiority of forgiveness to the liberationists' account of justice. Insofar as the gift of forgiveness creates a space where desire can flow down a path other than that marked by an endless and increasingly violent struggle to acquire what is due one's rights, it may indeed hold out more promise than the liberationists' vision of justice for liberating desire from capitalist discipline. Likewise, forgiveness does appear to more accurately reflect the character of God and the call of discipleship than justice so conceived.

Forgiveness as surrender?

Even as forgiveness transcends the shortcomings of the liberationists' account of justice, however, it is subject to its own particular vulnerabilities, on both the theological and practical fronts. The risk practically is that although forgiveness may create a space where something else is always possible, that "something else" may end up far more harmful than being locked in an interminable struggle for justice. For example, in surrendering claims to rights and renouncing the violence to enforce those rights, does not forgiveness risk further disempowering those who suffer injustice by encouraging an apathetic fatalism? And does not the dissolution of acquisitive desire amount to fostering resignation among those who have not had the opportunity to acquire even the most basic goods necessary for the sustenance of life? In other words, insofar as forgiveness is a refusal of justice as the guarantor of rights, it amounts to a refusal to cease suffering and this hardly appears liberating. Rather, it appears to be an invitation to injustice, an open door to impunity. Indeed, capitalism might relish just such a pacification program! Hence, interrupting the cycle of violence and conflict should not necessarily be equated with the emergence of genuine peace. If one side of a conflict surrenders or is destroyed, the fighting is interrupted, but genuine peace has hardly been achieved. And savage capitalism grinds on. This brings us to the theological questions that arise in the shadow of forgiveness. Theologically, forgiveness may correspond to the general logic of redemption and divine grace, but it remains to be seen how the primacy of forgiveness can avoid distorting the divine character such that God becomes the sanctioner of injustice with impunity. Likewise, the divine demand for justice that is so prominent in Scripture remains to be addressed.

These issues seriously threaten both the theological and practical integrity of forgiveness as a therapy that liberates desire from savage capitalism. If they cannot be satisfactorily addressed, then perhaps justice as the guarantor of rights is the best for which we can hope. Before attempting to answer them, however, these questions and doubts will be intensified as the focus shifts to the Latin American liberationists' treatment of forgiveness. For good reason, they have been particularly wary of calls for forgiveness and reconciliation.

Latin American liberationists on forgiveness

Although the liberationists are staunch champions of justice, they recognize that forgiveness is an integral part of the life of faith.[16] Indeed, the liberationists acknowledge that justice by itself does not accurately describe either the struggle for liberation or the Christian Gospel in its entirety. This section begins with a brief survey of what several prominent liberationists say about forgiveness in general. From these important if underdeveloped ideas a rather ambiguous and conflicted picture emerges. At times the primacy of justice appears to be on the verge of giving way to forgiveness, yet in the end the liberationists insist that justice remains the fundamental demand of the faith, with forgiveness subordinated to it. They are adamant that forgiveness becomes a possibility only after justice has been established. Consideration of the reasons for their suspicion of forgiveness concludes this section.

Beyond justice

Given the liberationists' abiding commitment, often at significant personal risk, to justice for the marginalized and oppressed majority of this world, some may be surprised to discover that justice does not have the last word in the liberationists' account of the struggle for freedom from oppression. On the contrary, justice does not stand alone at the pinnacle of the Christian life; it is accompanied by forgiveness. Leonardo Boff writes:

> Experience also teaches us that the actual achievement of justice is meager and fragile, though human life would be ignoble and impossible if we did not keep trying to achieve it. On the other hand justice alone is not enough to maintain peace. There must also be a gratuitousness and a self-giving that transcend the imperatives of duty. We need love and a capacity for forgiveness that go beyond the limits of justice.[17]

In a similar vein, Gustavo Gutiérrez develops the idea of God moving beyond justice. In a reflection on the Book of Job, he writes:

> What is it that Job has understood? That justice does not reign in the world God has created? No. The truth that he has grasped and that has lifted him to the level of contemplation is that justice alone does not have the final say about how we are to speak about God. Only when we have come to realize that God's love is freely bestowed do we enter fully and definitively into the presence of the God of faith. Grace is not opposed to the quest for justice nor does it play it down; on the contrary it gives it its full meaning. God's love, like all true love, operates in a world not of cause and effect but of freedom and gratuitousness. . . .

[T]he issue is not to discover gratuitousness and forget the demands of justice, but to situate justice within the framework of God's gratuitous love. . . . The world of retribution – and not of temporal retribution only – is not where God dwells; at most God visits it.[18]

He develops this idea of moving beyond justice even further in the midst of reflection on the biblical story of Jonah. After discussing God's stubborn desire to forgive the Assyrians, in spite of the fact that they had plundered and oppressed Israel, and in the face of Jonah's wish that they be punished and destroyed, Gutiérrez writes:

What Jonah finds unforgivable, if I may so put it, is the universal and unrestricted forgiveness of God. If this were a God who stayed on the level of justice, God's actions could be foreseen; but the God of the Bible, as the Book of Job says with unequaled power, is a God who loves gratuitously, a God who refuses to be contained by our categories and to submit to a standard of conduct based on a quid pro quo. God is an unpredictable God.[19]

Gutiérrez goes on to declare that God's will for reconciliation is greater than God's severity for those who have not practiced justice. This, however, ought not be interpreted as some sort of lapse in God, for ultimately it is forgiveness that gives life and liberty.[20] Indeed, he declares, "there can exist no Christian life, in fact no human life, without reconciliation and the capacity for pardon."[21]

This witness to the significance of forgiveness in the struggle for liberation finds a broad echo in the work of other liberationists. José Ignacio González Faus insists that the Christian God is just, not in the sense of destroying sinners but, rather, in the sense of transforming them. Likewise, he says, the Christian practice of justice is closer to pardon than it is to retribution or vengeance.[22] Segundo Galilea suggests that the theology of liberation is synonymous with a theology of reconciliation insofar as the liberation that it proclaims includes brotherhood, pardon, and reconciliation:

Christian reconciliation, the basis of brotherhood and peace, is the product of justice and people's willingness to obtain it. In situations that are riddled with conflict and openly unjust, as is the case in Latin America, reconciliation presupposes a struggle for justice and the use of moral and prophetic pressure to obtain it. That is not all, however. Reconciliation also presupposes *pardon*. It is not enough to have achieved justice or to be on the way toward achieving it. That process is inevitably marked by confrontation and conflict. . . . Vindictiveness and the desire for revenge may perdure. Christian pardon is the only thing capable of overcoming this attitude and achieving a reconciliation that is not only formal and juridical but also fraternal.[23]

155

Likewise, in the midst of an analysis of the doctrine of justification by faith, Elsa Tamez concludes that God's grace triumphs over justice, that God opposes every just sentence and instead offers pardon to all.[24] In recent years, Jon Sobrino has struck a similar chord as he has asserted that talking about the reality of God in terms of justice is not adequate and exhaustive of the Christian faith.[25] After all, he notes, Jesus announced the coming of the Kingdom of God in grace, not in vengeful justice.[26] As a result he has devoted significant attention to forgiveness and the "principle of mercy," suggesting that it is forgiveness and not justice that lies at the very heart of God:

> The acceptance that is Jesus' (and God's) forgiveness is their primordial love in going forth to seek the sinner instead of waiting like a judge, even the most just and benevolent of judges, for the sinner to come to them; in showing mercy rather than justice. . . . In sum, revelation says that human beings are sinners and that sin is supremely grave; but it also says that the opportunity for forgiveness is available. Indeed, revelation tells us that to be forgiving is not merely one characteristic of God among others, but the very expression of the divine essence.[27]

Consequently, the struggle for the liberation of the oppressed majorities of the world is not simply a struggle for justice. Authentic liberation is only possible if mercy and forgiveness are an integral part of that struggle.

The primacy of justice

From this brief overview, it would appear that the primacy of justice gives way to the recognition that God is quintessentially merciful and forgiving. It would appear that the demand for justice is not absolute, but is tempered by the gratuitousness of God. With perhaps the exception of Tamez, however, this is not the case. In spite of their comments to the effect that the mercy and forgiveness of God trump the demand for justice, liberationists remain committed to the primacy of justice. Justice remains the fundamental demand of faith; only after it has been established does forgiveness become a possibility. That this is the only way to correlate their strong statements on justice with these relatively underdeveloped comments on forgiveness is apparent when the comments on forgiveness are examined more closely. For example, in the passage cited earlier, Leonardo Boff says only that justice is not sufficient, that the duty of justice must be accompanied by forgiveness, which incidentally exceeds duty. The passages from Gutiérrez are a bit more ambiguous insofar as he seems to assert, on one hand, the primacy of forgiveness while on the other he refuses to allow forgiveness to mitigate in any way the imperative of justice. Thus he asserts that God transcends justice and that justice must be situated within the larger framework of God's grace. At this point a charitable reading might suggest that justice is subordinated to forgiveness;[28] the future God envisions is not one that is brought about by a strict rendering of justice. The assertion that

God is beyond justice, however, is weakened in the course of being developed as it is subject to several qualifications. For example, Gutiérrez states unequivocally that grace does not oppose or downplay the quest for justice and that although God does not "inhabit" the world of retribution, God does in fact "visit" that world. Here forgiveness appears to amount to little more than a check on justice, so that justice does not exceed its mandate and slip over into unrestrained vengeance. Moreover, his comments on forgiveness with reference to Jonah actually say more about the freedom of God from containment in any human conceptual scheme than the tempering of justice by mercy. His point is less that God exceeds justice than it is that humanity cannot always fathom God's justice, a point he reinforces when, in a discussion of Job, he clarifies how the renunciation of retribution in no way softens the demand for justice. "It should, however, be evident that in rejecting the theology of retribution Job has not been freed from the necessity of practicing justice, but only from the temptation of imprisoning God in a narrow conception of justice."[29] Particularly when viewed in light of the statement cited earlier, that where there is no justice there is no salvation, the comments on forgiveness only make sense when understood as a reminder that although justice is the primary demand of the struggle for liberation, it is not sufficient; forgiveness must accompany and complete that process.

Sobrino provides a particularly clear example of the way in which the recognition of the merciful and forgiving nature of the Christian life is subordinated to the struggle for justice. Indeed, Sobrino's account of forgiveness is remarkable for its display of the way in which forgiveness runs the risk in liberationists' work of being subsumed by justice to the extent that the two are virtually indistinguishable. At first glance, Sobrino appears to be one of the more forthright proponents of the primacy of forgiveness over justice in the liberation struggle. His bold proclamation of mercy and compassion seems worlds apart from the militant cries for justice of previous decades. However, the distance evaporates as Sobrino elaborates on mercy and the spirituality of forgiveness that accompanies it. Rejecting abstract treatments of mercy and forgiveness, Sobrino asserts that in a land suffering from terrible injustice, mercy takes the form of justice. The first priority of a Christian who seeks to be merciful is to defend the victims of injustice by struggling for justice; only after injustice has been replaced by justice can forgiveness be taken up. Christians, he says, "must defend the victims. What to do about the personal guilt of the offenders is also important but, at this point, secondary. What faith demands first is liberation from this sinful reality and the humanization of the victims and then, by derivation, the rehabilitation of the sinner and the humanization of the offender."[30]

At times even this sequence, whereby forgiveness follows justice as a distinct reality, collapses until there is little difference between justice and forgiveness. At one point, Sobrino writes, "Forgiving the sin of reality means converting it, setting up instead of the anti-kingdom, God's kingdom; instead of injustice, justice; instead of oppression, freedom; instead of selfishness, love; instead of death, life."[31] Forgiveness means converting injustice into justice. As such, it is indistinguishable from justice.

The collapse of forgiveness into justice is further exemplified in what Sobrino calls the "spirituality of forgiveness."[32] Forgiveness requires a particular spirituality, he says, one that has to integrate various aspects that are in tension. Specifically, the spirituality of forgiveness holds in tension the eradication of sin and the forgiveness of the sinner. This tension calls to mind the old phrase, "Hate the sin and love the sinner," but this is not radical enough. Although we must love the sinner, we must not only hate the sin but eradicate it as well, which may very well take the form of an objectively violent action against the sinner. This introduces into forgiveness a tension between love and destruction. "Liberation from oppression also means destroying the person oppressing, in his formal capacity as oppressor. . . . The spirituality of forgiveness must integrate this tension between love and destruction, and this can only be done with a great love which comprehends the destruction of the sinner as love."[33] Defending this forgiveness that destroys in the name of love, Sobrino appeals to Jesus:

> This spirituality is that of Jesus, who loves all people and is ready to forgive them all, but in a very precise way. Jesus loves the oppressed by being with them and loves the oppressors by being against them; in this way Jesus is for all. Through love of the oppressed, Jesus tells the truth plainly to the oppressors, denounces them, unmasks them, curses them, and threatens them with final dehumanization. But in this, Jesus is also paradoxically in favor of the oppressors. It is a paradoxical form of love.[34]

At this point it becomes impossible to distinguish forgiveness from justice. When forgiveness sanctions objectively violent action and can even threaten a sinner with "final dehumanization," it no longer looks any different than the justice that could resort to violence in the name of restoring violated rights.

The temptation at this point is to separate Sobrino from the other liberationists, who, like Boff and Gutiérrez, maintain a firmer distinction between justice and forgiveness, with the former serving as the foundation of the latter. Yielding to such a temptation, however, would be an error because Sobrino has only carried the primacy of justice to its logical conclusion. If one maintains the absolute demand of justice, then forgiveness is rendered moot. "If restorative justice is possible – if the wrong can be fully righted – then," observes Kyle Pasewark, "it is superfluous and even arrogant to speak of forgiveness. If justice is satisfied, what right does anyone have to claim the moral high ground of forgiveness?"[35] Just as the primacy of forgiveness abolishes justice as the guarantor of rights, the primacy of justice so conceived effectively nullifies a substantial account of forgiveness. At best, the forgiveness that follows on the heels of such justice amounts to, as Segundo Galilea suggested, an adjustment of attitudes, a refusal to hold grudges, an agreement that retribution will cease now that justice has been satisfied.[36]

The liberationists' resistance to granting forgiveness priority in the struggle against injustice is significant. Given the impact of their work and the witness of many of their lives, their resistance cannot be dismissed lightly. Even with its shortcomings, perhaps justice as *suum cuique* is the best hope there is for resisting capitalism? Perhaps there is good reason to risk the terror of justice instead of allowing it to be displaced by the aneconomic order of forgiveness? The liberationists' firm adherence to the primacy of justice prompts consideration of the reasons for their resistance to the subordination of justice to forgiveness.

Reservations concerning forgiveness

Although they say little explicitly about forgiveness, those reasons are not difficult to discern in the comments that liberationists make about calls for peace and reconciliation, concepts closely related to forgiveness in the Christian life. Their approach to peace and reconciliation is marked by a deep suspicion. Like the prophets of old, the liberationists are staunchly opposed to those who proclaim "peace, peace" when there is no peace. Therefore, liberationists assert that peace is, above all, a work of justice. Genuine peace is built upon the solid foundation of justice and the recognition of the rights of all. In other words, peace, no less than forgiveness, is subordinated to justice. A consequence of this lexical ordering of peace to justice is that:

> . . . the mediations of an evidently eschatological blessing, such as peace, are not necessarily or even primarily pacific, or of the same immediate nature as the end towards which they tend. To put it another way: the historical *oikonomia* of peace is not a series of pacific acts, or if you prefer, of acts whose *immediate* object is to introduce peace where there is conflict. . . . [A] facile, immediately rewarding peace . . . can present precisely the greatest obstacle to a deeper, more universal peace.[37]

Working for a true peace entails engaging in activity that may not immediately appear to have peace as its object. "Peacemaking is an essential task of Christians," writes Gutiérrez, "but if we are to grasp the scope of 'peacemaking' we must set aside a narrow view of peace as simply the absence of war or conflict."[38]

Care must be exercised not to read into this subordination of peace to justice a rejection of peace. On the contrary, liberationists wholeheartedly agree that Christians have, in the words of Ellacuría, a "clear vocation to peace."[39] What they recognize and resist are the manifold ways in which this calling to peace has been manipulated in support of a brutal status quo. Too often, calls for peace end up being little more than calls for the restoration of the "law and order" of the status quo. As such they amount to pleas for the poor not to disturb the comfortable and instead die quietly. Unsurprisingly, such a peace, the peace of clandestine graves, is vehemently rejected by the liberationists. On this view, the subordination of peace to justice is an effort to safeguard the genuine Christian vocation of peace from deadly distortions.

A similar effort can be glimpsed behind their comments on reconciliation. "Tranquility, stability, and reconciliation are," Juan Pico says, "suspect according to the theology of liberation, because they conceal the 'open veins' of the majority of the least of Jesus' brothers (cf. Mt. 25:45)."[40] Hugo Assmann notes that Christians in Latin America, under the influence of the importance of love in the Christian life, often display a deep fear of conflict of any sort, with the result that the Gospel is invoked to underwrite reconciliation at any price:

> Love tends toward reconciliation, dialogue, unity: this is basic in the Christian viewpoint. But can "love" be the ideology of peace at any price? Has this in fact been the Christian position in practice? In many ways it would seem that it has. Many Christians are simply incapable of accepting conflict as a fact, and as for deepening existing contradictions so as to bring out their real nature, this would be unthinkable for most. . . . We need to get rid of falsely conciliatory disfigurements of Christian thought and behavior. . . .[41]

Elsa Tamez attributes this affinity for a false reconciliation to the way that the classic doctrine of justification by faith has played itself out in Latin America.[42] The essential components of the doctrine, including the forgiveness of sins, liberation from guilt, and reconciliation with God, have been adopted in Latin America in a form that generally renders them good news for the oppressors while harming the poor. Specifically, justification by faith has had a decidedly negative impact on the life of the poor and their struggle for liberation by fostering a sense of impunity among those who enjoy power and privilege. The doctrine of justification by faith has meant that oppressors could be pardoned of their sins and relieved of their guilt without confronting the judgment of God or feeling the need for conversion or any change of practice. Moreover, as it has been propagated, the emphasis has been on the vertical dimension of humanity's relationship with God, while the implications of justification on the horizontal level of relations between persons have been neglected.

In a survey of the history of reconciliation in the Church, José Comblin has observed a similar tendency. In particular, he notes that calls for pardon and reconciliation have often been invoked by the Church in defense of the status quo maintained by the great empires and colonial powers.[43] Reconciliation has frequently been preached to the poor masses on behalf of the great powers, and more often than not it has entailed the sacrifice of the needs and aspirations of the poor for the sake of the status quo.[44] Accordingly, Comblin concludes that "the theme of reconciliation forms part of the ideology of the dominant classes, of the classes that occupy privileged positions."[45] The contemporary situation in Peru, according to Gutiérrez, is a perfect example. Writing about an amnesty law that shielded government security forces from accountability for various atrocities, he says, "Using words with a great human and Christian content, such as reconciliation and pardon, impunity for serious common crimes, even murder, has been legalized. . . . The so-called pardon has opened the door to new and loathsome abuses and crimes."[46]

160

The liberationists' fears with regard to reconciliation and forgiveness are also undoubtedly colored by the reaction of conservative elements within the Latin American Church to the spread of liberation theology in the 1970s and 1980s. Conservative forces began to articulate a "theology of reconciliation" that promoted an ethic of love and reconciliation instead of division and conflict between the rich and the poor. The highwater mark of this effort was reached in July of 1985 when what was known as the "Declaration of Los Andes" was produced at a gathering that included several of liberation theology's most outspoken Latin American critics. The Declaration asserts that a genuine liberation theology "supposes the reconciliation of the human person with God, with himself or herself, with others and with the entire creation."[47] It is not insignificant that this document was produced in Pinochet's Chile, released with the pretense of magisterial authority, and granted a degree of press and television coverage that the Chilean episcopacy did not always receive.[48] In its entirety, the Declaration amounted, in Ronaldo Muñoz's words, to "a virtual incitement to repression, even criminal repression."[49]

As was the case with calls for peace, liberationists are suspicious of calls for reconciliation because of the way such calls have been used to support oppression and discredit the struggle of the poor for liberation. Extrapolating from this, it is not difficult to ascertain the source of the liberationists' reluctance to allow forgiveness to temper the absolute demand for justice as the guarantor of rights. They are suspicious of anything that might gloss over the conflict that afflicts Latin America without resolving the underlying causes of that conflict and bringing to an end the horrendous suffering of the poor. Too often peace and reconciliation and forgiveness have been invoked by the dominant powers of this world in an effort to squelch resistance and change. They fear that the refusal to cease suffering that is forgiveness may amount to nothing more than a sheer refusal to cease suffering, that is, the perpetual suffering of the poor.

Given the distorted and oppressive history of forgiveness in Latin America, the liberationists' suspicion of calls for forgiveness cannot be blithely dismissed. On the contrary, those suspicions are all too justified. Hence, the burden of proof is on any account of forgiveness, particularly one that would discard justice in the traditional sense of *suum cuique*, to show how it is not simply another in a long line of proposals that effectively demands the poor relinquish their desire to rise above the misery in which the capitalist order submerges them. The refusal to cease suffering, that is, forgiveness must show itself to be more than simply a refusal to cease suffering, sheer resignation. In other words, forgiveness must actually show itself to be a fount of resistance to the capitalist order. To this display we now turn.

The therapy of forgiveness

What follows is not intended as an exhaustive treatment of forgiveness and the host of issues that surround it. Such a treatment both far exceeds the scope of this project and is available elsewhere.[50] Rather, this display focuses narrowly on forgiveness as a therapy of desire that funds Christian resistance to capitalism. Specifically, it takes up those technologies that constitute forgiveness as a means of liberating desire from capitalist discipline. Earlier I argued that some elements of the Church of the poor appear to be defying capitalist discipline and embodying Christianity as a fully material formation, as a true politics. Now I return to the "crucified people" who constitute the Church of the poor to argue that forgiveness is the name of that politics, that technology of desire, that therapy that founds Christian resistance to capitalist discipline. Included here is a consideration of the way justice is redefined and repositioned within the order of grace that is the Christian life.

God, grace, and the Church

Before taking up the particular technologies that constitute forgiveness as a therapy of desire capable of resisting savage capitalism's discipline, for the sake of clarity it is worth mentioning a few points that have been implicit in my argument thus far. First, although I have challenged the liberationists' vision of resistance rooted in statecraft and justice as *suum cuique*, the account of forgiveness advanced here shares a common starting point with the liberationists. Gutiérrez often says that the basic question of theology is not how to speak of God in a world come of age, but how to proclaim God in a world that is inhuman.[51] The argument on behalf of forgiveness takes as its starting point the same question. How can God be proclaimed in a world suffering from the madness that is savage capitalism? In other words, no less than the liberationists' cry for justice, the defense of forgiveness is fundamentally rooted in theological convictions. In contrast with much that passes for contemporary theological reflection on forgiveness, this appeal to forgiveness, no less than the liberationists' appeal to justice, is not a plea on behalf of the survival of humanity,[52] self-healing,[53] or even the most effective means of defeating capitalism.[54] The fundamental justification of forgiveness as a means of resistance to capitalism remains a claim about who God is and the way God in Christ is working in the world to overcome sin.

An important corollary of this foundation is that the therapy of forgiveness enacted by Christians is an outpouring of the divine gift of forgiveness. The implication that Christians should deal with sin as God deals with sin, namely by forgiving it, would be preposterous were it not for the accompanying conviction that Christ's Spirit is active, enabling Christians to participate in Christ's work of forgiveness. In other words, the therapy of forgiveness is a means of grace; it is not something that disciples initiate so much as discover already active and subsequently join.[55] Interhuman forgiveness, in other words, is a reflection of the divine gift of forgiveness not merely because it reflects God's intention that humans forgive, but because it is a continuation of the divine work, enabled by participation in Christ.

This way of putting matters raises the issue of the "conditionality" of forgiveness. Is forgiveness conditional? Is it contingent upon repentance or conversion?

When confronted with this question, the liberationists share the firm conviction that forgiveness is not something that can be earned. No one, even the repentant, deserves forgiveness. Consequently, if forgiveness is offered, it is always a matter of grace. Beyond this unequivocal starting point in grace, however, the liberationists reflect a certain ambiguity regarding the conditionality of forgiveness. Consistent with their assertion of the primacy of justice, the liberationists agree that there can be no forgiveness without justice. But does this mean that justice is a condition of forgiveness, that forgiveness can only be extended after justice has been fulfilled? The exact logic of this connection is not always clear. Some liberationists are adamant that forgiveness is conditional upon the offenders' conversion to justice. If, and only if, offenders have repented and satisfied the demands of justice, can they be forgiven. The passages cited earlier from Leonardo Boff and Segundo Galilea reflect this position. Forgiveness is a grace that arrives after justice has been satisfied. Other liberationists are less clear. At times, Gutiérrez clearly makes forgiveness contingent upon the fulfillment of justice, as was the case when he wrote that "without justice there is no salvation." Yet, elsewhere, specifically where God's gratuitous love is said to temper the force of retribution, forgiveness appears to be unconditional. Forgiveness, now understood as the limiting of retribution to no more than the demands of justice, is extended to all persons regardless of moral qualifications. Even more so than Gutiérrez, Sobrino reflects a certain complexity in this regard. At times he, too, presents forgiveness as a viable possibility only after justice has been fulfilled. Rehabilitation and humanization of the sinner, he wrote, can come only after the victims have been liberated and justice secured. At other times, however, there is no question that forgiveness is unconditional, as when he writes:

> It is the acceptance that is forgiveness that adequately and wholly discloses the fact that I am a sinner and gives me the strength to acknowledge myself as such and change radically. The conversion demanded so radically by Jesus is preceded by the offer of God's love. It is not conversion that requires God to accept the sinner; rather, just contrariwise, it is God's acceptance that makes conversion possible.[56]

This passage unambiguously asserts that forgiveness is not contingent upon any conversion or repentance. For all of its clarity, however, this passage is misleading because of the particular way the term forgiveness is used here. Forgiveness in this passage refers to what Sobrino calls forgiveness as welcome or acceptance, by which he means the love that approaches sinners in the first place and presents them with the demand for conversion (to justice).[57] Restated more congenially, as it is used here, forgiveness denotes the love which graciously provides offenders with both the opportunity and encouragement to change (fulfill the demands of justice) instead of simply annihilating them. Forgiveness as welcome is rendered essentially indistinguishable from the call for justice; Sobrino has once again effectively collapsed forgiveness into justice, a move that has the interesting effect of rendering forgiveness unconditional while simultaneously undermining its usefulness as a concept distinct from justice.

Sorting through the ambiguity of the liberationists' accounts, one reaches the conclusion that insofar as forgiveness is distinct from justice the liberationists make it conditional. Forgiveness emerges as a gracious possibility only after the demands of justice have been satisfied. Such a position, however understandable as an effort to protect forgiveness from distortion, is theologically problematic. Although there is no necessary temporal sequence between repentance and forgiveness, theologically forgiveness precedes repentance. Sometimes it is the offer of forgiveness by a victim that encourages the offender's repentance; at other times it may well be the offender's repentance that stimulates the victim's forgiveness. Whatever the temporal sequence, theologically repentance and conversion have as their condition of possibility the prior reality of God's gift of forgiveness in Christ. The God revealed in Jesus Christ freely and unconditionally forgives.[58] Repentance is not a prerequisite of God's giving the gift of forgiveness. On the contrary, it is God's forgiveness that makes repentance possible. The gift enables us to do that which we could not do. Because the Kingdom of God is at hand, one can repent.

Forgiveness enables repentance. In what follows I use stronger language. Forgiveness entails repentance. God's gift is not "out there", as it were, drifting in some (univocal) neutral space where humanity may or may not seize hold of it. Rather God's gift of forgiveness in Christ calls forth confession, elicits repentance, or evokes conversion. God's gift elicits the response of confession and repentance and the response (including extending the gift to others) is the sign of the gift's reception. Consequently, the question "Is forgiveness conditional upon repentance?" is largely a distraction.[59] If forgiveness is to have its full effect and desire is to flow once again in the sociality of love, then the gift of forgiveness will be met with the response of conversion and repentance. Repentance, therefore, is not a condition of forgiveness but rather the means of its reception. If there is no turning, no conversion, then it is clear that forgiveness has not been appropriated and the process of reconciliation has been curtailed. In the absence of repentance, the relationship between the parties, although not the same as if forgiveness had not been offered,[60] remains incomplete and broken. Full reconciliation and communion remain in the future. The absence of repentance, therefore, signals a refusal of the gift of forgiveness.

That forgiveness is enabled by participation in Christ suggests that it cannot be enacted by solitary individuals. The gift of forgiveness is made available through participation in Christ, which is to say in Christ's body, the Church. The gift of forgiveness is a communal endeavor. Here it is helpful to recall the example of the Cistercians. Although the enactment of Christianity as an ensemble of technologies of desire is not intrinsically bound to feudal monastic orders, the enactment of forgiveness is intrinsically social, communal. At the heart of the Christian therapy of forgiveness are technologies – confession, worship, obedience, and so forth – that are simply incoherent apart from the gathered community called Church. The liberationists speak of structural injustice to indicate that injustice is much more complex than individual acts of injustice. Forgiveness shares in a similar complexity. No less than sin, forgiveness has a structural dimension. Both receiving and extending the gift of forgiveness entail a host of technologies of desire – knowledges, instruments, persons, systems of judgment, and so forth – that extend beyond the individual. Put more simply, we need help identifying the sin that needs to be forgiven and we need help living forgiven and forgiving lives. In Christ the gift is given; in Christ's body, the Church, desire is provided the technologies that enable it to receive and return the gift, that liberate it from capitalist discipline. For this reason it is not incidental that the display of the therapy of forgiveness that follows revolves around the *Church* of the poor. It is in poor Christian communities' enactment of the gift of forgiveness that we are seeing desire healed and resistance to capitalism nurtured. In the Church of the poor we are seeing the true politics, an order of forgiveness, advanced against the capitalist order.

Lastly, that forgiveness is enabled by participation in Christ's body, the Church, does not imply that the specific form of the ensemble of technologies that constitute forgiveness is monolithic. As the history of Christianity shows, through the ages diverse technologies have been assembled for the sake of healing desire. From the adoption of the rabbinic practice of "binding and loosing," through the slow development of canonical penance, with its elaborate process of public confession and penance, to the emergence of penitential manuals and private confession, to contemporary forms of generalized confession and absolution, forgiveness has taken many different forms. The Spirit's continuation of Jesus' work by gathering communities where desire is liberated through the enactment of forgiveness is eternally innovative. Moreover, because the lives and situations in which sin and the need for forgiveness arise are irreducibly particular, there can be no single, prescribed system of forgiveness. Because there is no single way that sin has corrupted desire, there is no single way that desire is healed. Rather, the Spirit guides the process of forgiveness in accord with the complexities of a given situation.

Furthermore, as the liberationists noted, the efficaciousness of the various technologies in countering sin has not been uniform. Often forgiveness and reconciliation have been invoked to whitewash the impunity of the powerful to the detriment of the marginalized and increasingly excluded poor. Therefore, in an effort to minimize the possibility that it is just another subterfuge, the display of forgiveness as a therapy of desire that follows draws primarily on the witness of the Church of the poor as presented by the liberationists. First, the Church of the poor is displayed as a community that is engaged in the refusal to cease suffering that is forgiveness. Second, those technologies of desire that distinguish the therapy of forgiveness as a form of resistance to capitalist discipline are outlined.

The crucified people

Although the liberationists remain committed to justice as the enforcement of rights, many poor Christians involved in the struggle for liberation from savage capitalism are extending the gift of forgiveness to their oppressors. In other words, while the liberationists proclaim that liberation from capitalism will come about as more persons join the struggle for justice conceived in terms of modern rights, it appears that the Spirit may be generating resistance to capitalism and liberating desire from its distortions by gathering communities that are enacting the therapy of forgiveness.

The enactment of the therapy of forgiveness by some elements of the Church of the poor has not escaped the liberationists' notice. The recognition that many poor Christian communities are resisting capitalism by means of the refusal to cease suffering that is forgiveness has prompted several liberationists to compare the Church of the poor with the crucified Christ. Oscar Romero was the first to make this connection when, during a visit to a village that had been terrorized by the Salvadoran security forces, he proclaimed to the long-suffering poor that they were Christ crucified in history today.[61] Ignacio Ellacuría and Jon Sobrino, in particular, have developed this connection theologically in their accounts of the "crucified people." For both Ellacuría and Sobrino, the term refers to the hundreds of millions of Latin Americans who have languished and continue to languish in inhuman poverty. They prefer the designation "crucified people" to euphemisms like "the Third World" or "developing countries" because it highlights the fact that the poor majorities suffer actively inflicted death. As Sobrino explains:

> To die crucified does not mean simply to die, but to be put to death; it means that there are victims and there are executioners. It means that there is a very grave sin. The crucified peoples do not fall from heaven. If we followed the metaphor through, we should have to say that they rise from hell. However much people try to soften the fact, the truth is that the Latin American peoples' cross has been inflicted on them by the various empires that have taken power over the continent: the Spanish and Portuguese yesterday, the U.S. and its allies today; whether by armies or economic systems, or the imposition of cultural or religious views, in connivance with the local powers.[62]

The designation "crucified people," then, is first of all a historical designation referring to the people who have suffered and continue to suffer under the injustice of military dictators, formal democracy, and savage capitalism.

The term also carries theological significance. Echoing Romero, both Ellacuría and Sobrino make the connection between those who are crucified today and the crucified Christ. The poor, they assert, are the historical body of Christ today. "In Latin America," writes Sobrino, "the crucified people are the actualization of Christ crucified, the true servant of Yahweh."[63] Likewise, Ellacuría asserts, "This crucified people is the historical continuation of the servant of Yahweh, whom the sin of the world continues to deprive of all human shape, from whom the powerful of this world continue to strip everything, taking even life, especially life."[64]

This association of the crucified people with Christ crucified is further developed by means of a sustained mediation on the servant songs of Isaiah in light of contemporary Latin American reality.[65] The first thing that the servant songs say about the servant is that he is a "man of sorrows acquainted with grief" (53:3), which is the normal condition of the crucified people, who are afflicted by hunger, sickness, slums, illiteracy, unemployment, and so forth. This condition is intensified when they organize to "establish justice" (42:4–7), at which time they are met with repression and massacres. This additional violence in turn renders the people even more like the servant: "so marred was his appearance, beyond human semblance, and his form beyond that of mortals . . . he had no form or majesty, that we should look at him, nothing in his appearance that we should desire him" (52:14; 53:2). The ugliness of daily poverty is compounded by the disfigurement of bloodshed, torture, and mutilation. Consequently, like the suffering servant, the crucified people arouse loathing and fear and are despised and rejected: "many were astonished at him" (52:14) while others "hide their faces" from him (53:3), just as they do from the crucified people lest the crucified disturb the superficial happiness of those who have produced them and unmask the truth of our euphemisms – developing countries, new democracies and so forth.[66] It is said of the servant: "we accounted him stricken, struck down by God, and afflicted" (53:4). If the crucified bear their suffering in meek resignation, they are praised as models of piety and goodness, but if they protest their crucifixion and struggle against it, God is invoked against them and they are "numbered with the transgressors" (53:12), cursed as subversives, criminals, communists, terrorists, even atheists. Of the servant it is said, "By a perversion of justice he was taken away" (53:8). By arbitrary arrest and detention, by death squads and disappearances, by courts and laws that serve the market, the crucified are taken from their land, their homes, their families. The servant, although oppressed and afflicted, "did not open his mouth, like a lamb that is led to the slaughter" (53:7). Although the crucified have acquired voices in persons like Oscar Romero and the many murdered priests and nuns and leaders of the people, the great majority die in anonymity and obscurity. They are thousands and millions whose names we do not know; indeed, we do not even know their number. Moreover, the servant is innocent: "he had done no violence, and there was no deceit in his mouth" (53:9). The crucified have committed no crime; they certainly do not deserve the suffering inflicted by the vast array of force that is brought against them. As Sobrino writes:

> And truly, what crimes were committed by the Guatemalan Indians who were burned alive inside the church of San Francisco, in Huehuetenango, or by the peasants murdered at the River Sumpul or the children dying of hunger in Ethiopia, Somalia or Sudan? What guilt do they have for the greed of those who rob their lands or the geopolitical interests of the great powers?[67]

Finally, even in death the servant is despised: "They made his grave with the wicked" (53:9). Often the crucified do not have even that. They simply disappear.

Other times they are thrown on rubbish heaps or into the ocean or mass clandestine graves.

The parallels between the suffering servant and the crucified do not stop here, however, for no less than the suffering servant, the crucified people are also vehicles of God's salvation. The servant is chosen by God as an instrument of salvation: "I will give you as a light to the nations, that my salvation may reach to the end of the earth" (49:6), and of him it is said, "through him the will of the LORD shall prosper" (53:10). The crucified people are vehicles of salvation insofar as they are chosen mediators of God's good news to all of humanity. Just as the servant was chosen for the purpose of building a new land and a new people, God has chosen the crucified people as a vehicle of the Gospel and out of them God is building a new community. The preferential option for the poor is an expression of this. The crucified people are bearers of salvation insofar as it is precisely in and through them that God confronts oppressors with the good news of salvation. In this regard Gutiérrez remarks:

> Evangelization, the proclamation of the gospel, will be genuinely liberating when the poor themselves become its messengers. That is when we shall see the preaching of the gospel become a stumbling block and a scandal. For then we shall have a gospel that is no longer "presentable" in society. It will not sound nice and it will not smell good. The Lord who scarcely looks like a human at all (cf. the songs of the Servant of Yahweh in Isaiah) will speak to us then, and only at the sound of his voice will we recognize him as our liberator. That voice will convoke the *ek-klesia*, the assembly of those "called apart," in a new and different way.[68]

In other words, the crucified people, by virtue of God's election of them to bear the Gospel to the rest of humanity, are a sacrament of salvation.

The crucified people also model the suffering servant as the bearer of salvation inasmuch as they literally take on the sins of the world. Just as the suffering servant "bore the sin of many" (53:12), so, too, the crucified bear the weight of the world's sin. Although the First World conceals this truth from itself, the causes of the suffering of the Third World are to a great extent to be found in the First World. The poverty of the crucified is the price of other peoples' abundance; the death of the crucified is the price of others' lives.[69] The crucified people shoulder the brunt of the destructive consequences of the First World's rapacious desires, whether those consequences take the form of environmental degradation and resource depletion, starvation wages and harsh working conditions, or low intensity conflict and military bases. The blood and tears of the poor lubricate the gears of savage capitalism's market. This burden crushes them and they die like the servant. Hence, Ellacuría observes, Latin America has been left "like a Christ."[70]

Under the weight of this sin, however, the crucified people do not lash out. Instead, they offer mercy and forgiveness just as the suffering servant did. In spite of the burden of unjust suffering that they carry, the crucified people are ready to forgive their oppressors, as Sobrino notes:

> There is something that the First World often tends to forget. The Third World is open to forgiving its oppressors. It does not wish to triumph over them, but to share with them and open up a future for them. To whomsoever draws close to them, the poor of the Third World open up their hearts and their arms, and without realizing it, grant them forgiveness. By allowing them to come close, they make it possible for the world of the oppressor to recognize itself as a sinner, but also as forgiven. In this way, they introduce into the world of the oppressor a humanizing element which was absent [from it, namely] grace, because forgiveness is not a victory of the executioner but a gift of the victim.[71]

The crucified do not demand what is due; they offer forgiveness. Recall the story from the refugee camp in San Salvador recounted in the introduction. During a worship service, among the prayer cards placed on the altar in remembrance of slain relatives was one that read, "Our dead enemies. May God forgive them and convert them."[72] This is an example that is repeated countless times in the poor Christian communities of Latin America.

> As you approach a peasant refuge, a village devastated by war, or any community that has suffered persecution and martyrdom, one of the things that will strike you most is the difference between what you might logically expect in your encounter with the poor and oppressed here, and what actually occurs. Logically . . . it might happen that the poor would reject a visit from persons belonging structurally to the world of their oppressors, or that they would receive them with recriminations for having arrived so late (years late, centuries late) and for coming so casually (without having made a total decision of commitment to themselves, the victims). . . . But this is not what usually occurs. Elements of it can be present, but by and large, what happens is just the opposite. The poor in these localities fling wide the doors of their homes and their hearts to receive these strangers. They tell them of their afflictions, give them of the little that they do have, and show them how glad they are that they have come.[73]

The crucified people mirror the suffering servant and bring salvation by being merciful. In the midst of the terrible suffering that plagues Latin America, the Spirit has gathered the crucified people into the Church of the poor and freed their desire such that they can welcome those who oppress them and extend God's forgiveness.

The assertion that the crucified people are a contemporary manifestation of the suffering servant who extends the divine gift of forgiveness is a scandalous claim.

After all, exactly who constitutes the crucified people and how they reproduce the features of the servant are not immediately self-evident. Anticipating objections, therefore, the liberationists are careful to nuance this claim in several important ways. Chief among these is the acknowledgment that the relation between Christ and the crucified people is not one of absolute identity. The crucified neither replace nor repeat Christ's work. The advent of Christ was a unique event. Christ is the savior; the crucified do not usurp his place as the second person of the Trinity. Thus, the relation between the crucified of today and the crucified Christ is a matter of analogy and participation, not pure identity.[74] In the crucified people, the incarnation is analogously reproduced; the crucified bear a certain resemblance to Christ the suffering servant. They mediate the presence of that savior; they do not replace him. As the historical body of Christ, the crucified people remain subordinate to the head of that body, Christ. They remain in dialogue with Christ who continues to call, judge, and recreate them.[75]

Furthermore, the liberationists recognize that not all the crucified people resemble Christ or mediate his salvific presence to the same extent. Although all the crucified share a certain historical resemblance to Christ by the mere fact that they are both crucified by sin and loved preferentially by God,[76] the liberationists' strongest claims for the crucified people are correlated with a deeper moral resemblance. This moral resemblance is a matter of the crucified people being animated by the Spirit of Christ to continue Christ's work/passion in the world, which is to say, it is a matter of the crucified people being gathered into the Church of the poor.[77] The moral resemblance is manifest when the crucified people themselves convert, when they themselves make the option for the poor and follow Christ.[78] In this way, the link between the crucified people and the body of Christ is refined to encompass the crucified people who follow Christ, who bear the yoke of oppression "in a consciously Christian manner."[79]

In other words, the liberationists do not assert that all the poor and oppressed, simply by virtue of their poverty and oppression, constitute the body of Christ. On the contrary, they are well aware that neither do all the crucified resemble Christ in the moral sense nor do any resemble Christ all the time. Not all the poor respond to their situation in faith; not all extend forgiveness. Many fall prey to fatalism and resignation. Some put themselves at the service of the oppressors. Others are captured by the same disciplinary technologies that have corrupted the desire of their oppressors. The poor can become oppressors and subsystems of crucifixion can proliferate among them. In other words, there are no pure victims. Hence, even as they use the category of oppressor/oppressed, the liberationists recognize its limitations, particularly the risk of encouraging a Manichean division of the world that locates all good on one side – in the crucified people – and all evil on the other.[80]

In a similar vein, the liberationists note that all the crucified do not resemble Christ historically in the same way. Although the liberationists focus on socioeconomic oppression, such oppression does not exhaust the forms of crucifixion. Others are widespread, including those involving race, gender, culture, caste, and so forth. What unites these various forms of crucifixion is that they are all the consequence of sin (those forms of illness and poverty induced by natural catastrophe, for example, are not forms of crucifixion) and they undermine human dignity, especially the right to life.[81]

In light of the qualifications that attend the claim that the crucified people are the suffering servant who mediate God's salvation to the world, Sobrino concludes, "Without a doubt, not all the Third World is like this. In fact, it is only minorities who actively offer those values described here . . . who offer us in this way the grace of truth and conversion."[82] That this is the case, however, does not diminish the potency of their witness. The crucified people who are gathered as the Church of the poor are enacting God's forgiveness, not demanding what is due, in an effort to liberate desire from capitalist discipline. By so doing the Church of the poor is a testament to the truth that, in the words of José Ellacuría spoken after his brother's murder, "there is another way to live."[83] There is another way to live, beyond the madness of savage capitalism, beyond the madness of Deleuze's schizo desire, beyond even the terror of justice. To the therapy of desire that sets us on the path to this other way of living we now turn.

The judgment of grace

The crucified people that constitute the Church of the poor are extending God's gift of forgiveness, not demanding justice in the classic sense of *suum cuique*, in response to the oppression and injustice that afflicts them. But is this really a form of resistance to capitalism? Is the refusal to cease suffering that is forgiveness anything more than simply a refusal to cease suffering? What distinguishes the Church of the poor's enactment of forgiveness from the destructive forms that the liberationists rightly reject as little more than theological pacification programs – those forms of forgiveness that disempower victims and sanction impunity? For an answer we turn to the liberationists' account of several of the central technologies of desire that constitute forgiveness as those technologies are displayed in the Church of the poor. Specifically, we focus on three technologies – confession, repentance, and penance or reparations – that the liberationists testify are at the heart of the therapy of forgiveness as enacted by the Church of the poor.[84] It is the presence of these technologies that establishes the therapy of forgiveness as a form of resistance to capitalist discipline and distinguishes it from the destructive forms of forgiveness that the liberationists rightly reject. Through them, the Church of the poor is extending God's gift of forgiveness and redirecting desire toward its true end: the shared love that is friendship in God.

Before taking them individually, however, it is worthwhile considering them as a whole. For it is as a whole that we begin to perceive how the assemblage of knowledges, instruments, persons, systems of judgment, spaces and buildings that constitutes forgiveness as a therapy of desire avoids degenerating into a pious veneer spread over the impunity of the powerful. Taken together they reveal forgiveness to be a form of judgment. Confession, repentance, and penance are the path that the divine gift of forgiveness clears *beyond* sin. To confess and repent of sin, and to do penance, is to leave sin behind. To receive and return forgiveness, Sobrino notes, is to uproot sin.[85] As a tripartite movement of confession, repentance, and penance, the divine gift of forgiveness is the way God confronts and overcomes sin. Forgiveness, in other words, is God's judgment on sin. It is a positive movement that does not merely pardon or absolve but liberates and transforms, as José Comblin observes:

> . . . sin does not so much need forgiveness that cancels it or removes the punishment, but rather liberation. If human beings are victims of a sin that is stronger than their individual will, they need to be liberated from their sin. In this sense, grace is not an absolution, which cancels the sin and all the penalties laid down for the sin. Grace and forgiveness are instead the actual liberation movement through which people liberate themselves from the structures that crush them and take away their freedom.[86]

God's judgment of sin is real; forgiveness does not nullify that. On the contrary, it is the embodiment of that judgment.

Forgiveness is an embodiment of God's judgment of sin, however, as a judgment of grace. God does indeed judge sin, but not according to the traditional canons of justice. Such justice, as we have seen, does not accomplish reconciliation; rather it leaves us locked in struggle. For this reason, as the liberationists acknowledge, justice so conceived cannot be the final word about God. God judges sin not in order to uphold the canons of "what is due," but in order to heal all desire (of both victim and perpetrator) that it might participate in the joyous sociality of love. Forgiveness is a judgment that abandons none and seeks to reconcile all. As such it is a judgment of grace.[87]

This is nowhere more evident than in the cross and resurrection of Christ. That these mysteries are instances of God's solidarity with the victims of sin is a well-known theme of the liberationists. The cross is the consequence of Christ's incarnation in solidarity with the victims of the anti-Kingdom and the resurrection is an act of divine solidarity with those victims insofar as it is God's response, one that brings about the triumph of the victim over the executioner, to injustice and sin.[88] Viewed through the lens of solidarity alone, the cross and resurrection hardly illumine God's judgment as one of grace. Indeed, as manifestions of solidarity they are easily incorporated into the traditional logic of justice. In solidarity with the victims, God brings justice to bear against the victimizers. Solidarity with the victims, however, does not exhaust the mystery of the cross and resurrection, for God's judgment of sin manifest in the cross and resurrection of Christ involves not only a "no" to sin, but also a "yes" to a world that has to be reconciled.[89] Even as they are acts of solidarity with the victims of sin, the cross and resurrection are acts of atonement for the victimizers, as Leonardo Boff suggests:

The first to benefit in that kingdom are the victims of injustice, oppression, and violence. The powerful, the rich, and the proud will be toppled from their places. Thus they will be able to stop being inhuman. Freed from the schemes that made them oppressors, they too will have a chance to share in God's new order.[90]

Taking this a step further, Elsa Tamez asserts that the judgment of God is a judgment of life because the guilty are not abandoned to God's wrath. Speaking of the divine judgment on sin that is the cross and resurrection, she writes:

God was not guided by the standards of the just law – death for the assassin, life for the poor person. God's judgment, through love for the excluded, was carried out on the foundation of grace: unmerited grace for all. . . . The sentence of "death for the assassin" and "life for the poor person" is a just law, merited, but limited even for the poor themselves, because of their condemnation to the infinite repetition of their oppression. Therefore, the African theologian and political leader, Canaan Banana, son of a continent both exploited and discriminated against, affirms: "Distasteful as it might be to the victims of oppression, the oppressor has to be liberated along with the oppressed."[91]

Christ did not die for the just but for the sinner and the ungodly, argues Sobrino, and in this way the dichotomy between friend and enemy, oppressor and oppressed, is shattered.[92] Likewise, the resurrection reveals that God's intention for oppressors is reconciliation and love instead of condemnation. The risen one returns to those who betrayed and denied him, persecuted him and plotted his death, and extends his gracious love.[93] Thus, that the cross and resurrection are not only instances of divine solidarity with the victims of sin but also atoning acts indicates that the judgment that God levels against sin is a judgment of grace.

Insofar as the forgiveness extended by the crucified people gathered as the Church of the poor is a continuation of God's gift of forgiveness, it entails a judgment of grace leveled against sin. The liberationists are quick to point out that the forgiveness offered by the crucified people – in contrast with the forgiveness proclaimed by chaplains of the status quo – does not amount to a cheap grace that leaves reality untouched, unchanged, untransformed. Such forgiveness would hardly herald the liberation of desire from its capitalist captivity. Rather, the forgiveness extended by the crucified, insofar as it models the suffering servant, is a forgiveness that defeats sin. When the Church of the poor enacts forgiveness, it is not ignoring sin; it is striving to overcome it. The Salvadoran refugees who pray for the forgiveness of their enemies are not ignoring the fact that those enemies raped, tortured, and murdered their loved ones. The reconciliation that the Church of the poor hopes to facilitate through forgiveness involves the removal or elimination of the sin that ruptured communion in the first place. Recall Sobrino's assertion that forgiveness entails fighting against sin by destroying the structures of oppression

and violence, converting reality from injustice to justice, from oppression to freedom, from death to life. Although the liberationists misdescribe this judgment in
terms of justice instead of grace, they nevertheless bring to the fore the way in
which the forgiveness that the Church of the poor offers does not amount to a fatalistic capitulation to the capitalist regime but entails a judgment upon sin.

Honesty about the real

This judgment of grace takes the shape of a call for conversion. Traditionally, this
call has been articulated in terms of confession and repentance. The gift of forgiveness that overcomes sin is received by means of confession and repentance.
Genuine reconciliation between the oppressor and the oppressed, which is the
end of forgiveness, presupposes that the sin that divided them has been acknowledged and repented of. This is to say, the call for conversion, as a manifestation of
the judgment of grace that is the gift of forgiveness, is an invitation to enter into
certain technologies of desire that, through the operation of a host of knowledges,
persons, judgments, instruments, and so forth, identify the ways desire has been
distorted and reshape desire toward its true end. When speaking of these technologies, liberationists rarely use the traditional language of confession and
repentance; instead they speak of the need for truthfulness in the face of sinful reality ("honesty about the real"[94]) and for oppressors to convert. They are clear that
forgiveness presupposes acknowledging the truth about oneself and one's sin (personal and structural), including facing the reality of the harm that sin has wrought
on others, and then changing one's behavior. "Christianity calls for pardon, yes, but
a pardon based on truth," asserts Ignacio Martín-Baró.[95] Likewise, Segundo is
adamant, "conversion is required *in order that* Christians be reconciled."[96]

Confession is essential because liberation from sin and reconciliation with others
is not possible if one does not realize one is caught in sin and alienated from
others. Desire cannot be freed if it does not recognize its captivity. If the oppressors do not see the sinfulness of their actions, if they do not realize they are
embedded in sinful structures, there is no reason to seek reconciliation with and
accept forgiveness from the crucified people. For example, reflecting on the relation
between the North and the South, Sobrino observes that what is at stake in the
demand for truthfulness is whether "the North of the planet concedes the reality
of the South and is interested in building the human family, or whether its only
interest is in its own well-being, with the resulting declaration of the nonexistence
of the South and its lack of interest for the human family."[97] Nothing less than the
possibility of reconciliation and the renewal of communion hinges on a truthful
assessment of sinful reality and the obstacles it presents to that reconciliation and
communion.

That the confession of sin is an integral component of the forgiveness that the
crucified offer to their oppressors is evident in Sobrino's description of the way in
which the crucified people serve, in a manner analogous to the suffering servant, as
a light to the nations. Describing the current situation, Sobrino asserts that the First

World is submerged in the "sleep of inhumanity."[98] It hardly knows that the world of the poor exists, much less of its responsibility for their plight.

> The First World is not interested in the Third World, to put it mildly. As history shows, it is only interested in ways to despoil the Third World in order to increase its own abundance. People do not want to acknowledge or face up to the reality of a crucified world, and even less do we want to ask ourselves what is our share of responsibility for such a world. The world of poverty truly is the great unknown. It is surprising that the First World can know so much and yet ignore what is so fundamental about the world in which we live.[99]

Given the vast accomplishments of the First World, its stunning ignorance concerning the reality of the poor majorities can be accounted for only as a deliberate turning away from that reality.[100] Yet as the crucified people assert themselves on the stage of history, they become bearers of God's grace to the First World precisely as they confront that world with the truth about itself. As they emerge from the margins and excluded spaces they are awakening the First World from its inhuman slumber and helping it name its sin. Traditional piety, says Sobrino, has maintained that in order to know what sin is, one should gaze on the crucified Christ. Today this means standing before the crucifix composed of the crucified people and asking, what have we done?[101] In this way, the crucified people are a light for the nations that illumines the truth. This light, terrible in what it reveals, is nevertheless mercy's radiance. It dispels the darkness of sin and opens the way to healing and reconciliation.[102]

At this point an objection might be interposed. That truthfulness and confession are the fruit of mercy's radiance is hardly self-evident. In Latin America today, for example, in the face of the brutality and violence of the recent past, it is frequently asserted that forgetting, not full disclosure, is the way forward. Historical amnesia is proposed as the path to reconciliation. Should not Christians be about the formation of persons who forgive precisely by forgetting? Does not confession amount to little more than the opening of old wounds, wounds that if left alone would heal with the passing of time but if prodded will undoubtedly fester and rekindle the flames of conflict? There is significant force to this objection. Recalling and naming sin are not intrinsically therapeutic. Dwelling on sin can just as easily fuel hatred and violence as healing. Recalling the damage inflicted by the sin of another may prolong the anguish of the victim. Disclosure may ignite cries for "what is due" and so perpetuate the cycle of violence. In a similar manner, confronted with the truth about oneself, one may be filled with self-hatred and thus engage in self-destructive behavior or lash out at others for unmasking the truth about oneself. For these reasons, one should not be surprised, Sobrino cautions, if the offer of forgiveness is rejected and the sinner turns on the one offering it with even greater fury.[103]

Setting aside for the moment the difficulties with confession this objection highlights, the liberationists reject the counsel of forgetfulness for several reasons. First, it supposes that the crucified people can simply put out of mind the afflictions of injustice. The counsel of forgetfulness asks, in effect, that the void created in families and friendships by the absence of the persons who have been murdered or "disappeared," and the anguish of all those who survived the cruelty visited on their flesh in hideous prisons, endless interrogations, and refined tortures (probably more than the number who died), as well as the trauma of the countless persons who were threatened, harassed, and persecuted, and who, for the sake of their lives and the lives of their loved ones renounced their ideals and principles and fled, be dismissed from the memory.[104] Confronted with the magnitude of the suffering, Ignacio Martín-Baró asserts that forgetting is not possible. "All this damage is of such magnitude that it becomes almost ingenuous or cynical to act as if it can be forgotten overnight."[105] In other words, the counsel of forgetfulness is incredible; it mocks the depth and seriousness of the suffering inflicted by sin. Second, if forgetfulness were possible, it would render forgiveness unnecessary in the same way that the possibility of justice would. If the offense could be forgotten, then what would need to be forgiven? That the offense cannot simply be ignored and forgotten provides forgiveness with both its necessity and its condition of possibility. Finally, as the prior objections suggest, forgetting fails because the wound of sin does not heal if left untreated. "It is commonly argued that dwelling on the past only serves to reopen old wounds," writes Luis Peréz Aguirre. "That assumes wounds have been closed. They have not, and the only way to close them is to achieve a genuine . . . reconciliation based on truth and justice with reference to our history."[106] Sin that has not been named and confessed is sin that maintains its hold on bodies, individually and collectively. The past that is buried in the call for forgetfulness, Martín-Baró observes, is still alive. It is alive not only in persons and groups – victims and victimizers – but also in the social structures that inflicted the suffering then and are still standing now.[107] As those who endured the nightmare of the Latin American national security states of the past few decades know only too well, silence and the refusal/failure/inability to name sin were critical elements in the perpetuation of the reign of terror. The counsel to forget is not the path toward healing; it is an invitation to impunity. It does not change anything. On the contrary, it only leaves the field open to the forces of oppression that already dominate our world.[108] In this way, forgetting does not really free anyone from the sin and suffering of the past; rather, it only insures that the past will continue to stalk the present and undermine genuine reconciliation.

Although the counsel of forgetfulness is a dead end, the intuition that prompts it, namely, that disclosure and confession are not intrinsically healing, is an important one, one that prompts recognition that the technology of desire that is confession entails remembering in a particular way. When situated within the gift of forgiveness, confession becomes a way of remembering that ironically, and in contrast with a forgetting that closes off the future precisely by its inability to let go of the past, sets both the offender and victim free from the past for the sake of the future. As a part of the judgment of grace that is forgiveness, the confession of truth does not exacerbate either the wound of sin or the cycle of violence that is the wound's effect. This is to say, confession of sin involves the recollection of sin in such a way that such recollection does not appear as a threat.

Accomplishing this nonthreatening recollection entails what Duquoc calls "an invitation to the imagination."[109] Confession is an invitation to renarrate our lives, to renegotiate our identities under the impact of a truer story than the story of our sin.[110] Here it may be helpful to recall the way in which the Cistercian liturgy assembled memory. Confession is a process whereby we learn a new and truer way to locate our lives and our desire. We learn to tell the story of our lives as the story of God's gift of forgiveness.

In other words, nonthreatening recollection is possible only because it occurs in Christ. Confession is a redemptive moment in a judgment of grace because through it our lives are remembered in Christ. When we are gathered in Christ's body, through liturgy, Word, the lives of saints, and so forth we learn to remember well, which is to say that our memory becomes first the memory of God, of God's gift of forgiveness in Christ, and of the return of that gift through its extension to others.[111] Recall the sense in which Christ's atoning work was an innovative movement. Christ has borne the burden of (past) sin and opened a path to a future beyond all sin. The resurrection of the crucified one and his return with the gift of forgiveness to those who rejected him are a sign that sin does not have the final, destructive word in our lives but that something new and different and holy is possible. Corrupt desire must not always be corrupted by past corruption. With the resurrection of Christ, our sinful past is raised, not in the sense that it is undone, but in the sense that it is redeemed. Therefore, confession is possible. What once could only be recalled at the risk of renewed violence, is now remembered in Christ as redemption, as the moment of God's overcoming of sin, as the beginning of a new life and the promise of a future unhindered by past sin.[112] Thus, the invitation to confess is nothing less than "an act of love for the offender" that opens the way to reconciliation.[113]

Conversion and the revolution of the forgiven

Of course, the mere disclosure of sin, the mere recognition of the ways desire is disciplined, is hardly sufficient to usher in this new future.[114] Therefore, the healing of desire and journey towards communion that were begun with confession continues with repentance. Insofar as forgiveness is God's way of eliminating sin, it entails that those who confess their sin also leave that sin behind, that they break with personal and social sin and act in new ways. Once the ways in which desire has been warped have been identified, the therapy of desire that is forgiveness requires that the technologies that brought about those distortions be actively renounced. In this regard, the liberationists speak of the need for oppressors to undergo conversion:

> The thrust of the Spirit does not end with the discovery of the battered
> victim lying in the ditch. It drives us, to make a commitment to that

victim, to enter actively upon his or her pathway, to make a commitment to his or her liberation. This element of the foundational experience has led us to an in-depth understanding of *metanoia*, the Christian conversion.[115]

Referring to Jesus' proclamation "Repent and believe in the Gospel" (Mark 1:15), Sobrino argues that oppressors must undergo a radical change in their lives if they are to participate in the Kingdom that liberates people and creates human fellowship.[116] Indeed, as was noted earlier, this conversion amounts to nothing less than the destruction of oppressors in their capacity as oppressor. "We must free him from this evil," says Sobrino, "and this is what forgiveness tries to do: convert and re-create the sinner."[117] Likewise, Duquoc notes that "forgiveness may be gratuitous but it is not arbitrary: it calls for a change of attitude on the part of the offender or sinner, who enters into a new relationship with the person who forgives. This goes by the name of conversion."[118] Gutiérrez is more explicit about the character of this conversion when he suggests that it amounts to an entering upon the way of "the neighbor, the oppressed person, the exploited social class, the despised ethnic group, the dominated country."[119] In other words, the conversion that is repentance is a matter of entering into solidarity with the crucified people. When the oppressors repent they are in effect renouncing the option for the wealthy that characterized their previous lives and opting instead for the poor. That this renunciation and option should be a part of the divine grace that is forgiveness should be unsurprising. After all, Gutiérrez notes, the clemency of God is not arbitrary; it demands behavior that gives life to others.[120]

The imperative of repentance or conversion is reflected in the crucified people's gift of mercy to their oppressors. Recall that the Salvadoran refugees' prayer of forgiveness for their enemies was a prayer for conversion. The crucified people, even as they bring to light the sinful character of reality, also mediate the power for the oppressor to change. As they extend the offer of forgiveness they invite conversion. The grace and mercy that they present to the First World is the grace to change, to embark on a new path that leads to life and reconciliation. Thus, says Sobrino, when the First World faces the crucifix that is the crucified people, the challenge that confronts them does not stop with the naming of sin but continues in the form of the questions, "What am I doing to take them down from the cross? What ought I to do that a crucified people may rise again?"[121]

The call for conversion, for confession and repentance, is not directed solely at those who oppress the crucified people. The resistance to the capitalist order that the crucified offer in the form of the therapy of forgiveness is "the revolution of a forgiven people."[122] Central to the therapy of desire that is forgiveness functioning as a source of resistance to capitalist discipline is the Church of the poor not only offering the gift of forgiveness, but receiving it as well. Returning the gift by extending it to others is contingent upon first having received the gift. Hence, the crucified people who constitute the Church of the poor are called to conversion too. Indeed, theirs is a dual conversion of sorts. On one hand, they experience conversion as they accept forgiveness and confess and repent of their sin. As previously noted, they, too, must make the option for the poor. In particular, the poor are faced with the challenge of repenting of their lack of faith in God that leads to a pervasive hopelessness and resignation in the face of oppression. "These people are living proof of the absence of God's reign," writes Sobrino, "and the first thing asked of them is faith. They must believe that their present situation is not the last possibility open to them because it is not the last possibility open to God."[123] Moreover, they need to repent of the ways in which their lives, too, are caught up in behaviors that replicate the structures that uphold the oppressive order. In this regard, Sobrino observes that in the Church of the poor:

> . . . the rediscovery of the great structural sin and structural forgiveness has helped people rediscover their own worlds of sin and forgiveness. Structural oppression has helped people discover typical oppressions within communities, *machismo*, the authoritarianism of leaders, refusal to take responsibility, selfishness, and lust for domination. Often people recognize simply: We have behaved a little like the great oppressors.[124]

They recognize that they are not immune to the distortions of desire that the dominant order inflicts. They, too, are tempted by violence, greed, and the will to power. And for the crucified people, no less than for the great oppressors, conversion in the form of confession and repentance is the means through which forgiveness is appropriated, through which sin is overcome and desire liberated.

But there is a second dimension to the crucified people's conversion. Not only does conversion entail a movement away from sin; it includes a movement toward the other as well. The gift is received only in love being returned as the gift is extended to others. Recall that as desire is healed, it is rendered no longer a proprietary force but rather exists in the modality of donation. As desire receives, it learns to give. From the experience of being forgiven – from the memory of their own sin and forgiveness by God – springs the crucified people's desire to forgive.[125] But this learning to give in response to what has been received requires a further conversion in the sense that extending forgiveness to one who has inflicted harm, especially if that harm has taken a particularly heinous form, such as the starvation of one's children or the torture, rape, and murder of one's friends and family, requires an extraordinary conversion. When the crucified people offer forgiveness to their oppressors they, in effect, give away any claim they have to a full rendering of what is due. Extending God's judgment of grace, they relinquish their claim to the rights that have been violated (and the justice that would enforce them) and hence their power over the offender. Indeed, forgiveness is the renewal of desire as generosity that absorbs the debt created by offense and reaches out in a renewed effort at love, friendship, communion. In particular, notes Gutiérrez, forgiveness requires that the forgiver trust the one who is being forgiven – no small demand, given the gravity and longevity of oppression in Latin America.[126] In other words, forgiveness requires of the crucified people not only a renewed faith in God, but also a new confidence in humanity. Not only does forgiveness entail desire learning to receive and be embraced, it also involves desire learning to give and embrace. In this way, forgiveness involves a conversion in the one who forgives as much as in the one who is forgiven.

No salvation without reparations?

Consistent with their effort to safeguard forgiveness and reconciliation from becoming a license for oppression, the liberationists assert that God's judgment of sin is not complete with confession and repentance, but continues with penance and the making of reparations. The liberation of desire and renewal of the harmonic sociality of desire are contingent not only upon the distortions of desire being identified and renounced, but also upon the injured being compensated. According to the liberationists, Christianity grants forgiveness and acknowledges reconciliation only after reparations have been paid. "Even the most traditional morality," writes Martín-Baró, "only speaks of reconciliation when joined with the 'offer of compensation'; that is, the recognition of wrong committed, and of 'atonement through acts,' which is to say, reparation."[127] Luis Peréz Aguirre, likewise, insists that there is no forgiveness without compensation for injustice:

> Here it may be helpful to consider the experience of the churches. They never granted forgiveness or acknowledged a sinner's reconciliation with the community until the sinner had fulfilled certain basic requirements – and then only if he had examined his conscience, repented of his sin, expressed a firm resolve not to sin again, acknowledged his fault before the community and before God, and had done penance to atone for the harm he had done. Nowhere in the gospels does forgiveness, or mercy as its source, mean indulgence for evil, injustice, or offense. In all cases, reparation for evil, compensation for injustice, and indemnification for offense, are conditions for reconciliation.[128]

Although Gutiérrez never directly addresses the issue of penance and reparations, he does cite approvingly the work of Bartolomé de Las Casas. Las Casas was a priest and *encomendero* in Hispaniola when he came into contact with a group of Dominicans who, as part of a campaign against the mistreatment of the natives, began to preach the duty of restitution. "In recent days," wrote the Dominican Pedro de Córdoba, "we have preached straight out against the [culprits], declaring to them the state of damnation in which they live and the obligation they have of making restitution, not only for what they have acquired in the way of temporal goods, but also for the harm they have caused in the course of that acquisition."[129] Indeed, at one point a Dominican refused to hear Las Casas' confession because he held natives in bondage. In 1514 Las Casas had a dramatic "conversion," after which he became an advocate for the oppressed indigenous peoples. About this experience Gutiérrez writes, "It was an acute awareness of the duty of restitution that sparked Las Casas's conversion experience, from which his radical change of life emerged. . . . [I]t was by this duty that he was impelled to renounce his *encomienda*."[130] Thereafter, the obligation of restitution became a pillar of Las Casas' work. Indeed, he went so far as to assert that reparations are a condition of salvation: "On peril of losing their souls, all who start wars of conversion . . . are bound to restore to the devastated pagan peoples whatever they took in war, permanent or perishable, and make up for whatever they destroyed. Make up totally."[131] Lest there be any misunderstanding, he follows this with a forthright declaration that "without restitution, without complete restoral, they cannot be saved."[132] Years later, as bishop, Las Casas instructed the clergy in his diocese that when they heard confessions, they were not to grant forgiveness to *encomenderos* until they freed the Indians and restored their ill-gotten gains.[133] Finally, toward the end of his life, Las Casas wrote to the confessor of the Spanish king Philip II, arguing that restitution demanded nothing less than the immediate manumission of all the Indians, the withdrawal of the Spaniards from the Indies, and the rehabilitation of the native societies that flourished prior to the Conquest.[134] Although Gutiérrez is clear that there can be no simple appropriation of Las Casas today, it is also clear that his witness is recognized as a genuine manifestation of the Gospel. Hence, it is reasonable to infer that Las Casas' call for reparations and restitution is a model of the liberationists' understanding of the proper functioning of forgiveness.

In light of what has been said thus far, the inadequacies of the liberationists' account of reparations and penance are not difficult to discern. By making forgiveness contingent upon reparations, it does not faithfully reflect the way God has revealed the Kingdom in and through Christ. Forgiveness is extended by God and, as the liberationists themselves suggest, by the crucified people who worship God as well, prior to any human effort at amendment or reparation for sin. In this regard, it is odd that even as the liberationists staunchly oppose theories of atonement that hinge upon the satisfaction of a debt created by sin, their articulation of the obligation of reparations appears to follow the same logic of satisfaction.[135] Penance and reparations amount to nothing more than the satisfaction of an obligation incurred by sin. Forgiveness is contingent upon the satisfaction of the debt created by the violation of the human rights of the crucified. Once the debt has been paid, once reparations have made up for the damage inflicted by sin, then forgiveness is forthcoming.

Moreover, their account fails to escape the terror of justice. The liberationists' demand for reparations stems from their insistence that forgiveness be subordinated to justice as the guarantor of rights. According to the liberationists, ultimately reparations are simply the outgrowth of the justice upon which forgiveness and reconciliation must be established. The reparations awarded to the victim by the offender, Silvio Campana argues, are "the fruit of justice."[136] Likewise, Gutiérrez writes in his reflections on Las Casas' uncompromising call for restitution, "Restitution seeks to reestablish the justice that has been wronged by plunder and extortion."[137] Restitution is a matter of shoring up the canons of justice, of rendering what is due, of restoring and securing the rights that have been violated.

The demand for reparations as the way to re-establish a violated justice, how-ever, cannot succeed. As indicated previously, the irreversibility of injustice renders such efforts impossible. There are no reparations that can, in the words of Las Casas, "make up totally" for the massive and enduring injustice that the crucified people have suffered. As Martín-Baró rightly observes, "It is clear that nobody is going to return his youth to the imprisoned dissident; or her innocence to the young woman who has been raped; or integrity to the person who has been tor-tured. Nobody is going to return the dead and the disappeared to their families."[138] If, as Silvio Campana asserts, forgiveness is dependent upon the victims feeling that they have been restored from the damage inflicted by the offense, then reconcilia-tion is inconceivable and the best that we can hope for is a justice that manages to constrain the unending spiral of violence and counter-violence in which we are trapped.[139]

The difficulties with the liberationists' construal of reparations and penance, however, do not lead to the conclusion that such technologies have no place in the therapy of desire that is forgiveness. On the contrary, as a judgment of grace that seeks to eliminate sin, the therapy of forgiveness includes reparations. No less than confession and repentance, penitential activity aimed at countering the effects of sin is an important component of forgiveness. What the difficulties with the liber-ationists' account do suggest is that reparations, if they are to be both theologically adequate and practically efficacious, must be construed as something other than a component of justice as the guarantor of rights. In order to both reflect the true nature of God and avoid the terror of justice, penitential activity must be recast as a response to and appropriation of the grace that is the gift of forgiveness and its goal must be reconceived as the renewal of human communion instead of the reassertion of claims to what is due rights. This is to say, if it is to escape the spiral of violence that plagues a justice erected on the foundation of rights, penance must be guided by a merciful logic that does not demand the impossible – the reversal of the past – but miraculously creates new possibilities for the future out of the ruins of sin that is the past.

Conceived as the embodiment of the merciful logic that undergirds the gift of forgiveness, penance becomes an extension and growth of solidarity. "Under pre-sent circumstances," writes Sobrino, "solidarity with Latin America constitutes a kind of reparation by First World [Christians] for what was done in the past."[140] Penance as solidarity does not aim at the restoration of rights and the rendering of what is due victims. Rather, it strives for the renewal of friendship, the sociality of love, between those who were formerly divided as victim and victimizer, oppressed and oppressor. Specifically, penance is the lifelong process of completing what was begun with repentance. The deconstruction of desire in its agonistic, propri-etary (capitalist) modality that occurs in confession and repentance is accompanied by the construction of new participatory relations in penance. If confession is about identifying the bonds that hold desire captive and repentance is a matter of severing those bonds, penance is the positive, life-giving movement whereby desire learns to enter into non-possessive, non-proprietary, non-agonistic relations with others. As such, penance is the renewal of desire in its mode of donation, whereby it desires to enter into a non-possessive, participatory, peaceful communion with others. In other words, penance is fundamentally unitive and not distributive. It functions primarily to bring about the unity and reconciliation of persons, not to see that goods are distributed in accord with justice as the guarantor of rights.

That it is fundamentally a unitive process, however, does not preclude the possibility that penance might involve the distribution and redistribution of goods. As the liberationists' account of integral liberation reminds us, reconciliation with God and humanity is not limited to a spiritual dimension but encompasses the material realm as well. In other words, the unity of persons, the sociality of desire, that forgiveness intends and penance fosters is not something that occurs in isolation from the way in which material goods are used and distributed. It is not the equivalent of some sort of psychological or "spiritual" bond that "transcends" (ignores) real social and material divisions. On the contrary, human communion is a material effect of material processes. Indeed, one of the primary ways that capitalism corrupts desire and breaches human communion is through the particular ways it misuses and maldistributes goods. Where some dine on delicacies and watch their weight while the poor pick through their trash, there is no communion, regardless of whatever feelings of good will or charitable gestures the rich may dispense to the poor. In spite of the sincere but facile professions of solidarity with their poor sisters and brothers made by the guilty consciences of some benefactors of the current capitalist order, the great social and material gulf that continues to separate them from the crucified people belies genuine unity and reconciliation. Hence, penance will undoubtedly entail the redistribution of goods. Indeed, the liberationists stress that entering into solidarity with the poor entails voluntary poverty, the loving renunciation of privilege and assumption of the condition of the poor for the sake of struggling against it.[141]

The unitive nature of penance does not diminish the importance of the distribution of goods in the course of desire's liberation from capitalism. What it does do is highlight the way in which such redistribution is governed, not as it is in the liberationists' account by the logic of rights, but by the conciliatory logic of forgiveness. This is to say, penitential redistribution is neither an attempt to satisfy the proprietary desire of the victim by rendering what is "by right" its due nor is it an effort to restrain the proprietary desire of the offender by re-establishing the equilibrium of rivalrous desires. Rather, penitential redistribution proceeds as part of the effort to heal desire of its proprietary and agonistic distortions and renew the harmony of desire in the communion of love.[142] Accordingly, penitential redistribution is not undertaken in accord with calculations of what will "make up totally" for past sin, but rather is guided by what is needed to reconcile oppressor and oppressed.

That penance is not meant to enforce "rights" but facilitate reconciliation means that it is not a process entered into by offenders alone but requires the participation of the victims as well. Because its end is the renewal of communion, penance requires both the offender and the victim to give. In particular, it requires that the victim give up claims to vengeance and rights. Only if the victim's desire is renewed in the modality of gift or donation, only if it flows as generosity to embrace the penitential offender can penance attain its end, reconciliation and the renewal of communion. Thus, notes Sobrino, the solidarity that has developed in recent years between First World Christians and the Church of the poor in Latin America is not a unilateral action on the part of the penitent but a "bearing with one another in faith," a mutual giving and receiving.[143] Even as penitent Christians of the First World have offered aid, support, accompaniment, and in some cases their lives to their crucified sisters and brothers, they have in turn been welcomed, embraced, and renewed in their faith.[144] The liberation of desire occurs only as the conviviality of desire flourishes once again, which is contingent upon the victims embracing those who sinned against them and ruptured the bonds of friendship.

Forgiveness in absentia?

That this is the case, that the attainment of the end of penance involves the participation of both offender and victim, raises several difficulties. Chief among these is that presented by those situations where one or more parties are unable or unwilling to participate in the process. In such situations there is no reconciliation and the therapy that is forgiveness is, at least temporarily, prevented from coming to full fruition. This, however, does not mean that the therapy of forgiveness should be abandoned. On the contrary, such situations call for imagination and creativity in discerning how the process might continue in the hopes that at some point in the future the possibility of reconciliation might yet be revived and consummated.

In the case where, perhaps because they are not a part of the Christian community or have been poorly formed by that community, one of the parties is unaware of the need for forgiveness, the situation may call for evangelism and instruction. In the case of those unwilling either to forgive or be forgiven, the hope is that over time, with patient witness, nurture, and guidance, the stubborn will receive the gift. Meanwhile, the process of forgiveness can continue with victims learning to love their enemies and offenders entering into solidarity with other victims of sin.[145] In the case of the death of either victim or offender, or perhaps where either or both are too numerous, the therapy of forgiveness acquires an eschatological dimension.[146] Again in this case the therapy of forgiveness may continue to heal the desire of those present in preparation for a future, perhaps eschatological, reconciliation. Such preparation will again take the form of victims learning the posture of embrace and of offenders entering into solidarity with other crucified people.

This solution, however, seems to create another absence. The necessity of interhuman reconciliation appears to have eclipsed divine forgiveness. In particular, God's mediating role seems to have been foreclosed. Does not God in Christ, as the ultimate victim, stand in for all victims and thus grant forgiveness on their behalf?

Furthermore, is not the Church, as an extension of Christ, empowered to forgive sin on behalf of others?

Where this objection falters is in the way in which, even as it acknowledges Christ as the embodiment of all victims, it nevertheless subtly distances Christ from all victims, as though divine forgiveness were something distinct from the forgiveness extended by and through the crucified people. It supposes that Christ replaces or substitutes for all the victims in such a way that those who desire forgiveness need no longer seek out or enter into solidarity with their victims but need only deal directly with God. Yet, as the liberationists remind us, there is no reconciliation with God that does not pass through this world, a world littered with the crosses of the crucified people. Reconciliation with God does not happen apart from reconciliation with humanity. In other words, God does not shoulder aside the victims to pronounce an empty and formal acquittal on the oppressors.[147] On the contrary, it is precisely the crucified people gathered in the Church of the poor who extend God's gracious forgiveness to oppressors. Christ neither replaces the victims as this objection suggests nor is he replaced by them as this objection fears. Rather, Christ stands with the victims. Hence, victimizers can penitentially turn toward their victims, seeking reconciliation, because of the hope that in such an encounter Christ is indeed present, enacting his judgment of grace, releasing desire from its captivity to sin, enabling reconciliation.[148]

The same difficulty confronts the claim that the Church can forgive sin on behalf of others. Insofar as the Church is the Church of the crucified people, it can enact the forgiveness of the sin that afflicts the crucified people. Insofar as the Church is indeed constituted by the victims, it can extend forgiveness and reconciliation can occur.[149] But the Church cannot enact forgiveness and seek reconciliation by proxy. The Church, for example, cannot forgive on behalf of his victim, the Guatemalan soldier who is not a Christian for torturing an indigenous organizer who worships traditional Mayan gods. If the Church did pronounce forgiveness, it would be hollow, for sin was not overcome and reconciliation was not effected between victim and victimizer. It would be an example of the forgiveness that the liberationists rightly fear. More than this, it would be yet another example of the Church silencing the victims and revealing its own distance from the Christ who stands with the victims. In this situation, when confronted with the sin of "third parties" as it were, the Church should proclaim the good news of the gift of forgiveness and facilitate its enactment. Indeed, as the prior account of the therapy of forgiveness suggests, even the Church's offer of forgiveness for the ways in which the actions of that soldier fractured communion with Christians would entail the soldier's turning to his victim and seeking reconciliation.

The liberationists challenge proponents of forgiveness to show how forgiveness is more than a theological pacification program. What prevents the refusal to cease suffering that is forgiveness from being nothing but the refusal to cease suffering? How does the therapy of forgiveness enacted by the crucified people liberate desire? Beginning with their own account of the crucified people gathered in the Church of the poor, I have argued that what may distinguish the crucified people's enactment of the gift of forgiveness as a form of resistance to capitalist discipline is the presence of three technologies of desire – confession, repentance, and penance – that liberate desire from the agony of capitalist discipline by conforming desire to the gift of Christ, that is, by renewing and reforming desire in the modality of donation, of gift. There is one more stroke to my argument, but before taking it up, the lingering issue of justice bears consideration.

The redemption of justice

The heart of my argument is the claim that forgiveness is the form of Christian resistance to capitalism. To advance this claim, I have pitted forgiveness against the liberationists' conception of justice as a guardian of rights. Does this mean that justice has been banished from the Christian life? Along the way, I have hinted that this cannot be so. After all, as the liberationists rightly remind us, justice has far too prominent a position in Scripture and the tradition to be discarded. Indeed, it is precisely its dismissal that has contributed to the ongoing crucifixion of so many for so long under the sign of the cross. The therapy of forgiveness, therefore, does not entail expunging justice from the Christian life. Rather, it calls for a conception of justice other than the liberationists' (modern) account of justice as the guarantor of rights. Forgiveness, one might say, redeems justice.

This redemption begins with repositioning justice within the aneconomic order of the divine gift of forgiveness. Although this move is suggested by several liberationists, only Elsa Tamez consistently carries it through. She argues that justice is a consequence and not a condition of God's grace. Humanity, she holds, does not earn redemption by fulfilling the precepts of justice; on the contrary, salvation comes through faith in Christ, whose death and resurrection manifest God's displacement of justice with grace and forgiveness. As a consequence of Christ's atonement, humanity is empowered to do justice. As Tamez writes:

> Incorporated into the new logic of the Spirit, whoever has this faith forgets neither his or her past as a victim excluded by sin, nor the possibility that he or she too subjects others to exclusion. Such persons know that they have been accepted by God purely by the merciful solidarity of God, not because they are just. . . . When the solidarity of the Triune God – as friend and as brother or sister – is received by faith, this presence of God through the Spirit turns into a permanent critical appeal to conscience in the paths of justice.[150]

Having received the Spirit, those who have been forgiven are animated to set forth on the path of justice. Justice does not, as the liberationists suggest, set things right and then forgiveness steps in to squelch the flames of vengeance and resentment. On the contrary, it is forgiveness that sets things right, and then in the soil that forgiveness has prepared, justice blossoms. Forgiveness is the condition of possibility for justice.

Yet if this justice is to avoid immediately submerging humanity in the terror that haunts justice as the guarantor of rights, it is not sufficient that justice be positioned within the aneconomic order of grace; it must also be reconceived as something other than an essentially distributive operation that secures rights and mediates the clash of proprietary desire. After all, merely reversing the liberationists' preference for justice over forgiveness only postpones the onset of the terror that plagues justice and ensures that its efforts to resist capitalism fail. Therefore, the redemption of justice calls for a justice beyond justice, a justice that is neither recognizable to the progenitors of the classic conception of *suum cuique* nor assimilable with the modern discourse of rights.

Actually, we might call this alternative a justice before justice because its roots can be found in the biblical tradition. Indicative of the tension and ambiguity that attends their work on matters of justice and forgiveness, even as the liberationists cast justice as a matter of distributing goods in accord with the modern logic of rights, they acknowledge that the biblical witness concerning justice transcends such a conception. For example, Sobrino makes the following observation about the practice of Jesus:

> . . . we can say that the basic value of Jesus is doing justice. But here we should not understand it as retributive or vindictive justice designed to give all persons and situations what is due them by virtue of what they are. Justice is meant here in the Old Testament sense. It is the liberation of Israel. Yahweh is just, not because he gives all their due, but because he tries to re-create human beings and situations, to "save" them.[151]

The biblical understanding of justice cannot be reduced to a matter of rendering what is due nor is it primarily a matter of protecting rights against encroachment by the community and others. Rather, justice is fundamentally a matter of recreation and reconciliation, of living in communion and love.[152] Consequently, says González Faus, the traditional understanding of justice as "rendering what is due" must be radically transformed.[153] Prior to its christological transformation, justice as the pursuit of what is due mediates what are essentially impoverished and agonistic relations between persons: persons approach one another as either wolves feeding on or supreme beings warding off each other. Yet with the advent of Jesus as the justice of God, justice sheds its battledress and becomes subservient to genuine community between human beings.

These insights, unfortunately, are not sustained; eventually the liberationists corral them into line with their conception of justice as the guarantor of rights. Nevertheless, such comments do gesture in several ways toward a more promising notion of justice, one that transcends the endless struggle of proprietary desire for what is due in accord with its rights. First, they suggest that justice flows from God's redeeming activity in the world. In this sense there can be no opposition between justice and forgiveness; they are but two names of the single love of God that desires to draw humanity into communion. Justice and forgiveness are not opposing logics; rather they share a single end – the return of all love, the sociality of all desire, in God. Justice attains its end by enacting forgiveness to overcome sin. Forgiveness overcomes sin to attain its true end, which is justice. In this way, forgiveness implements perfect justice (Aquinas) and the rule of God's justice is forgiveness (Anselm).[154]

Besides gesturing toward the dissolution of the opposition between justice and forgiveness, the liberationists' insights suggest that an alternative conception would cast justice as a matter of sustaining the sociality of love, the communion of desire in God. This redeemed or perfect justice is about fidelity to a relationship.[155] It is not principally a matter of calculating and distributing what is due; rather, it is concerned with maintaining the unity that God establishes with and among humanity as humanity is liberated from sin. In other words, redeemed justice nurtures desire in such a way that once it has been liberated from sin, it continues to flow as it was created to do, as ceaseless generosity in harmony with others in the communion of the divine life. Justice nurtures the conviviality of desire; it sustains the friendship of humanity in God.

In this sense, justice that has been redeemed recovers the meaning of Aquinas' general virtue of justice in that it is fundamentally a principle of unity. It seeks to maintain communion by fostering cooperation in the pursuit of holiness, by nurturing solidarity in a common good much more substantial than anything modern rights language, even when theologically fortified, presupposes. Whereas modern rights narratives presuppose no shared conception of the good beyond the recognition of rights, redeemed justice recovers the sense of Aquinas' general justice as rooted in a shared desire of God. Its deliberations are oriented by a common love (dare I say worship?), not by calculations of what is due persons by virtue of their rights in the absence of a shared love. Redeemed justice is not a matter of protecting the rights of strangers but of nurturing the communion of saints.

This redeemed justice also includes within its purview distributive and commutative operations, which are forms of rendering what is due.[156] Yet such commutative and distributive operations function to maintain the communion in love. That is, the rendering of what is due is always determined in accord with what, under the impact of the Spirit, is discerned best to promote the communion of humanity in divine love. This is to say, the redemption of justice effects the transformation of the meaning of *suum cuique*. No longer is rendering what is due a matter of the division of resources among rivalrous desires; rather, it is about the arrangement of the resources of life in such a way that the divine donation of love that is desire continues to flow, ever intensifying the conviviality that is the communion of humanity in God.

In other words, as it is adapted by Christianity, *suum cuique* is transformed from a logic of debt, equivalence, and retribution to a logic of liturgy. Augustine argued that Christianity embodied the true politics because unlike pagan Rome, it alone worshipped the triune God. It alone was a truly just community because only it offered God the sacrifice of worship, praise, and obedience that was due God. And of course this is *not* because Christians are somehow able to fulfill the classic canons of *suum cuique* where pagans are not, but because Christians are incorporated into Christ, who through his donation of love to the Father transforms the operation of *suum cuique* by an act of substitution or recapitulation that miraculously (which is to say, graciously) renders the impossible possible, namely our praise and worship of God. As God in Christ bears the burden of sin, the classic logic of *suum cuique* explodes as the divine refusal to render unto sinners what is due sin ironically creates the possibility that they may now return to the fold of perfect justice, where God is duly worshipped.

At this point, the complementarity of redeemed justice with the therapy of forgiveness is readily apparent. This complementarity, however, is not necessarily benevolent. After all, such a reconceptualization of justice renders it susceptible to the same vulnerabilities that attend forgiveness. Perhaps all that this so-called redemption has accomplished is the evisceration of justice. Perhaps this justice, by renouncing rights and refusing a strict accounting of what is due in accord with the modern logic of rights, only strips those who suffer under savage capitalism of the few feeble defenses they have. Is it possible that this justice, and the forgiveness that accompanies it, only tighten the coils of the serpent around desire? To this disturbing possibility we now turn.

The refusal to cease suffering: the risk of forgiveness

When viewed from a certain angle, my argument has made strikingly little progress. I began by asserting that forgiveness is the Christian form of resistance to capitalism, and a couple hundred pages later, I am really no closer to proving this claim than when I began. For all of the ink spilt in the analysis of contemporary capitalism, in exposing the futility of justice as the guarantor of rights and the limitations of the Latin American liberationists' revolutionary vision, in presenting the Church of the poor as an embodiment of the therapy of forgiveness, doubt lingers. Hinkelammert's query continues to prick the conscience, ¿Capitalismo sin alternativas? The question remains, does forgiveness really underwrite resistance to capitalism? The nagging suspicion is that it does not. As Sobrino notes, "It may seem to some readers, rightly enough, that the language of 'mercy' is too soft, even too dangerous, an expression of what the crucified people need."[157]

The therapy of forgiveness does indeed appear too soft, even dangerous. I have referred to it as "the refusal to cease suffering" because it expects the victims of injustice to forego certain means of overcoming that suffering – namely, justice as the guarantor of rights and the violence to enforce it – and can there be any doubt that foregoing such means is tantamount to a refusal to cease suffering? Therefore, insofar as forgiveness funds Christian resistance to capitalism, it is an odd and risk-laden form of resistance. It is an odd and risk-laden form of resistance because it is haunted by the possibility, always lying in wait just over the horizon, that forgiveness really is nothing more than the refusal to cease suffering. This abiding uncertainty, the possibility that forgiveness is ultimately *only* a refusal to cease suffering, constitutes the risk of forgiveness, which is the focus of this final section. My goal here, however, is not the futile one of attempting to "theorize away" the uncertainty and risk that currently attends the therapy of forgiveness enacted by the Church of the poor. This risk is impervious to theoretical reduction and for the time being must simply be endured, which is to say that there is nothing that can be said that will mitigate the uncertainty that envelops forgiveness.[158] All I can do is clarify the nature of this risk in the hopes that it remains a risk, uncertain, as yet undecided. In other words, if a theoretical display such as this cannot prove that the refusal to cease suffering that is forgiveness is not ultimately just a refusal to cease suffering, it can nevertheless labor to see that the question remains open, that the contrary conclusion – that forgiveness is not capable of generating and sustaining resistance – is not prematurely (which is to say, theoretically) pronounced.

Toward this end, I begin by distinguishing the suffering that is the refusal to cease suffering that is forgiveness, from suffering that is sheer resignation. Specifically, I identify what distinguishes forgiveness as resistance from the mere disempowerment of victims and endorsement of suffering. In essence, I defend the therapy of forgiveness by suggesting that Christianity embeds the crucified people in a way of life that, if true, not only renders the refusal to cease suffering intelligible, but redemptive. Of course, this defense remains a formal one and hence does not dispel the risk. Therefore, I conclude by suggesting on what the truth of forgiveness as the Christian form of resistance to capitalism ultimately turns and how that truth will be decided.

Disempowerment or a crucified power?

The liberationists' analysis of forgiveness suggested that it runs the risk of disempowering victims. Insofar as it expects the crucified people to forego the justice of asserting their rights, this certainly appears to be the case. Yet, if, as Ellacuría suggested earlier, the Church of the poor is not just another worldly power but rather embodies a different kind of power, then appearances may be misleading.

At the heart of the therapy of forgiveness lies the conviction that sin, and the unjust suffering that is a consequence of sin, are defeated precisely by its being borne. Reflecting on the cross, Sobrino observes that "what God's suffering makes clear in a history of suffering is that between the alternatives of accepting suffering by sublimating it and eliminating it from the outside we can and must introduce a new course, bearing it."[159] The gift of forgiveness is precisely resistance as the bearing of sin. It is the incarnation of the truth that Christianity liberates desire from capitalism not simply by opposing its destructive force with an equally destructive force but rather by meeting it with a refusal, a refusal to cease suffering by shifting that suffering on to others by embracing the terror of justice.

This refusal is costly. For the crucified people it entails renouncing the power of justice as the guarantor of rights, and for the forgiven oppressor it entails renouncing the power of privilege by entering into solidarity with the crucified people.

The cost of forgiveness is nothing less than the deliberate setting aside of claims and instruments that are usually invoked in the name of warding off suffering and combatting sin.

This renunciation, however, is not synonymous with disempowering the victims of injustice. As the liberationists note, forgiveness has too often been distorted into a counsel of passivity and fatalism. Too frequently those submerged in repressive and violent situations are admonished to forgive in "Christian love," patiently and (preferably) quietly, enduring the torments of their oppressors instead of rebelling. Yet the therapy of forgiveness that the crucified people embody, while unquestionably requiring patience and endurance, is not an instance of long-suffering resignation. On the contrary, it is the form of resistance that is taken by a different kind of power, a crucified power. It is the resistance to sin offered by a power-in-vulnerability,[160] by a desire that exists in the mode of donation, of sheer generosity, and, hence, ceaselessly desires to embrace the enemy and renew communion. The crucified people's offer of forgiveness marks the advent of a different kind of appeal to overcome sin. The appeal to a justice erected on a logic of rights and backed up by whatever force can be mustered is replaced with the appeal of renewed communion and harmony between peoples in the divine life. Granted, this may not appear to be a particularly potent form of resistance, but the weakness of forgiveness' power or, more accurately, the power of weakness that is forgiveness, should not be equated with the disempowerment that shadows calls for forgiveness and reconciliation devoid of the judgment of grace.

Furthermore, on account of its intrinsic connection with the agency of the crucified people, the cruciform power that is forgiveness ought to be distinguished from discourses that disempower victims. The appeal to the forgiving power of God advanced here does not originate in a Church comfortably situated within the status quo, nor does it amount to a plea by oppressors to the oppressed for mercy. On the contrary, the crucified power that is forgiveness emanates from the Church of the poor, from the margins and the excluded spaces of savage capitalism. Thus, what separates the therapy of forgiveness from discourses that inevitably and perhaps intentionally intensify the fatalistic resignation of those who suffer injustice is its inescapable connection with the agency of the crucified people gathered as the Church of the poor. Specifically, the therapy of forgiveness is founded on the merciful power of the God who in Christ underwent a partisan incarnation. It is an instantiation of the divine forgiveness that is made available by the poor Christ, the Christ found with and among the poor. The therapy of forgiveness, in other words, far from suppressing the agency of the crucified people, is intimately linked to those "who hardly anyone believed would be active subjects of social and political struggle."[161]

To the extent, and only to the extent, that the therapy of desire that is forgiveness is an instantiation of a crucified power intrinsically related to the crucified people gathered and empowered by God in Christ as protagonists in history, may it overcome the risk of disempowering victims.

Endorsing suffering or suffering against suffering?

Besides the risk of disempowering victims, forgiveness faces the risk of encouraging or at least endorsing suffering. To the extent that the therapy of forgiveness can be characterized as the refusal to cease suffering, this risk is patently obvious. Not so obvious is the way in which the therapy of forgiveness is an instantiation of suffering against suffering.

The therapy of forgiveness amounts to a refusal to cease suffering not only because it refuses certain resources in the struggle against capitalism, but also because it risks the intensification of suffering and even death. The effort to liberate desire from capitalist discipline by means of the therapy of forgiveness provokes repression and persecution. Just as the powers and principalities could not abide Christ's giving the gift of divine forgiveness, capitalism cannot tolerate the Church of the poor extending that gift to others, and so it moves immediately to reterritorialize the space that the Church of the poor has created and to discipline every desire that would escape its control. A Church that offers charity, that superficially tends to the wounds inflicted by capitalism, would be tolerated, but a Church that enters into the world of the crucified and names sin, facilitates the turning from sin, and fosters solidarity is met with strong action, as Sobrino observes in a reflection on the parable of the Good Samaritan:

> This world is ever ready to applaud, or at least tolerate, works of mercy. What this world will not tolerate is a church molded by the principle of mercy, which leads the church to denounce robbers who victimize, to lay bare the lie that conceals oppression, and to encourage victims to win their freedom from culprits. In other words, the robbers of this anti-merciful world tolerate the tending of wounds, but not the true healing of the wounded. . . . When the church does these things, it is threatened, assaulted, and persecuted.[162]

A Church that embodies mercy, that seeks to heal desire from the wounds of oppression, incurs the wrath of the capitalist regime. "The true people of God," wrote Ellacuría, "in a world dominated by sin cannot help but be persecuted, because as people of God it wants to be the negation of sin and the builder of a Reign that to a great extent is the negation of existing structures." He goes on to quote Archbishop Romero, "Christ invites us not to fear persecution, because, believe me, brothers and sisters, the one who is committed to the poor must share the same fate as the poor. And in El Salvador we already know what the fate of the poor means: to disappear, to be tortured, to be apprehended, to appear as corpses."[163] The bearing of sin that is forgiveness is not only a matter of laying aside the justice of rights; it involves actively taking up the cross, sharing the same fate that Christ did when he initiated the liberation of desire from all sin.

This, however, should not be misconstrued as an endorsement of suffering. The therapy of forgiveness enacted by the Church of the poor does not encourage the active pursuit of suffering and persecution. Indeed, the liberationists warn against confusing the liberating and redeeming task of the crucified people with a cult of suffering. Gutiérrez, for example, cautions that "amid all our admiration and respect for martyrdom we must not forget the cruelty that marks such an event, the abhorrence that the conditions giving rise to these murders should make us feel. Martyrdom is something that happens but is not sought."[164] Likewise, Sobrino asserts, "Christian spirituality . . . is not a spirituality of the cross or of suffering. It is a spirituality of honest, consistent, and faithful love – a wide-awake love that knows the necessary risks it is taking. Christian spirituality is the spirituality of a crucified love."[165] This crucified love does not seek out suffering; rather, it seeks the suffering in order to restore communion. Desire that has been liberated does not seek to be wounded; rather, it reaches out to those who wound in the hopes of joining them in the circle of charity that is the divine life. Far from encouraging suffering, the therapy of forgiveness struggles against unjust suffering. It is a matter of, in the words of Leonardo Boff, "suffering born of the struggle against suffering."[166] The therapy of forgiveness is about entering into suffering, bearing it, in the hope of bearing it away.

For this reason, the refusal to cease suffering that is the therapy of forgiveness cannot rightly be construed as attributing redemptive significance to suffering. The suffering of the crucified people and those who enter into solidarity with them is not beneficial. Oppression and crucifixion, Javier Jiménez Limón reminds us, neither liberate nor redeem.[167] The redemptive power of the therapy of forgiveness resides not in the suffering itself but in the gracious generosity and vulnerability to the one who is/was an enemy. Redemption is found in the embrace that breaks down the walls of hostility and reconciles crucified and crucifier. Any suffering incurred as a consequence of adopting this posture is exactly that: a contingent, historical consequence and not of the liberative and redemptive heart of God that gives rise to the posture that is forgiveness. That this redemptive power is crucified points not to the necessity of suffering as the path to reconciliation but to the stubborn persistence of sin and the brutal resilience of capitalism in producing both crosses and executioners, in distorting the joyous sociality of desire into agonistic rivalry. Furthermore, that the crucified people extend forgiveness is not an indication of their fatalistic embrace of a terrible fate, but a sign of hope that suffering will not prevail. That the Spirit continues to empower the Church of the poor to refuse to cease suffering is a sign that one day all the stones shall be rolled away and communion in love resurrected.

If and only if the therapy of desire that is forgiveness really is an instance of suffering signifying that suffering will be overcome does it circumvent the risk of amounting to nothing more than a sheer embrace of suffering.

A wager on God

The risk of forgiveness is that it only disempowers the Church of the poor and prolongs their suffering by depriving them of recourse to what is due. The risk of forgiveness is that it is not able to fund resistance to the capitalist order. The risk is that the refusal to cease suffering that is forgiveness is only a refusal to cease suffering. On the other hand, the therapy of desire that is forgiveness may fund resistance to capitalism. It may embody a crucified power that amounts to suffering against suffering. But how do we know if this is true? No theory can verify it.

Ultimately the refusal to cease suffering that is Christian forgiveness is an act of hope. The arguments advanced on behalf of forgiveness and the witness of the Church of the poor come down to this. The enormity of the suffering and sin that stains history precludes any stronger conclusion than that offered as hope.[168] There simply is no guarantee that forgiveness is ultimately anything more than a refusal to cease suffering.[169] It is possible that the crucified people are only a brilliant example of a misguided faith and love joined together in a futile effort to turn the tide of their own blood as it washes over history. It may well be the case that justice as *suum cuique* is the best that can be accomplished. The risk of forgiveness must simply be borne in patient hope that mercy will indeed triumph over sin and death.

The truth of the therapy of forgiveness as a form of resistance to capitalism, to echo Foucault, is in the future. It is in a future where the tears are wiped away, where those who are hungry now are filled, where those who build homes inhabit them and those who plant vineyards partake of their fruit. This is to say, the truthfulness of forgiveness as the Christian form of resistance to capitalism is contingent upon the consummation of redemption, when suffering will indeed cease. In this regard, Gutiérrez speaks of the need for the Gospel to be "veri-fied." By this he means that the Gospel becomes true as it actually happens in history.[170] Forgiveness as resistance, then, remains to be verified.

But this verification is not simply a matter of evaluating the effectiveness of Christian forgiveness in alleviating suffering and achieving reconciliation. Forgiveness is not first and foremost a tactic, like conflict resolution, for bringing people together.[171] This is the point of characterizing forgiveness as the refusal to cease suffering. While reconciliation is the goal of forgiveness, at times it may not prove very effective at attaining that goal and bringing suffering to an end. As suggested previously, it may only intensify the suffering as it provokes a hostile response that leads to persecution and martyrdom. At such times, the true politics that is the gift of forgiveness may amount to little more than surviving, maintaining the presence of grace that is the offer of the gift of forgiveness.[172] Forgiveness, therefore, is best characterized as a matter of how Christians live in the absence of reconciliation.[173]

How then is the therapy of forgiveness to be evaluated? That it cannot be evaluated on the basis of its immediate effect shifts the burden of truth to its foundation: the divine gift of forgiveness. The therapy of forgiveness is anchored in the conviction that God has acted decisively in Jesus Christ to liberate desire from sin and that that victory is now being enacted by Christ's Spirit. Hence, the therapy of forgiveness is not foremost a tactic to resolve conflict, but is fundamentally a matter of witness. The therapy of desire that is Christian forgiveness is not simply one of a handful of social strategies the Church has at its disposal for the sake of reducing conflict; rather, it is primarily a witness to God and what God in Christ is doing in the world to overcome sin. Christians forgive as a witness to the God who is acting in history to halt the suffering of sin and liberate desire from all that would inter-rupt the flow of charity precisely by forgiving. The refusal to cease suffering that is forgiveness is ultimately an act of hope in God. Forgiveness, in other words, is a wager on God. In a reflection on the Book of Job, Gutiérrez observes that God has made a wager on humanity. "In sending his Son," he writes, "the Father 'wagered' on the possibility of a faith and behavior characterized by gratuitousness and by a response to the demand that justice be established. When history's 'losers' . . . follow in the steps of Jesus, they are seeing to it that the Lord wins his wager."[174] With regard to the therapy of forgiveness this insight can be inverted. When his-tory's losers, the crucified people, follow in the steps of Jesus and forgive their enemies, they are wagering on God. They are wagering that God is who the Gospel proclaims God to be, the one who defeats sin and wipes away every tear, not with the sword of a justice that upholds rights but with the gift of forgiveness in Christ.

Fukuyama and his neoconservative cohorts can declare that history has attained its end with the triumph of capitalism because the true end of history remains momentarily fugitive. Although the tomb is empty, the Lamb who was slain has yet to return in final victory. In the meantime, the crucified people, awaiting his return and the consummation of the judgment of grace, refuse to cease suffering.

Notes

1 It is perhaps worth reiterating a point I made earlier, namely that the claims I advance here for Christianity and now more specifically, about Christ, need not eclipse God's work in Israel. Christ's work, for example, is only rightly understood in the context of Yahweh the Triune God. For more on this way of characterizing the Trinity, see R. Kendall Soulen, "YHWH the Triune God," *Modern Theology* 15 (1999): 25–54.

2 Note that I do not mean to preclude the possibility that God acts beyond the borders of Christian communities. Here I am in agreement with the liberationists in rejecting any "ecclesiocentrism" that would confine God's activity in history to the Christian Church.

3 Christian Duquoc, "The Forgiveness of God," *Concilium* 184 (1986): 35.

4 The classic example is Gustaf Aulén, *Christus Victor* (Eugene, OR: Wipf and Stock, 1998). For a Latin American reading, see Franz Hinkelammert, *Sacrificios Humanos y Sociedad Occidental* (San José: DEI, 1998), 69–86.

5 What follows draws heavily on D. Bentley Hart, "A Gift Exceeding Every Debt: An Eastern Orthodox Appreciation of Anselm's *Cur Deus Homo*," *Pro Ecclesia* 7 (1993): 333–349; as well as John Milbank's unpublished essay, "Forgiveness and Incarnation." See also, Hans Urs Von Balthasar, *The Glory of the Lord II: Studies in Theological Style: Clerical Styles* (San Francisco: Ignatius Press, 1984), 211–259.

6 Hart, 348.

7 Ibid.

8 Duquoc, "The Forgiveness of God," 39.

9 Ibid., 40.

10 Jon Sobrino, *The Principle of Mercy* (Maryknoll, NY: Orbis Books, 1994), 63–64.

11 Gutiérrez, *A Theology of Liberation*, rev. ed. trans. Caridad Inda and John Eagleson (Maryknoll, NY: Orbis Books, 1988), 24.

12 Clodovis Boff provides a poignant example of this when he recounts meeting a bishop in one of the more impoverished regions of Brazil. The bishop, he said, was distraught and upon being questioned told Boff of his recent encounter on the steps of the cathedral with a woman who was accompanied by three small children and a baby clinging to her neck. The bishop saw that the children were fainting from hunger and the baby appeared dead so he encouraged the woman to give the baby some milk. When she replied that she could not and the bishop insisted, the woman opened her blouse. "Her breast was bleeding; the baby sucked violently at it. And sucked blood. The mother who had given it life was feeding it, like the pelican, with her own blood, her own life." See Leonardo Boff and Clodovis Boff, *Introducing Liberation Theology*, trans. Paul Burns (Maryknoll, NY: Orbis Books, 1987), 1–2.

13 For more on "donation" as a mode of being, see John Milbank, "Can a Gift be Given? Prolegomena to a Future Trinitarian Metaphysic," *Modern Theology* 11 (1995): 119–161. See also Nicholas Lash, *Believing Three Ways in One God* (Notre Dame: University of Notre Dame Press, 1993), 91–106; John Milbank, "Stories of Sacrifice," *Modern Theology* 12 (1996): 27–56.

14 Franz J. Hinkelammert, "Economía y Teología: Las Leyes del Mercado y la Fe," *Pasos* 23 (1989): 1–10. It should be noted that capitalism can handle (commodify) those forms of forgiveness, quite popular today, that do not, in fact, amount to a rejection of the proprietary logic that sustains capitalism.

15 Leonardo Boff, *The Lord's Prayer*, trans. Theodore Morrow (Maryknoll, NY: Orbis Books, 1983).

16 Because Latin American liberation theology is not monolithic, there are exceptions. José Miranda, for example, sees little but destruction for oppressors. See his *Marx and the Bible*, trans. John Eagleson (Maryknoll, NY: Orbis Books, 1974), 83, 96, 128.

17 Leonardo Boff, *Way of the Cross – Way of Justice*, trans. John Drury (Maryknoll, NY: Orbis Books, 1980), 54–55.

18 Gustavo Gutiérrez, *On Job*, trans. Matthew J. O'Connell (Maryknoll, NY: Orbis Books, 1987), 87–88. For an important critique of Gutiérrez's reading of Job, see Terrence Tilley, *The Evils of Theodicy* (Washington, DC: Georgetown University Press, 1991), 99–102.

19 Gustavo Gutiérrez, *The God of Life*, trans. Matthew J. O'Connell (Maryknoll, NY: Orbis Books, 1991), 39; Gustavo Gutiérrez, "Perdonar es dar vida," *Paginas* 13 (April 1988): 8.

20 Gutiérrez, "Perdonar es dar vida," 6–7.

21 Gustavo Gutiérrez, "Peru: An Interview with Gustavo Gutiérrez," *LADOC* 19 (September/October 1988): 25.

22 José Ignacio González Faus, "Justicia" in *Conceptos Fundamentales de Pastoral*, eds. Casiano Floristan and Juan-José Tamayo (Madrid: Ediciones Cristiandad, 1983), 522; see also Rafael Aguirre and Francisco Javier Vitoria Cormenzana, "Justicia," in *Mysterium Liberationis: conceptos fundamentales de la teología de la liberación*, eds. Ignacio Ellacuría and Jon Sobrino (Madrid: Editorial Trotta, 1990), 576–577.

23 Segundo Galilea, "Liberation Theology and the New Tasks Facing Christians," in *Frontiers of Theology in Latin America*, ed. Rosino Gibellini (Maryknoll, NY: Orbis Books, 1979), 176 (italics in original).

24 Elsa Tamez, *The Amnesty of Grace*, trans. Sharon H. Ringe (Nashville: Abingdon Press, 1993), 160, 162.

25 Jon Sobrino, *Spirituality of Liberation*, trans. Robert R. Barr (Maryknoll, NY: Orbis Books, 1988), 121.

26 Jon Sobrino, *Jesus in Latin America* (Maryknoll, NY: Orbis Books, 1987), 123.

27 Jon Sobrino, *The Principle of Mercy*, 90–91.

28 I call this a charitable reading because Gutiérrez does not actually mention forgiveness. He mentions grace, which may or may not be the equivalent of forgiveness.
29 Gutiérrez, *On Job*, 91.
30 Sobrino, *The Principle of Mercy*, 60–61.
31 Ibid., 61.
32 Ibid., 64–65.
33 Ibid., 65.
34 Ibid.
35 Kyle Pasewark, "Remembering to forget: A politics of forgiveness," *Christian Century*, 112 (July 5–12, 1995): 684.
36 This last point, the surrender of vengeance, should not be dismissed lightly. Indeed, it is no small accomplishment and would provide the liberationists' account of forgiveness some standing were it not traditionally understood as justice's raison d'être.
37 Juan Luis Segundo, *Signs of the Times: Theological Reflections*, ed. Alfred T. Hennelly, trans. Robert R. Barr (Maryknoll, NY: Orbis Books, 1993), 47 (italics in original).
38 Gutiérrez, *The God of Life*, 126.
39 Ignacio Ellacuría, "Violence and Non-Violence in the Struggle for Peace and Liberation," *Concilium* 195 (1988): 73.
40 Juan Hernández Pico, "Revolución, Violencia, y Paz," in *Mysterium Liberationis: conceptos fundamentales de la teología de la liberación*, eds. Ignacio Ellacuría and Jon Sobrino (Madrid: Editorial Trotta, 1990), 602. The mention of "open veins" is a reference to the famous work by Eduardo Galleano, *The Open Veins of Latin America*, trans. Cedric Belfrage (New York: Monthly Review Press, 1973). Translation is mine.
41 Hugo Assmann, *Theology for a Nomad Church*, trans. Paul Burns (Maryknoll, NY: Orbis Books, 1976), 98.
42 Tamez, *The Amnesty of Grace*, 19–24.
43 José Comblin, *Liberación y Reconciliación* (Chile: CESOC, 1987), 61.
44 The Central American Kairos Document, signed in April 1988 by members of the various Churches in Central America, aptly reflects Comblin's point: "In Central America we frequently hear calls to reconciliation made by the Churches who seem to place themselves above the parties in the conflict, appealing to love and to Christian brotherhood and sisterhood. Such calls seem at first glance to be very Christian, but if we seek to come to a careful spiritual understanding, we find that they are not. . . . The Central American conflict is played out between a violent and heavily armed oppressor and the helpless majorities who have been oppressed and massacred for centuries. It is a conflict that can be described only in terms of a struggle between justice and injustice, good and evil, life and death. In this context the idea of reconciling good with evil not only represents a misapplication of the Christian idea of reconciliation, it is also a twisting of the Christian faith. Our duty is to put an end to evil injustice, oppression, and sin, not to come to an agreement with them. We must not reconcile good with evil, life with death. . . . The peace that the world offers is a 'reconciliation' that covers up injustice and oppression. Real peace is the outcome of justice, not the result of arrangements negotiated with injustice" (§80–82). The text is found in Carmelo Alvarez, *People of Hope* (New York: Friendship Press, 1990), 79–106.
45 Comblin, *Liberación y Reconciliación*, 63. Translation is mine.
46 Gustavo Gutiérrez, "Shame," *LADOC* 26 (November/December 1995): 24.
47 Communio, "Declaration of Los Andes," in *Liberation Theology: A Documentary History*, ed. Alfred T. Hennelly (Maryknoll, NY: Orbis Books, 1990), 449.
48 Ronaldo Muñoz, "An Open Letter to Cardinal Alfonso López Trujillo," in *Liberation Theology: A Documentary History*, ed. Alfred T. Hennelly (Maryknoll, NY: Orbis Books, 1990), 452. Note that this was not an official Church document of any kind. However, given the way it was released, the spokesperson for the Chilean episcopacy felt the

need to go on the public record stating that the declaration had nothing to do with the Chilean episcopacy.

49 Ibid.

50 I have been greatly aided by the lengthy treatments of forgiveness developed in L. Gregory Jones, *Embodying Forgiveness* (Grand Rapids, MI: William B. Eerdmans Publishing Co., 1995); Miroslav Volf, *Exclusion and Embrace* (Nashville: Abingdon Press, 1996); and Rowan Williams, *Resurrection* (Harrisburg, PA: Morehouse Publishing, 1982).

51 Gustavo Gutiérrez, *The Power of the Poor in History*, trans. Robert R. Barr (Maryknoll, NY: Orbis Books, 1983), 57.

52 For an example of a plea for forgiveness based on the necessity of the preservation of society, see Donald Shriver, *An Ethic for Enemies* (New York: Oxford University Press, 1995).

53 For an example, see Lewis Smedes, *Forgive and Forget: Healing the Hurts We Don't Deserve* (New York: Harper & Row, 1984).

54 Indeed, forgiveness probably is not the most effective means of defeating capitalism, if one were unconcerned with what emerged in its place.

55 Robert J. Schreiter, *Reconciliation* (Maryknoll, NY: Orbis Books, 1992), 43–45.

56 Sobrino, *The Principle of Mercy*, 90.

57 Ibid., 92, 89; Jon Sobrino, *Christology at the Crossroads*, trans. John Drury (Maryknoll, NY: Orbis Books, 1978), 55–57; Jon Sobrino, *Jesus the Liberator*, trans. Paul Burns and Francis McDonagh (Maryknoll, NY: Orbis Books, 1993), 95–97.

58 See Jones, *Embodying Forgiveness*, 101–134.

59 The real question is, "Why does it appear that the gift of forgiveness can be rejected?" But, of course, the answer to this question is the mystery of iniquity, which is not a mystery at all, but rather a surd.

60 James McClendon, *Systematic Theology: Ethics* (Nashville: Abingdon Press, 1986), 227.

61 For the text of Romero's homily see "Homilía de Monseñor Oscar A. Romero, Arzobisop de San Salvador en Aguilares (19 de Junio de 1977)," *Estudios Centroamericanos* 344 (1977): 431–433.

62 Sobrino, *The Principle of Mercy*, 50.

63 Ibid., 51. See also Jon Sobrino, "Los pobres: crucificado y salvadores," in *La Matanza de Los Pobres*, by María López and Jon Sobrino (Madrid: Ediciones HOAC, 1993), 361.

64 Ignacio Ellacuría, "Discernir 'el signo' de los tiempos," *Diakonia* 17 (1981): 58. Translation is mine.

65 What follows draws from Ellacuría, "The Crucified People," 593–599; Sobrino, *The Principle of Mercy*, 51–53; and Sobrino, *Jesus the Liberator*, 254–271. All biblical references are to the NRSV text of Isaiah.

66 Sobrino, *Jesus the Liberator*, 256–257.

67 Ibid., 258.

68 Gutiérrez, *The Power of the Poor in History*, 22.

69 Sobrino, *The Principle of Mercy*, 70, 79; Sobrino, *Jesus the Liberator*, 260–261.

70 Ignacio Ellacuría, "Quinto Centenario de América Latina, ¿descubrimiento o encubrimiento?" *Revista Latinamericana de Teología* 7 (1990): 278. Translation is mine.

71 Sobrino, *The Principle of Mercy*, 79–80; cf. 56.

72 Ibid., 63.

73 Ibid., 98. For another example see The Amanecida Collective, *Revolutionary Forgiveness: Feminist Reflections on Nicaragua* (Maryknoll, NY: Orbis Books, 1987), 80–110.

74 Sobrino, *Jesus in Latin America*, 160.

75 Williams, *Resurrection*, 84.

76 Sobrino, *Jesus in Latin America*, 164.

77 Ellacuría, "The Crucified People," 553.

78 See Gustavo Gutiérrez, *A Theology of Liberation*, xxvi; Sobrino, *Spirituality of Liberation*, 123.

79 Sobrino, *Jesus in Latin America*, 165.

80 Ellacuría, "The Crucified People," 592. Of course, the universality of sin does not legitimate a leveling of sin that would allow the oppressors off the hook on the grounds that the oppressed are sinners too. This is why the liberationists continue to use the categories. See also Volf, *Exclusion and Embrace*, 82f.

81 In this regard, Sobrino is instructive when he writes, "Always and everywhere, many different classes of wounds, physical and spiritual, cry out for healing. Their size and depth vary by definition, and mercy must re-act to cure them all. However, the Church must not succumb to a reckless universalization here, as if all cries expressed the same wound." *The Principle of Mercy*, 22.

82 Sobrino, *The Principle of Mercy*, 81.

83 Quoted in Sobrino, *The Principle of Mercy*, 81.

84 In what follows it is not possible to display the technologies enacted by the Church of the poor in the same detail that attends an account of the Cistercians. There are several reasons for this. Not much work has been done in this area. Sobrino's account is the most extensive treatment to date of the Church of the poor's offer of forgiveness. Second, for various and sundry reasons, the Church of the poor does not keep written records of their life together like the Cistercians did. Third, and perhaps most importantly, the Church of the poor is not as centralized and thus much more diverse than the Cistercians. Hence, it is more difficult to generalize. For example, some of the poor Christian communities have frequent contact with priests and religious, while others may rely on a delegate of the Word and only see a priest once a year. Still other communities may not even have delegates of the Word. As a consequence, it is not hard to imagine that there will be a tremendous diversity in the way forgiveness is enacted, with some communities relying more heavily on formal, sacramental means and others developing more localized and informal technologies.

85 Sobrino, *The Principle of Mercy*, 95.

86 José Comblin, "Grace," in *Mysterium Liberationis: Fundamental Concepts of Liberation Theology*, eds. Ignacio Ellacuría and Jon Sobrino (Maryknoll, NY: Orbis Books, 1993), 528.

87 Note that this does not in any way foreclose on the eschatological dimension of judgment. For more on this see Miroslav Volf, "The Final Reconciliation: Reflections on a Social Dimension of the Eschatological Transition," *Modern Theology* 16 (2000): 98; David Brown, "No Heaven Without Purgatory," *Religious Studies* 21 (1985): 447–456.

88 Ibid., 210; Sobrino, *Jesus in Latin America*, 149, 151.

89 Ibid., 135.

90 Boff, *Way of the Cross – Way of Justice*, 29.

91 Tamez, *The Amnesty of Grace*, 161.

92 Sobrino, *Jesus the Liberator*, 231; Sobrino, *Christology at the Crossroads*, 213.

93 Sobrino, *Christology at the Crossroads*, 183.

94 See Sobrino, *Spirituality of Liberation*, 13–22.

95 Ignacio Martín-Baró, "Reparations and Democracy," in *Towards a Society that Serves its People*, eds. John Hassett and Hugh Lacy (Washington, DC: Georgetown University Press, 1991), 140.

96 Segundo, *Signs of the Times*, 49 (italics in original).

97 Sobrino, *The Principle of Mercy*, 78. Note the way in which Sobrino easily slips from discussing the Church of the poor to poor persons in general to entities like "the North" and "the South" or the "First World" and the "Third World," a characteristic he shares with many liberationists. This is symptomatic of the fundamental weakness I have traced in the liberationists' work in the previous chapters – namely, they do not sufficiently attend to the ways in which both the coherence of particular discourses of justice and forgiveness as well as the viability of their enactment are dependent upon communities that share more substantial bonds than anything that unites the rich and

the poor, the First and Third Worlds, or the North and the South. In other words, because they reduce Christianity to a conglomeration of transcendental principles or values that are shared with all humans simply by virtue of their being human (which, as we recall from the second chapter, they theorize in terms of the dissolution of the traditional theological concept of "pure nature" and which they would distance from traditional forms of rationalism by locating the universal point of access not in the mind or reason but in the praxis of solidarity with the poor), they feel no need to restrain their speech by identifying it with particular communities or technologies of desire. That this is the case does not necessarily diminish the usefulness of the liberationists' observations and insights when those observations and insights are adapted to more modest speech, to speech that recognizes its dependence on a particular, substantive community.

98 Ibid., 78, 1.

99 Ibid., 5.

100 Ibid., 49, 70.

101 Ibid., 95; Jon Sobrino, "Companions of Jesus," in *Companions of Jesus*, by Jon Sobrino, Ignacio Ellacuría *et al.* (Maryknoll, NY: Orbis Books, 1990), 32.

102 Ibid., 55.

103 Ibid., 64. See also Volf, *Exclusion and Embrace*, 237–239.

104 Martín-Baró, "Reparations and Democracy," 138.

105 Ibid., 139.

106 Luis Peréz Aguirre, "Reconciliation and Forgiveness," *Fellowship* 64 (1998): 8.

107 Martín-Baró, "Reparations and Democracy," 138.

108 Ellacuría, "The Crucified People," 588.

109 Duquoc, "The Forgiveness of God," 41.

110 Foucault, it will be recalled, held that Christian confession was a sort of martyrdom, a sacrifice of the self. He could not conceive of confession as a matter of self-reception in a world that only exists in the mode of donation – through God's ceaseless giving. This is no doubt due to his embrace of the univocity of being, which precludes the possibility that identity is not self-contained (the underlying theme of Foucault's work being the ways in which this autonomous self has been captured throughout history) but could in fact be *given* and *received* through participatory relations of analogous being.

111 L. Gregory Jones, "Behold, I Make All Things New," in *God and the Victim*, ed. Lisa Barnes Lampman (Grand Rapids, MI: William B. Eerdmans, 1999), 173–176.

112 While redemption entails remembering now, eschatologically it may well involve not forgetting, but the divine gift of non-remembering. This is so because time and memory only persist via participation in the divine and evil, which as a lack does not participate in divinity, will pass. It will not be remembered. For this reason I spoke of injustice as irreversible but not indelible. It cannot be undone, but its mark will not always be present, its effect always be felt. Eschatologically, the tears will be wiped away (Isaiah 25:8). To make evil indelible and therefore eternally remembered, would be to take sin *too* seriously, just as forgetting *now* fails to take sin seriously enough. For more on this, see Jones, "Behold, I Make All Things New," and Milbank, "Forgiveness and Incarnation."

113 Sobrino, *The Principle of Mercy*, 58.

114 As the current popularity of confession suggests, the disclosure of sin is not intrinsically oppositional to capitalism. On the contrary, from the proliferation of "true confession" phone lines and "tell-all" autobiographies, to the ubiquitous talk shows, solemn press conferences, and remorseful interviews, confession and disclosure may be quite profitable.

115 Roberto Oliveros Maqueo, "History of the Theology of Liberation," in *Mysterium Liberationis: Fundamental Concepts of Liberation Theology*, eds. Ignacio Ellacuría and Jon Sobrino (Maryknoll, NY: Orbis Books, 1993), 9.

116 Sobrino, *Christology at the Crossroads*, 57–59.

117 Sobrino, *The Principle of Mercy*, 63.

118 Duquoc, "The Forgiveness of God," 42.

119 Gutiérrez, *A Theology of Liberation*, 118; Gustavo Gutiérrez, *The Truth Shall Make You Free*, trans. Matthew J. O'Connell (Maryknoll, NY: Orbis Books, 1990), 5, 56.

120 Gutiérrez, "Perdonar es dar vida," 9.

121 Sobrino, *The Principle of Mercy*, 96.

122 González Faus quoted in Sobrino, *The Principle of Mercy*, 66. See also 96–97.

123 Sobrino, *Christology at the Crossroads*, 57.

124 Sobrino, *The Principle of Mercy*, 66.

125 Ibid.

126 Gustavo Gutiérrez, *Sharing the Word Through the Liturgical Year*, trans. Colette Joly Dees (Maryknoll, NY: Orbis Books, 1997), 65.

127 Martín-Baró, "Reparations and Democracy," 140.

128 Aguirre, "Reconciliation and Forgiveness," 8.

129 Cited in Gustavo Gutiérrez, *Las Casas*, trans. Robert R. Barr (Maryknoll, NY: Orbis Books, 1993), 41.

130 Ibid., 364–365.

131 Bartolomé de Las Casas, *The Only Way*, ed. Helen Rand Parish, trans. Francis Patrick Sullivan (New York: Paulist Press, 1992), 171.

132 Ibid., 173.

133 See Bartolomé de Las Casas, *Witness: Writings of Bartolomé de Las Casas*, ed. George Sanderlin (Maryknoll, NY: Orbis Books, 1992), 159–161.

134 See Las Cases, *Witness*, 168–173; Gutiérrez, *Las Casas*, 336, 390–395.

135 For arguments against satisfaction/sacrificial theories of atonement, see Comblin, *Reconciliación y Liberación*, 19–24; Tamez, *The Amnesty of Grace*, 156–159; Hinkelammert, *Sacrificios Humanos y Sociedad Occidental*, 9–94. For an analysis of the way that satisfaction/sacrificial logics play into the hands of capitalism, see Hinkelammert, "Economía y Teología: Las Leyes del Mercado y la Fe," 7–10.

136 Silvio Campana, "La justicia come fuente liberadora para la reconciliación y perdón," *Paginas* 134 (1995): 17.

137 Gutiérrez, *Las Casas*, 364–365.

138 Martín-Baró, "Reparations and Democracy," 139.

139 Campana, "La justicia come fuente liberadora para la reconciliación y perdón," 16.

140 Sobrino, *The Principle of Mercy*, 159–160. The significance of solidarity as an act of penance should not be underestimated. As it is frequently used, there is little recognition that solidarity is a deeply problematic concept when not located within a narrative of grace and conversion. Too often calls for solidarity rest on the faulty assumptions that there exists a clear distinction between oppressor and oppressed and that it is something relatively easy to enter into. Sobrino's association of genuine solidarity with penance suggests that for liberationists solidarity is a much more complicated endeavor. As we have seen, the liberationists recognize that there is no simple dichotomy between oppressor and oppressed. As a consequence, genuine solidarity can only be a product of God's judgment of grace. It is made possible by the sanctifying grace of God that converts oppressors, cleanses them of their sin, and enables them to embrace and be embraced by those who were their enemies. For this reason it is associated with penance. For more on the problematic nature of solidarity, see Kenneth Surin, *Theology and the Problem of Evil* (Cambridge: Blackwell Publishers, 1986), 119–122.

141 Gutiérrez, *A Theology of Liberation*, 172. See also Second General Conference of Latin American Bishops, *The Church in the Present-Day Transformation of Latin America in the Light of the Council*, "Document on the Poverty of the Church," §4–6. Text is found in *Liberation Theology: A Documentary History*, ed. Alfred T. Hennelly (Maryknoll, NY: Orbis

Books, 1992), 114–119; Gutiérrez, *We Drink from Our Own Wells*, trans. Matthew J. O'Connell (Maryknoll, NY: Orbis Books, 1984), 122–127; Gutiérrez, *The Power of the Poor in History*, 34, 54–55; Sobrino, *The Principle of Mercy*, 54; Ignacio Ellacuría, "The Kingdom of God and Unemployment in the Third World," *Concilium* 160 (1982): 91–96.

Note that according to the liberationists the call to voluntary poverty takes many different forms and is not lived out the same way by everyone. See Second General Conference of Latin American Bishops, "Document on the Poverty of the Church," §6; Jon Sobrino, *The True Church and the Poor*, 326.

142 Note that such a redistribution will undoubtedly entail, among other things, a reconstrual of such practices as ownership and possession in accord with what it means to be connected to others in a shared love of the common good. Incidentally, such redistribution may bring us closer to earlier Christian understandings of the distribution and possession of goods. For more on this, see Milbank, *Theology and Social Theory*, 12–17; Joan Lockwood O'Donovan, "Historical Prolegomena to a Theological Review of 'Human Rights'," *Studies in Christian Ethics* 9 (1996): 55–61; Joan Lockwood O'Donovan, "Natural Law and Perfect Community: Contributions of Christian Platonism to Political Theory," *Modern Theology* 14 (1998): 19–42.

143 Sobrino, *The Principle of Mercy*, 146, 165.

144 Ibid., 165.

145 As the liberationists noted, not all the crucified people offer forgiveness. The case of victims who are unwilling to forgive is complex. When faced with unforgiving victims, it is important to remember that forgiveness is a process that may entail spiritual growth on the part of the victim as much as for the one who has inflicted harm. The victim needs to be freed to forgive as much as the offender needs to be forgiven. Therefore, the first response of the Christian community to the unforgiving should be a nurturing patience and compassion. For helpful reflections on these matters from the perspective of the struggle to liberate women from abuse, see Marie Fortune, "Forgiveness: The Last Step," in *Abuse and Religion*, eds. Anne L. Horton and Judith A. Williamson (Lexington, MA: Lexington Books, 1988), 215; Mary D. Pellauer and Susan Brooks Thistlethwaite, "Conversations on Grace and Healing: Perspectives from the Movement to End Violence Against Women," in *Lift Every Voice: Constructing Christian Theologies from the Underside*, eds. Susan Brooks Thistlethwaite and Mary Potter Engel (San Francisco: Harper San Francisco, 1990), 169–185.

146 See Volf, "The Final Reconciliation," *passim*.

147 Williams, *Resurrection*, 22.

148 See Williams, *Resurrection*, 16.

149 Note that this opens new possibilities for understanding how forgiveness and reconciliation with the dead may come about. Contrary to the tenets of the Enlightenment, the Church is not a voluntary association of discrete individuals. Rather, persons who join the Church become part of a trans-temporal body, and as such are joined with all those who were previously and shall in the future be part of that body. Therefore, the Church may both extend and seek forgiveness for the unforgiven sins of the past in which it has been entangled. It is the same party who committed the wrong then that is seeking forgiveness now; it is the same party who suffered wrong then who is being asked to forgive now. To the extent (and *only* to the extent) that the Church today is an extension of the faithful departed, it may both offer and seek forgiveness on behalf of the faithful departed. See Elliot Dorf, "Individual and Communal Forgiveness," in *Autonomy and Judaism*, ed. Daniel Frank (Albany, NY: State University of New York, 1992), 202f.

150 Tamez, *The Amnesty of Grace*, 166.

151 Sobrino, *Christology at the Crossroads*, 119.

152 Josep Vives, "El ídol y la voz. Reflexiones sobre Dios y su justicia," in *La justicia que brota*

de la fe, eds. J. I. González Faus, R. Sivatte, X. Alegre, *et al.* (Santander: Editorial Sal Terrae, 1982), 120.

153   What follows is drawn from José Ignacio González Faus, "Cristo, Justicia de Dios. Dios, justicia nuestra. Reflexiones sobre cristología y lucha por la justicia," in *La justicia que brota de la fe*, eds. J. I. González Faus, R. Sivatte, X. Alegre, *et al.* (Santander: Editorial Sal Terrae, 1982), 143–145.

154   Milbank, "Forgiveness and Incarnation," 34–50; Hart, 341.

155   Karen Lebacqz, *Justice in an Unjust World* (Minneapolis: Augsburg Publishing House, 1987), 83.

156   Although as I have already suggested, such operations, once they have been repositioned with the divine aneconomic order of grace, would hardly be recognizable as calculations of what is due in the classic sense of *suum cuique*.

157   Sobrino, *The Principle of Mercy*, viii.

158   For more on the imperviousness of suffering to theoretical resolution, see Surin, *Theology and the Problem of Evil*. Also helpful in this regard is Tilley, *The Evils of Theodicy*.

159   Sobrino, *Jesus the Liberator*, 245–246.

160   The phrase "power-in-vulnerability" is taken from Sarah Coakley, "Kenōsis and Subversion: On the repression of 'vulnerability' in Christian feminist writing," in *Swallowing a Fishbone? Feminist Theologians Debate Christianity*, ed. Daphne Hampson (London: SPCK, 1996), 84.

161   Ignacio Ellacuría, *Conversión de la Iglesia al reino de Dios* (San Salvador: UCA Editores, 1985), 158. Translation is mine.

162   Sobrino, *The Principle of Mercy*, 23.

163   Ellacuría, *Conversión de la Iglesia al reino de Dios*, 112–113. Translation is mine.

164   Gutiérrez, *We Drink from Our Own Wells*, 116–117.

165   Jon Sobrino, "Spirituality and the Following of Jesus," in *Mysterium Liberationis: Fundamental Concepts of Liberation Theology*, eds. Ignacio Ellacuría and Jon Sobrino (Maryknoll, NY: Orbis Books, 1993), 694.

166   Leonardo Boff, *Passion of Christ, Passion of the World*, trans. Robert R. Barr (Maryknoll, NY: Orbis Books, 1987), 117.

167   Javier Jiménez Limón, "Suffering, Death, Cross, and Martyrdom," in *Mysterium Liberationis: Fundamental Concepts of Liberation Theology*, eds. Ignacio Ellacuría and Jon Sobrino (Maryknoll, NY: Orbis Books, 1993), 710.

168   For more on the way the reality of negation checks testimony of affirmation, see Surin, *Theology and the Problem of Evil*, 142–153.

169   On the tenuous and uncertain character of Christian hope, a hope that abides somewhere between optimism and pessimism, see Nicholas Lash, *Theology on the Way to Emmaus* (London: SCM Press, 1986), 202–215.

170   Gutiérrez, *The Power of the Poor in History*, 59–60.

171   Schreiter, *Reconciliation*, 25–27.

172   Ernest W. Ranly, writing from Peru, makes a similar point in his essay "Christian Spirituality of Nonviolence as Reconciliation," in *The Wisdom of the Cross*, eds. Stanley Hauerwas *et al.* (Grand Rapids, MI: William B. Eerdmans Publishing Co., 1999), 115–130.

173   See Volf, *Exclusion and Embrace*, 109.

174   Gutiérrez, *On Job*, 103.

INDEX